PRAISE FOR BEYOND70

This beautifully written, designed, and illustrated volume sheds light on the abundant creativity and zest for life of twenty-one vibrant artists, performers, writers, and musicians. As someone who made art in her "spare time" during a long academic career, and who is now a full-time artist, I am inspired and moved by such fascinating and diverse interviews. **The stories illustrate how everything in one's life forms the foundation for creativity in one's older years.** These women provide a road-map for my next exuberant, joyful, creative decades. A fervent *thank you* to Stacy Russo and her collaborators.

—JANET CATHERINE BERLO, Art Historian, Artist, and Memoirist of *Quilting Lessons*

BEYOND 70 is full of captivating stories. Artists, musicians, writers, filmmakers, performers, and more share their challenges and joys. They uplift. **This beautiful collection honors women's voices through their wisdom, transformation, and willingness to try something new at any age.** In many ways, these lives are just beginning.

—CINDY RINNE, Fiber Artist and Author of *The Feather Ladder*

These insightful pages celebrating courageous women's stories are at once admirable and inspiring. **Enduring spirits manifest** in the intriguing, beautiful art shared with us in this book.

—SYLVIA H. GOULDEN, Artist; President, Collage Artists of America

BEYOND 70 makes me feel as though I have an elixir inside my body, rushing with exhilaration! Reading these life stories and viewing the art of women over age 70 is hopeful and exciting. **Late in life creativity? This is something to live for and look forward to!**

—LUCRETIA TYE JASMINE, Freelance Writer/Artist,
Co-producer of *Feminist Magazine*, L.A.'s weekly radio show on KPFK

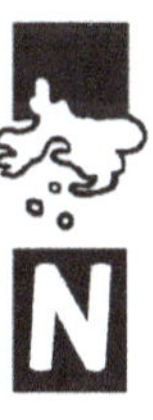

BEYOND 70

THE LIVES OF CREATIVE WOMEN

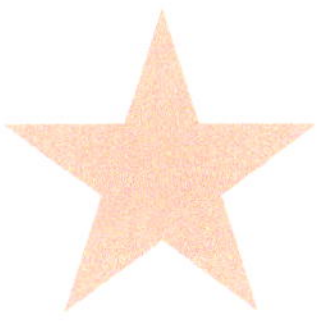

STACY RUSSO

NAUSET PRESS
WAREHAM, MASSACHUSETTS

BEYOND 70: The Lives of Creative Women

Published by Nauset Press

nausetpress.com

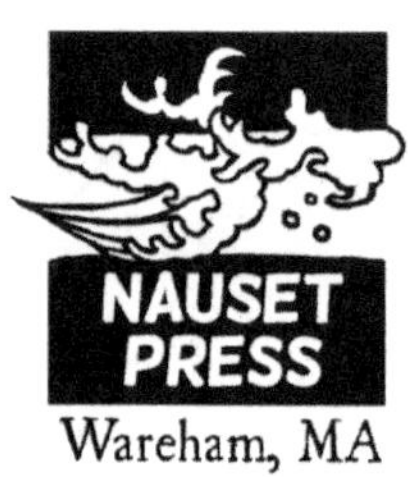

Wareham, MA

Cover and Book Design: Nauset Press.

Cover image: Rosemary Ollison, *Confusion in a Black and White World*, circa 2000, ink on paper, 12"x18"

ISBN: 979-8-9859692-1-4

Library of Congress Control Number: 2023931681

PHOTO CREDITS:

PAGES 17, 51-55: © SCOTT MCCUE PHOTOGRAPHY

PAGES 18, 57-60: © LARRY MELKUS

PAGES 19, 61-67 (ARTWORK): © JULIE FEINSTEIN ADAMS

PAGE 23: © DOUG STREMEL

PAGE 44: OPENER, © DAVID CONTE

PAGE 50: OPENER, © JORDAN DEBREE

PAGE 68: OPENER, © ADINA ALLEN

PAGE 75: OPENER, © KEVIN J. MIYAZAKI

PAGE 81: OPENER, © TAMI BAHAT

PAGE 83: © ERIC MINH SWENSON

PAGE 87: OPENER, © NANCY RUBIN

PAGE 87: © NANCY BUNDT

PAGE 89: © JAMES MAIDHOF

PAGE 91: ©JEREMY WANGLER

PAGE 98: OPENER, © MARY WHEATLEY

PAGES 101-102: © GREG STOVALL

PAGE 110: OPENER, © LLUVIA HIGUERA

PAGE 141: OPENER, © ANITA BOWEN

PAGE 146: OPENER, © CLAUDIA MAGAS (LADIES, LORDS PHOTOGRAPHY)

PAGE 156: © KYLE MCEVOY

PAGE 157: OPENER, 162: © ADRIANNE MATHIOWETZ

ALL OTHER IMAGES ARE PROVIDED BY THE ARTISTS

FOR MY MOM,
WHO WAS FILLED WITH
JOY, LOVE, HOPE, AND
CURIOSITY HER WHOLE LIFE.

MOM, I CELEBRATE
ALL THE LAUGHTER WE SHARED!

CONTENTS

8 Introduction
12 About the Interview Process

INTRODUCTORY GALLERY

15 Ofelia Esparza, *Mictlan Sur*
16 Suzanne C. Oullette, *Still Life with My Father's Silver Bowl*
17 Suellen Cox, *Frida Kahlo—Cuatro Libros*
18 Judy Bowman, *Waiting For My Set I*
19 Frances Porter, *Is Graffiti Art?*
20 Pat B. Allen, *Fool with His Shield*
21 Della Wells, *Who Me, Chicken*
22 Malka Nedivi, *Covered with a Blanket*
23 Rita Blitt, *Confluence*
24 Young Yun Summers, *Flowers from Kitchen*
25 Kathleen Horne, *Beyond 70 - 2 Waves of Life*
26 Phyllis I. Thompson, PhD, *Miss Lucy*
27 Yreina D. Cervantez, *Danza Ocelotl*
28 Nancy Wang, outtakes from *Monkey Moon*
29 Wendy Tigerman, *Rockin' It*
30 Paula Chamlee, from the series *High Plains Farm*
31 Rosemary Ollison, *Women of Color Embracing Their Individuality Proudly and Boldly, Taking Their Place in the Universe, Part A*
32 Gwyn Kirk, *Greeting Cards*
33 Launa D. Romoff, *Pacifico*
34 Kath Bloom, *Kath performing with guitarist David Shapiro*
35 Sandra Gail Lambert, *A Certain Loneliness*

THE INTERVIEWS

37 OFELIA ESPARZA
44 SUZANNE C. OUELLETTE
50 SUELLEN COX
56 JUDY BOWMAN
61 FRANCES PORTER
68 PAT B. ALLEN
75 DELLA WELLS
81 MALKA NEDIVI
87 RITA BLITT
92 YOUNG YUN SUMMERS
98 KATHLEEN HORNE
104 PHYLLIS I. THOMPSON, PhD
110 YREINA D. CERVANTEZ
119 NANCY WANG
125 WENDY TIGERMAN
130 PAULA CHAMLEE
137 ROSEMARY OLLISON
141 GWYN KIRK
146 LAUNA D. ROMOFF
152 KATH BLOOM
157 SANDRA GAIL LAMBERT

162 Discussion Questions
164 Endnotes
164 Acknowledgments

INTRODUCTION

ARE YOU READY to discover the inspiring life stories of creative women who are age seventy and beyond? The interviews collected here offer a bright light for all of us regardless of our age. A gift that comes from reading personal stories is that our minds and hearts may change. Societal constructs we have been living under start to evaporate. This includes stereotyping we may project on others or internalize, causing harm to ourselves. Age discrimination works in the same menacing way as other forms of discrimination and injustice: people are grouped together, denied their individuality, and subjected to stereotyping. Once we deconstruct the group and listen deeply to people's individual stories, we may be dazzled by what we find. Be prepared for some wonderful discoveries that may impact how you view others and how you imagine your own life now and in the future.

Are you also ready to witness the profound and powerful force of creativity? One of my early inspirations for this project was the late visual artist Luchita Hurtado. She was interviewed by *Ursula* magazine about her long career and current art practice at the age of ninety-eight. Her work was still evolving, and climate justice was the focus of her art in the final years. "'The most interesting thing for me now is to make sure that the planet is going in the right direction,'" Hurtado stated. She also commented on her work as an artist in relation to her age: "'As far as physical strength and ability goes, I'm very weak, of course, because of my age, but I still can paint, I can still draw. And so that's my contribution.'"[1] I've discovered that stories like Hurtado's are all around once you begin to look for them.

WITNESS THE PROFOUND AND POWERFUL FORCE OF CREATIVITY

While completing this manuscript, I was delighted to open *The New York Times* one Sunday morning to see Barbara Dane, the folklorist, singer, and co-founder of Paredon Records, was interviewed about her life at age ninety-three. She stated, "'When I was 89, I made the record that I would liked to have made years ago.'"[2] Dane also shared she was working on her memoir. That same month, the paper featured pioneering conceptual artist Lorraine O'Grady at age eighty-six. Oh yes, just like Dane,

O'Grady was busy too. She was preparing for her first retrospective show.[3]

Another example of abundant late life creativity is found in Emily Urquhart's memoir about her father Tony Urquhart, the Canadian painter. She comments on her father's creativity in his eighties: "My father was struggling with his memory, and his pace had slowed, but his work – or, rather, his vocation, as he called his daily art practice – continued unabated, revealing creativity to be an act as inevitable and constant as death itself."[4] We can see from these examples the hopeful and very real evidence that creativity could care less about age. As human beings, we can celebrate in knowing that creativity is pleased to show up at different times, including late in life, and would be happy to be a life partner if we so desired.

CREATIVITY ... WOULD BE HAPPY TO BE A LIFE PARTNER IF WE DESIRED

I discovered stories like these of individuals with rich life experiences who were still prolific and engaged in their creative lives when I was working on an earlier collection of interviews with activists.[5] During that project, I had the honor of interviewing the poet Judy Grahn and the late ecofeminist artist Helène Aylon, who were both beyond age seventy at the time. Grahn and Aylon each had amazing vitality and creativity. Grahn was engaged in writing projects and immersed in the founding of the Commonality Institute to promote her work and legacy; Aylon was preparing for a solo exhibition and spoke about her future art and travel plans. Those interviews and the discovery of Luchita Hurtado's creative life as she approached her one hundredth birthday sowed the seeds for this book. I did some preliminary research and found there were plenty of other stories out there and women who were ready to share their life journeys and how they were living and/or imagining their creativity beyond age seventy. I decided to focus solely on women, since the value of women's lives is so often tied to youthful beauty or child-rearing possibilities. I knew how hopeful and inspiring a collection of these stories would be. They demonstrate how restrictive, harmful, and wrong it is to judge a woman's worth so narrowly.

THE VALUE OF WOMEN'S LIVES IS SO OFTEN TIED TO YOUTHFUL BEAUTY OR CHILD-REARING

While spending time with the women featured in this book, I noticed there is something quite magical about interviewing a person in their sixth or seventh decade or beyond. Patterns and rhythms that travel over a long distance emerge. The only way to experience these aspects on a large scale is with time. This does not mean a younger person's story cannot carry transformation, wisdom, and its own cycles and rhythms, but there is something different about stories that arrive in the third act of a long and full life. This realization was only magnified during this project when I had the good fortune of speaking to so many voices who have long journeys behind them and future horizons to imagine. When Judy Bowman shared with me that she had a gap of several decades in which she did not make art, I knew it was a startling revelation that packed much more of a punch than a gap of five or ten years. It speaks to resilience and how long we can hold a dream within us and see this dream return and be realized.

A CLEAR EMERGENCE OF THREE DISTINCT ARCS TO THE LIFE OF AN ARTIST

When being asked questions about a long life, one needs to also discern the most important moments from such a life, which is not necessarily an easy task. I asked every woman in this collection a version of the question, "Please tell me about your artistic life." When I think of answering this question myself at age fifty-one, there is a much richer landscape to cross than how I would have answered at thirty or forty. I'm certain this terrain will only grow deeper if I'm blessed with a long life like the women I interviewed.

DRAWING IS ENERGY MADE VISIBLE

As I progressed through this project, I also saw a clear emergence of three distinct arcs to the life of an artist. These arcs could only have been discovered from interviewing older creatives. The first arc is demonstrated by an individual such as Rita Blitt. Rita, who was age eighty-nine when I interviewed her, is a formally trained artist who has practiced art her entire life. A second arc is found in the lives of artists such as Phyllis I. Thompson, PhD and Judy Bowman, who went to art school and started their early career within the arts but took considerably long breaks, possibly decades, from creating art. The third arc is found in the stories of Launa D. Romoff, Suellen Cox, and others, and it involves women who never thought they were artists and had no formal training earlier in life. These women started practicing art and embracing their identities as artists much later, often during or close to the stage of life the late anthropologist and scholar on aging, Mary Catherine Bateson, called "... active engagement that falls roughly between ages fifty-five and seventy, depending on circumstances."[6] Some of these women were awakened to their artistic life by a mentor and received some form of instruction; others, such as Della Wells, remain completely self-taught.

It's interesting to note that for women in the third arc, several told me they didn't think they were artists earlier in life because they couldn't draw. This speaks to the need for an expansion of how art is taught and encouraged from a young age. The artist Pat B. Allen, one of the women I interviewed for this project, offers a definition for drawing in her book *Art is a Way of Knowing: A Guide to Self-Knowledge and Spiritual Fulfillment through Creativity*: "Knowing 'how to draw,' being able to represent objects with a degree of realism, is commonly assumed to be the measure of a true artist. Actually, drawing is energy made visible."[7] How liberating!

There are some variations here and there to the three arcs of the life of an artist that I outlined above, yet a clear presence of one of these arcs is found in most of the stories. Discovering the three arcs added a wonderful dimension to the project. I thought of you—the readers of these stories—and how this diversity of the life of an artist will hopefully give everyone something to connect with. Perhaps in your own life, you have a through line of a passion or calling that you have never moved away from since childhood. Or maybe there is something important you have set aside for many years, and this makes you feel as if something is missing or unbalanced in your life. It could also be that there is something you never imagined yourself doing, such as creating art, traveling, or cultivating a lush garden, and you will discover—just possibly—that you can, and you will!

These discoveries also made it clear to me that to provide a meaningful and perhaps holistic story of a long life, one cannot only focus on the later chapters. Bateson imagined human life as a house. The "use of a new room in a house depends on what is already there," she believed, just like entering a new life cycle. "It is often only in its final pages that a story reveals its meaning, so the choices made in later decades may reflect light back on earlier years," Bateson further explained. I agree with Bateson, which is why you will not only discover what the women artists are doing currently and what they imagine for the future, but you will travel back to their childhood and through other important periods of their lives to reach what Bateson calls an "inclusive composition."

While interviewing the diverse voices for *BEYOND 70*, I was not prepared for how this project would impact my life. I imagined I was already liberated from constricting views on age and aging, yet I realized I had internalized ageism and I was allowing fear to dictate some thoughts and decisions. I made different personal discoveries about aging that surprised me. I'll share with you a significant one. For many years, I had a personal goal and dream of pursuing my PhD. Not too long before embarking on this project, I believed I had waited too long. "Let your dream go," I told myself, "and learn to be okay with it." But, like many big dreams, it wouldn't let go of me. The dream reappeared during this project. As I complete this manuscript and sit here writing this introduction, I'm in the first class of my doctoral program. I look ahead with a huge smile considering, if all goes well, I will not yet be sixty when I graduate. Here I am in my fifties, and I've realized I'm so young! What falsehoods I've been told! Thank you to the phenomenal women of *BEYOND 70* for offering their wisdom to me.

Dear reader, as you meet these amazing women through their life stories, may you experience the wonder and inspiration I did.

Stacy Russo

Santa Ana, California
Summer 2021

ABOUT THE INTERVIEW PROCESS

A NOTE ABOUT the interview process is important because not all interview projects are conducted in the same way. This project was completed within an ethical social justice framework.

In 2012, I attended an exhilarating week-long workshop for educators through the Voice of Witness organization in San Francisco. The workshop, titled "Amplifying Unheard Voices," bridged the powerful connection of oral history and social justice. As a librarian, professor, and writer, I signed up for this workshop because of my love for personal stories that arrives through oral history, autobiography, and memoir. I had no expectations for the workshop; I flew to the Bay Area open to whatever possibilities I would discover. The workshop ended up changing my life as a writer.

BEYOND 70 is my fourth book with interviews and the third book that is entirely an interview collection. With all my interview projects, which I think of as story-gathering projects, I do my best to follow the ethical guidelines of interviewing that come from my own activism and social justice beliefs, as well as those I learned through my time with Voice of Witness and the subsequent reading of several volumes of the organization's published oral histories. Many factors come into play here, but the ultimate belief I work within is that the stories always remain the narrators' stories; they are not mine to change and embellish. I ask open questions and allow people to tell their stories the way they want and not how I or anyone else may desire. Each story is received as a gift.

I WANT YOU TO EXPERIENCE EACH STORY AS POWERFULLY AND DIRECTLY AS POSSIBLE

There is a raw and rare beauty to interviews. Interviews are not personal essays, although they may sometimes read that way. The interviews in this book capture moments in time that are relayed verbally and then transcribed and lightly edited. Transferring the interview from a verbal to written format for a book does require that some changes be made for ease of readability. In addition, to keep the interviews around the same length, choices often need to be made about what to remove and what to retain.

With each interview in this collection, I sent the portion of the interview I would like to include back to the woman for her review. Although interviews do provide this "moment in time" essence mentioned above, as human beings, we can have good days and bad days. We can say something we regret or remember something we forgot to say. We can be nervous, distracted, joyful, sad, and a plethora of other things. Out of respect and kindness for the women interviewed, it was important to make sure they were okay with the parts of their interviews I wished to include. I also wanted them to check for any errors and sometimes clarify or elaborate on statements they made.

You will discover the interviews are not in a question-and-answer format that moves between the interviewer and interviewee's voices. I want you to experience each story as powerfully and directly as possible. I hope you will feel yourself immersed as if each woman is speaking directly to you. Enjoy!

INTRODUCTORY GALLERY

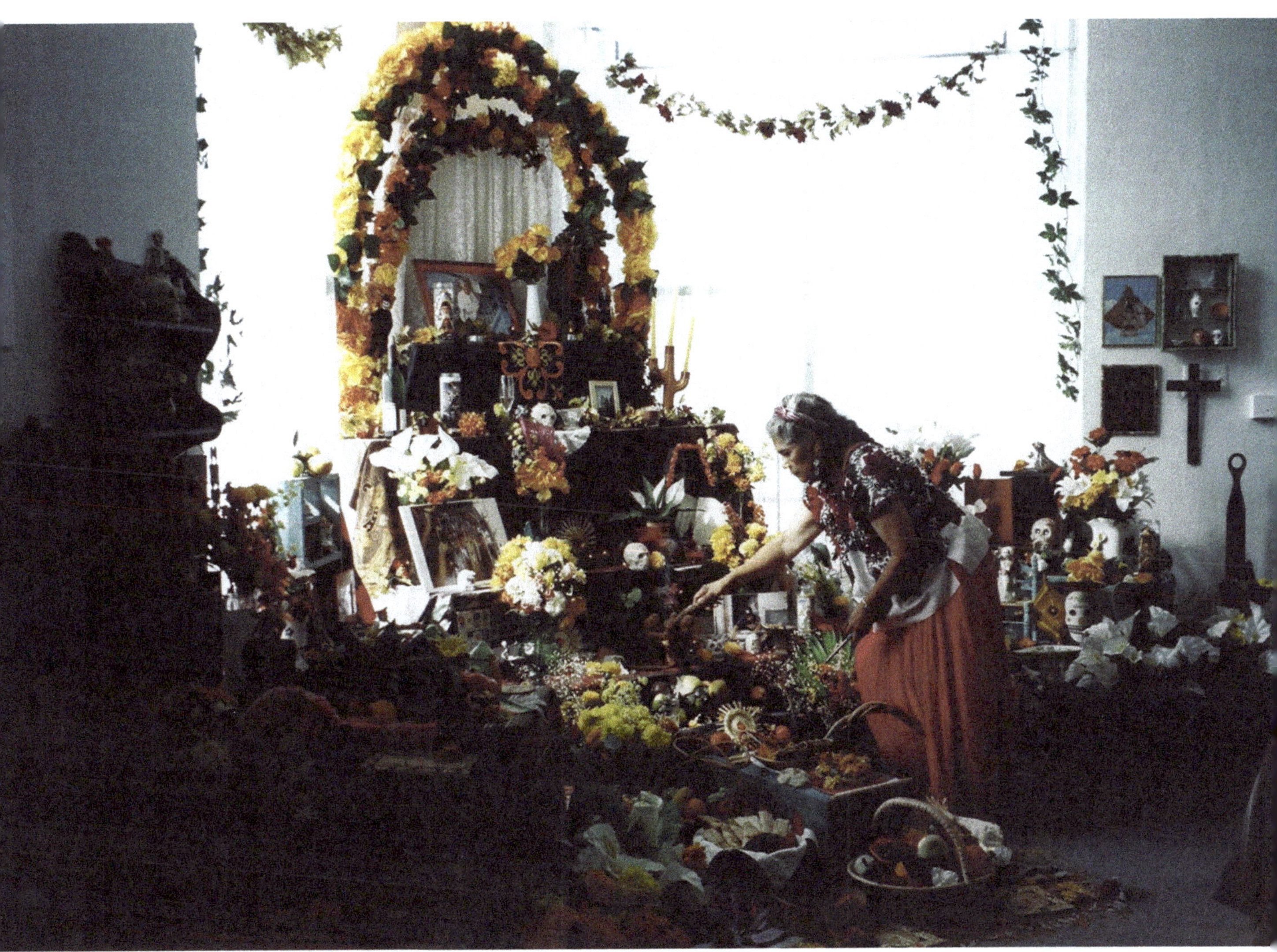

Ofelia Esparza, *Mictlan Sur* at Self Help Graphics, Commemorating the *25th Anniversary Celebrating Day of the Dead* in California, initiated by Self Help Graphics & Galeria de La Raza, 2000

Ofelia Esparza

See the interview on page 37

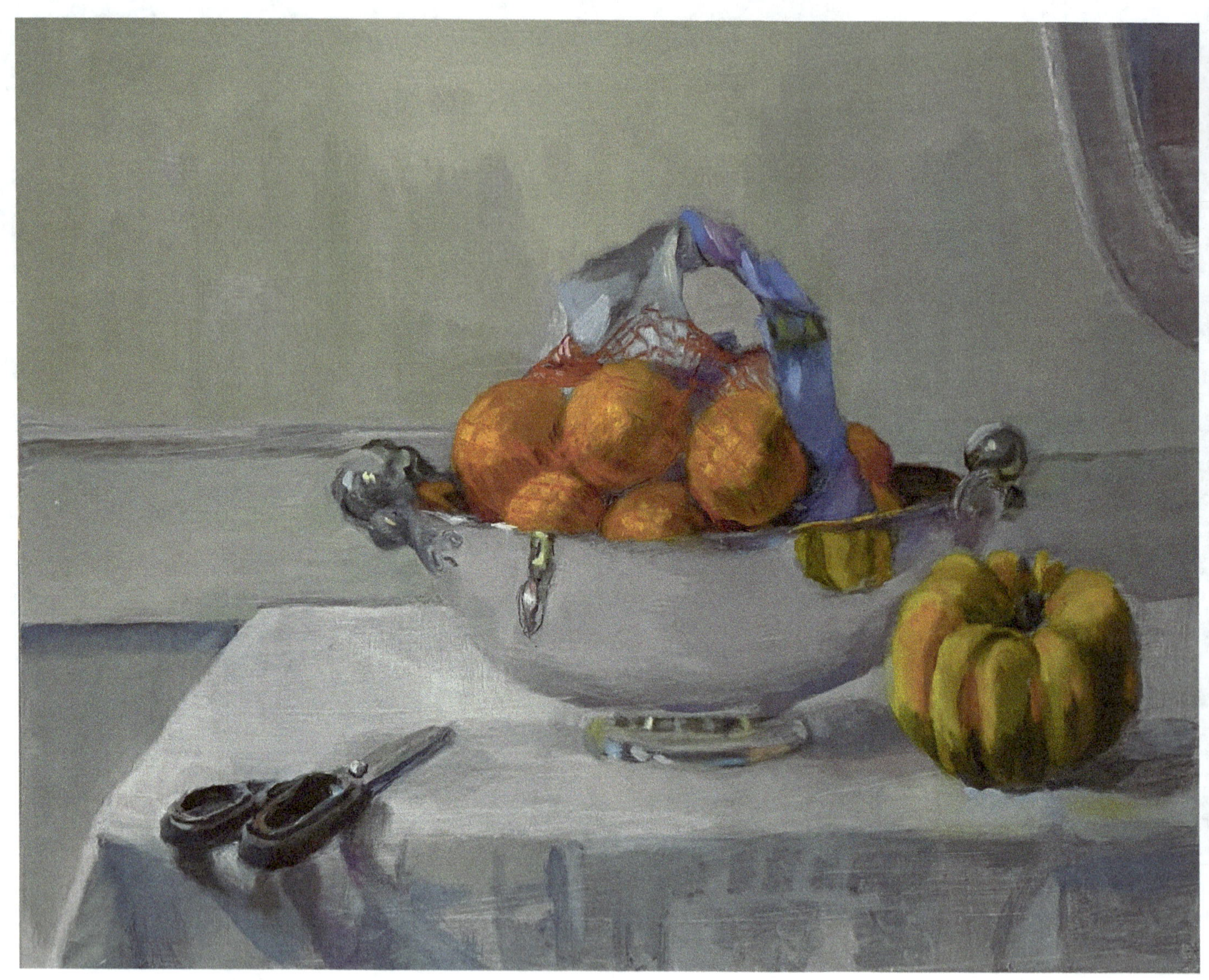

Suzanne C. Oullette, *Still Life with My Father's Silver Bowl*, oil on panel, 16" x 20", 2021

Suzanne C. Oullette

See the interview on page 44

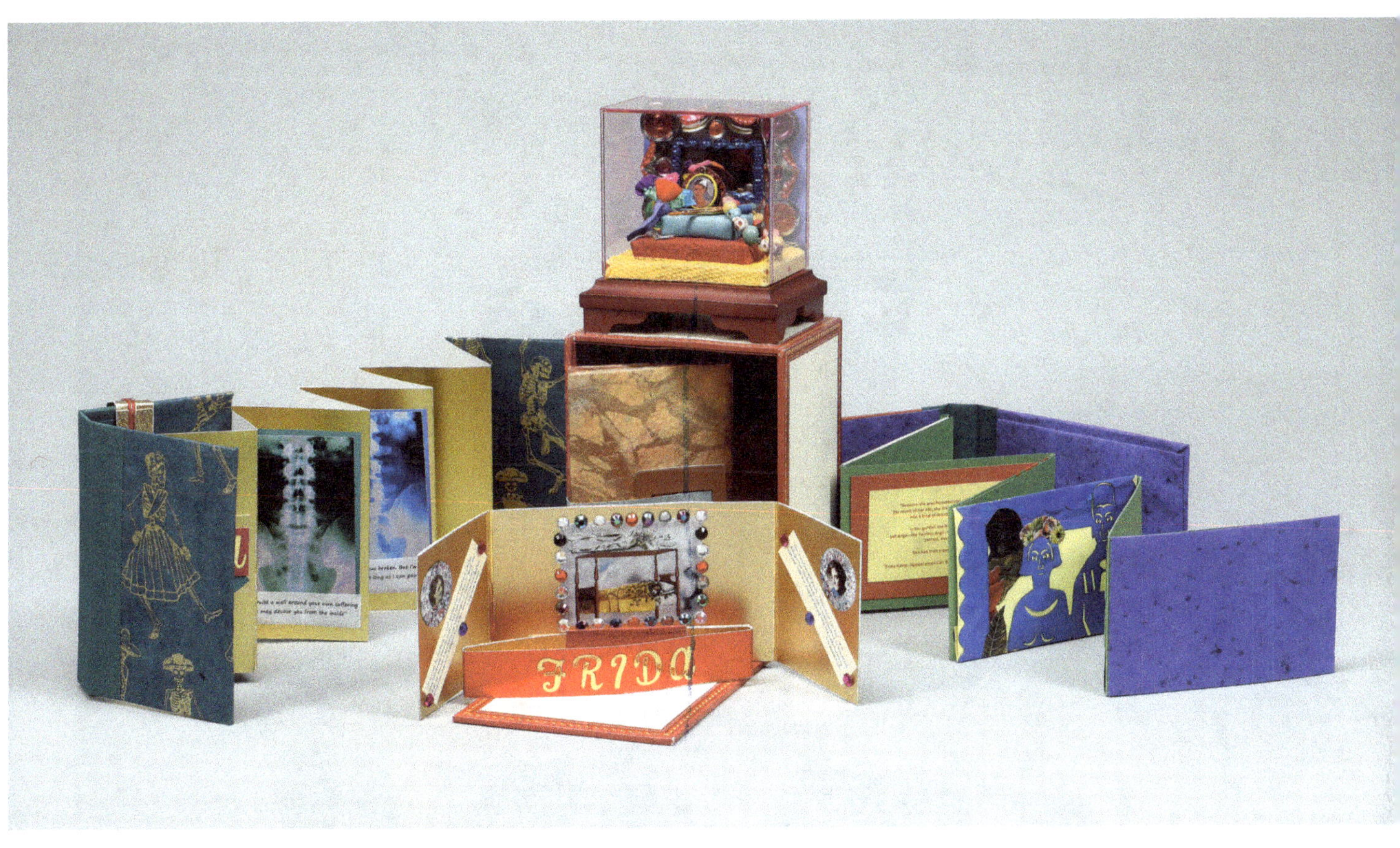

Suellen Cox, *Frida Kahlo—Cuatro Libros*, October 2021

Suellen Cox

See the interview on page 50

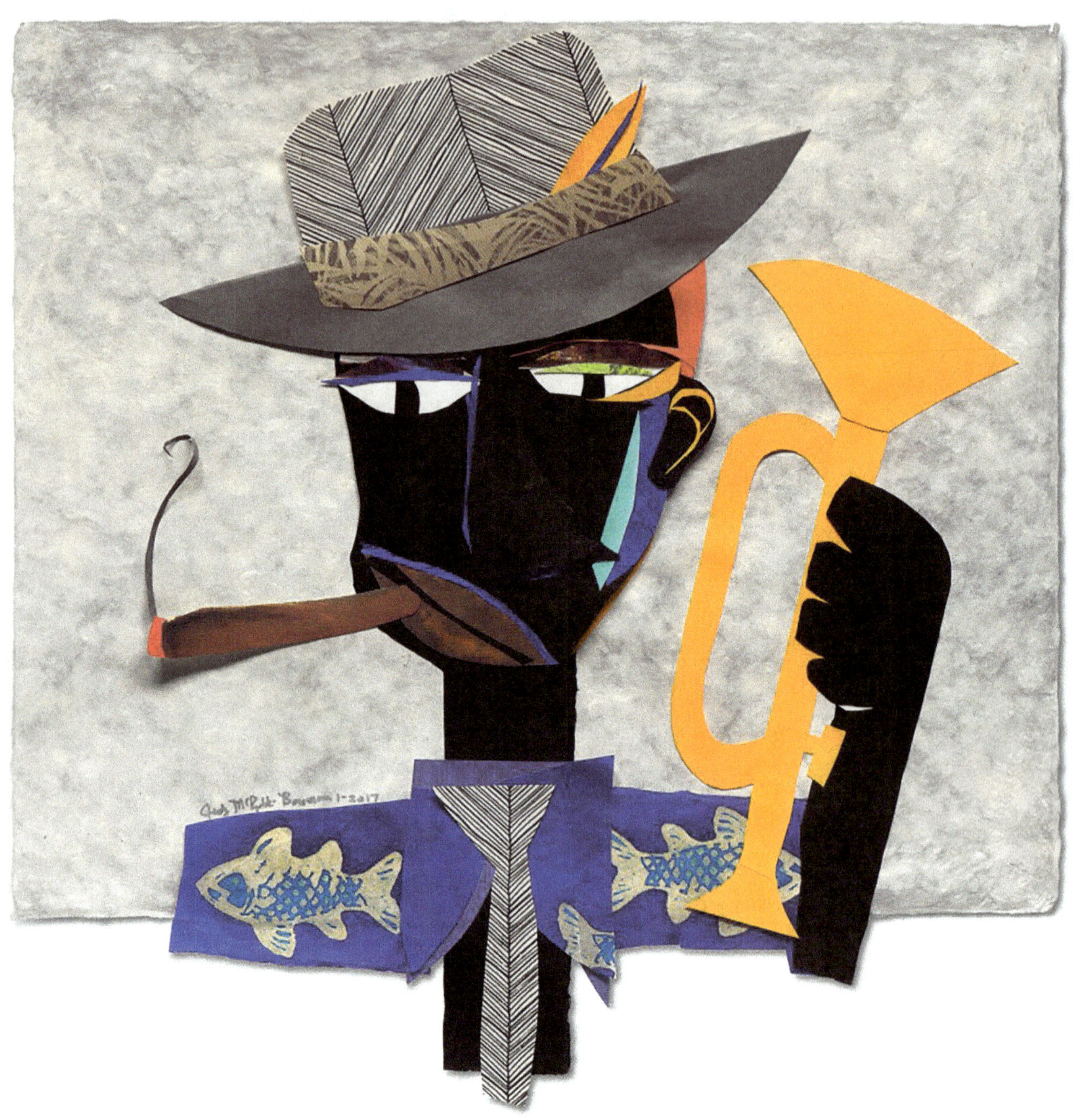

Judy Bowman, *Waiting For My Set I*, mixed media collage, 2017

See the interview on page 56

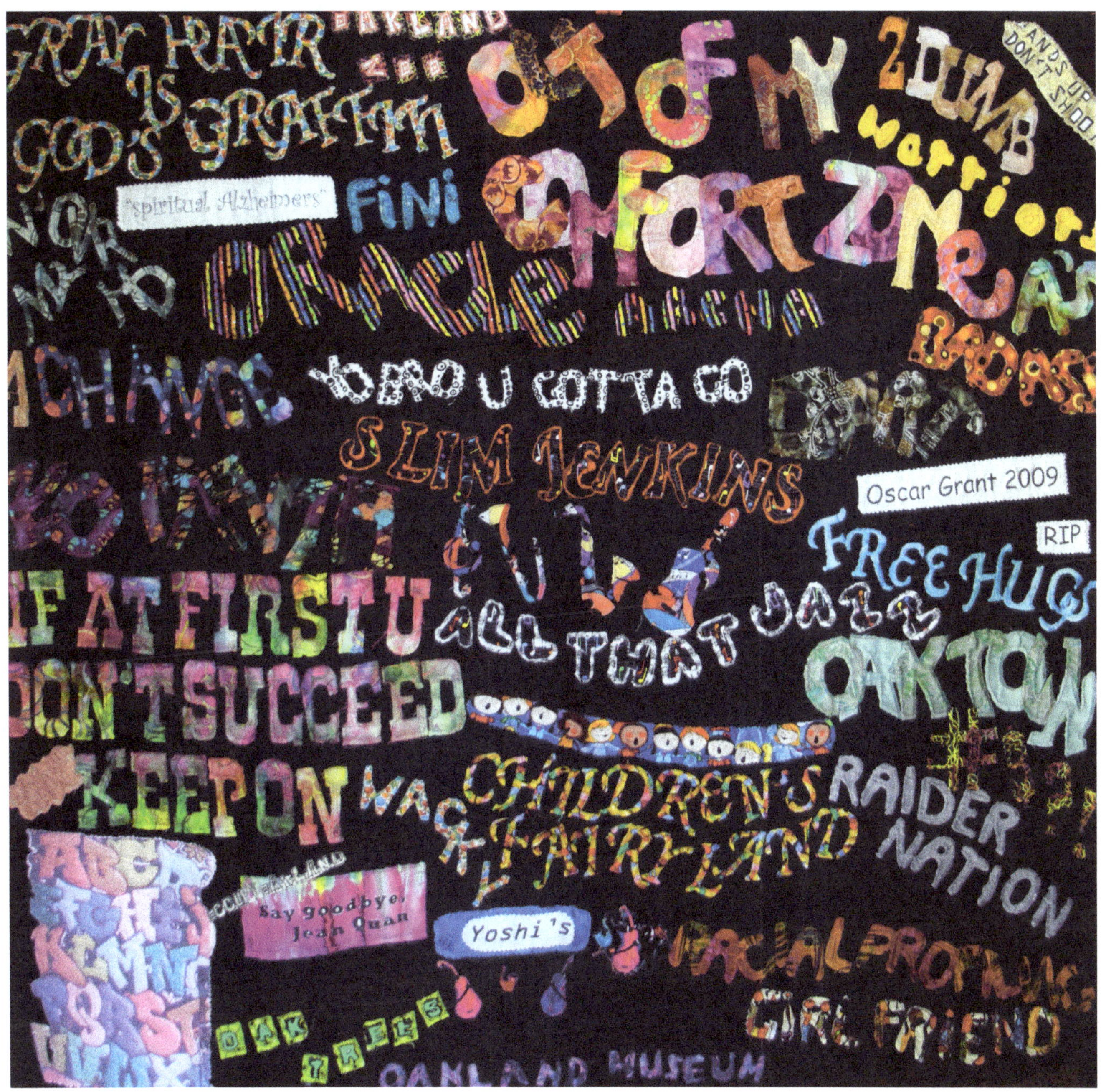

Frances Porter, *Is Graffiti Art?*, quilt, 2016

Frances Porter

See the interview on page 61

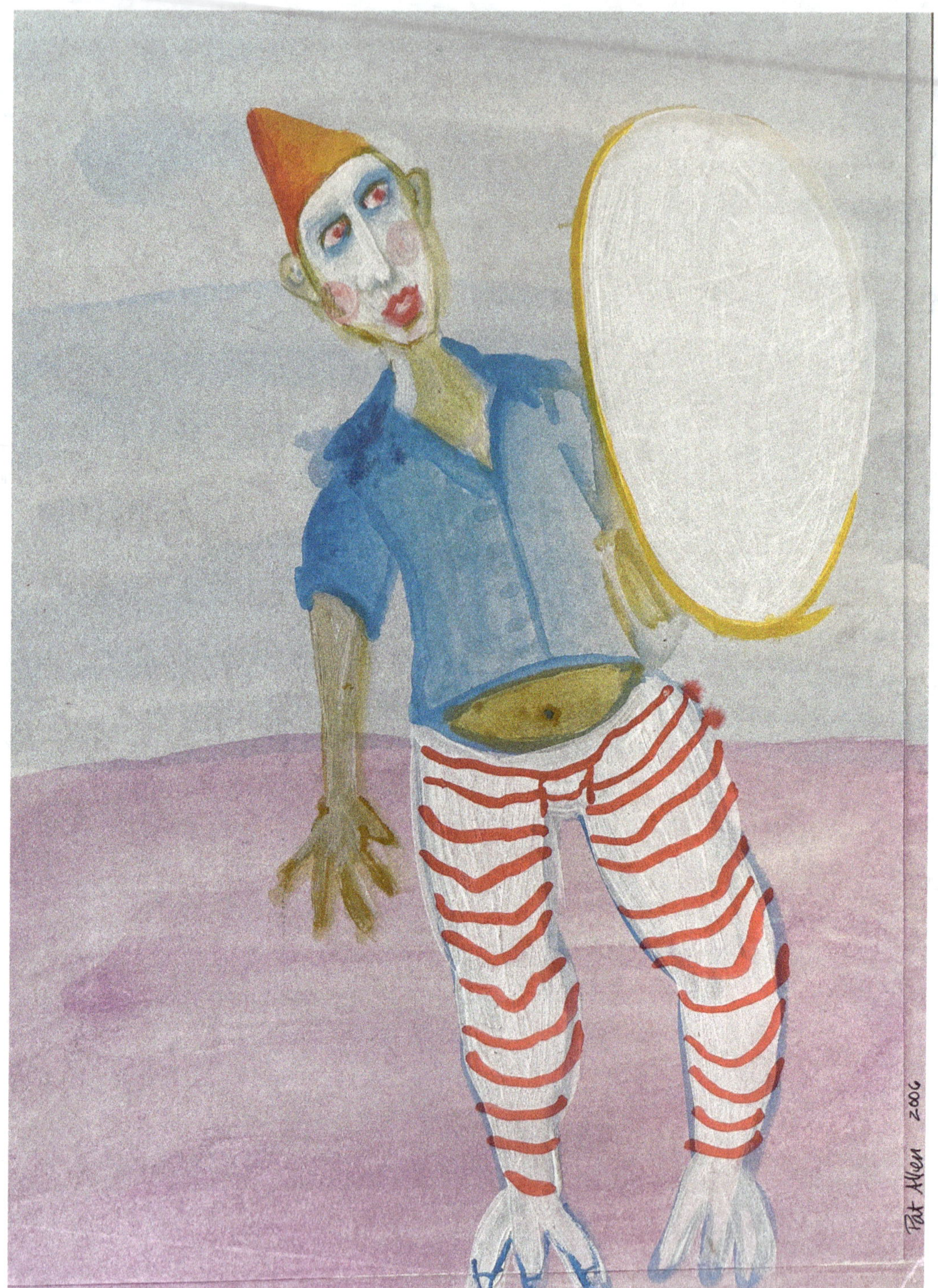

Pat B. Allen, *Fool with His Shield*, watercolor on board, 7.5" x 10.5", 2006

Pat B. Allen

See the interview on page 68

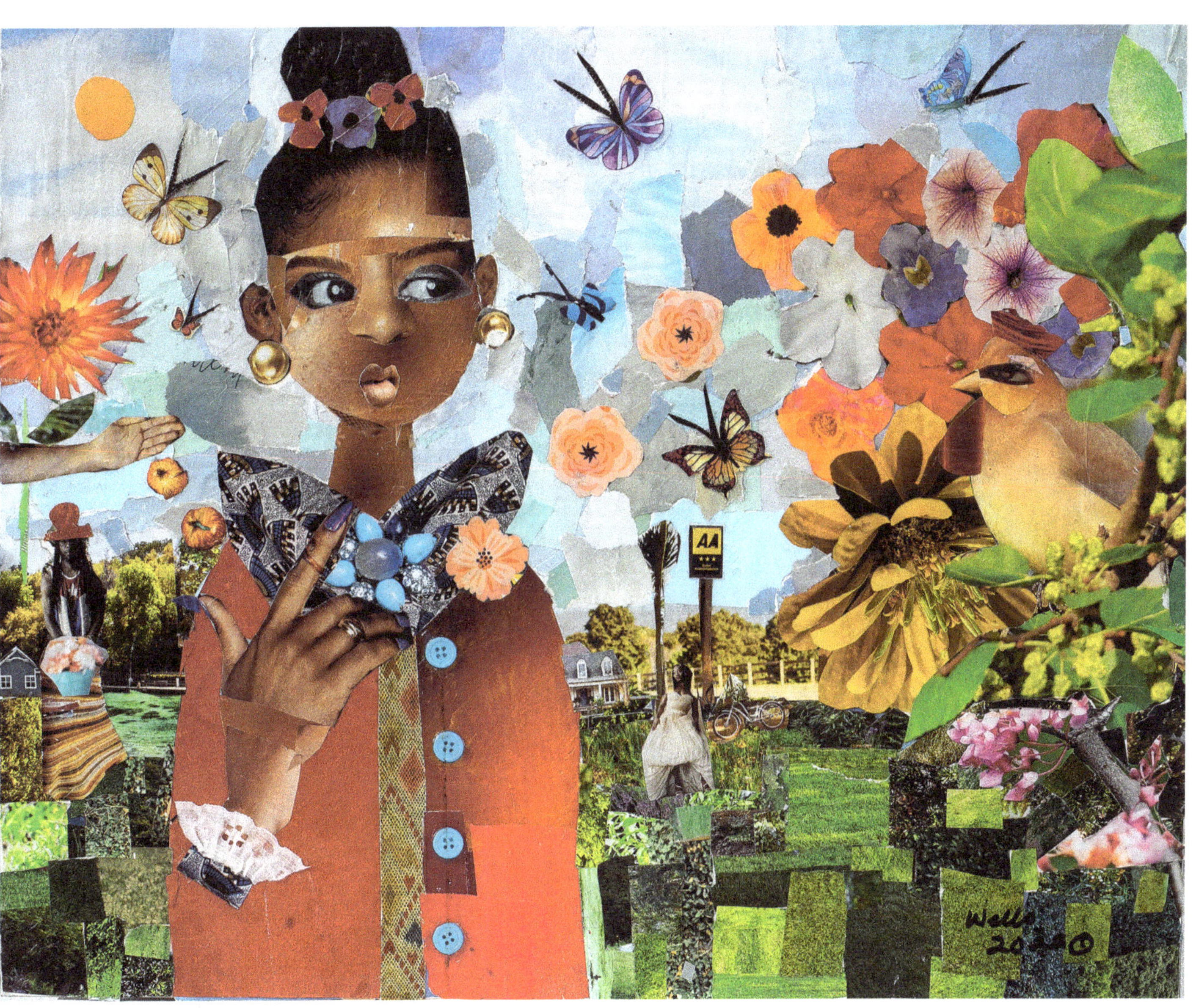

Della Wells, *Who Me, Chicken,* collage, 16" x 20", 2022

See the interview on page 75

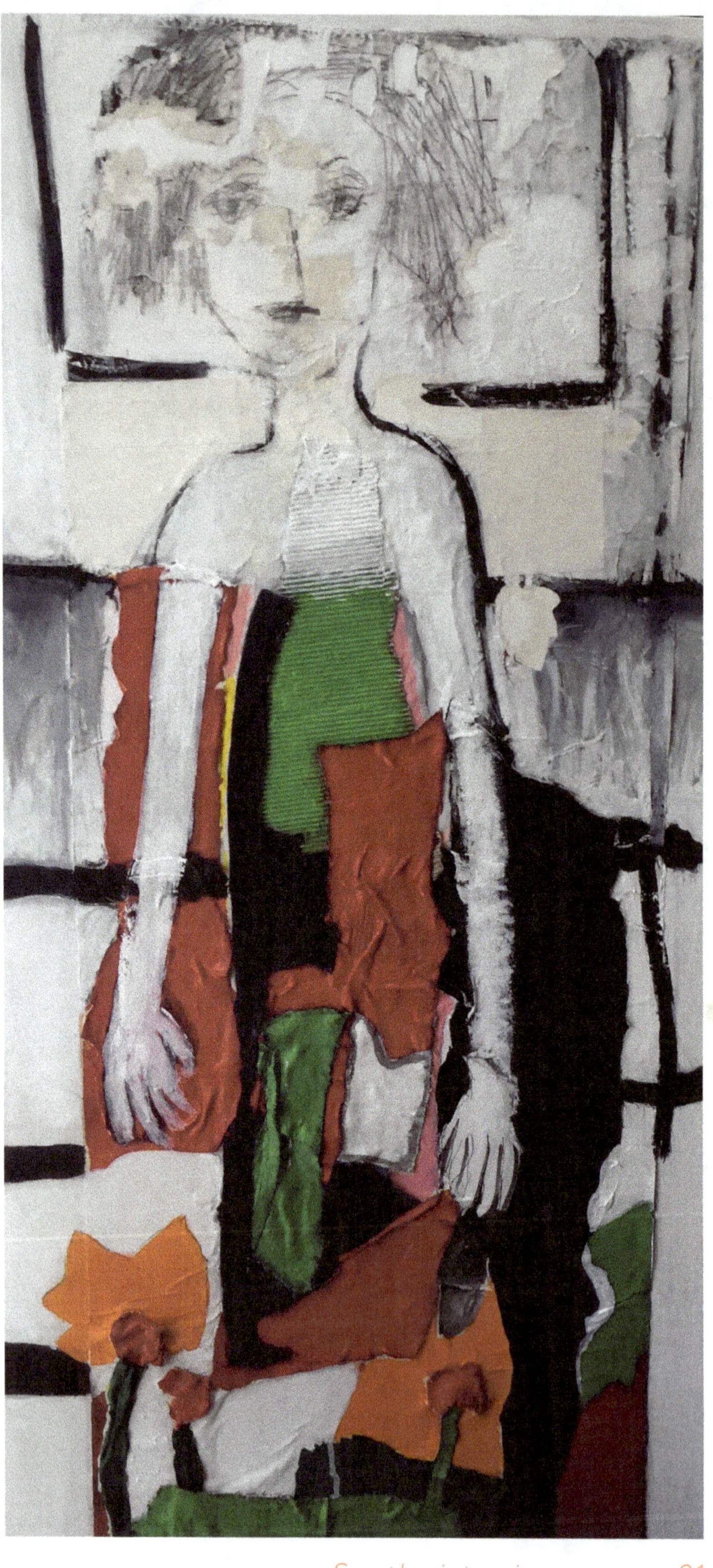

Malka Nedivi, *Covered with a Blanket*, mixed media on framed canvas, 2015

MALKA NEDIVI

See the interview on page 81

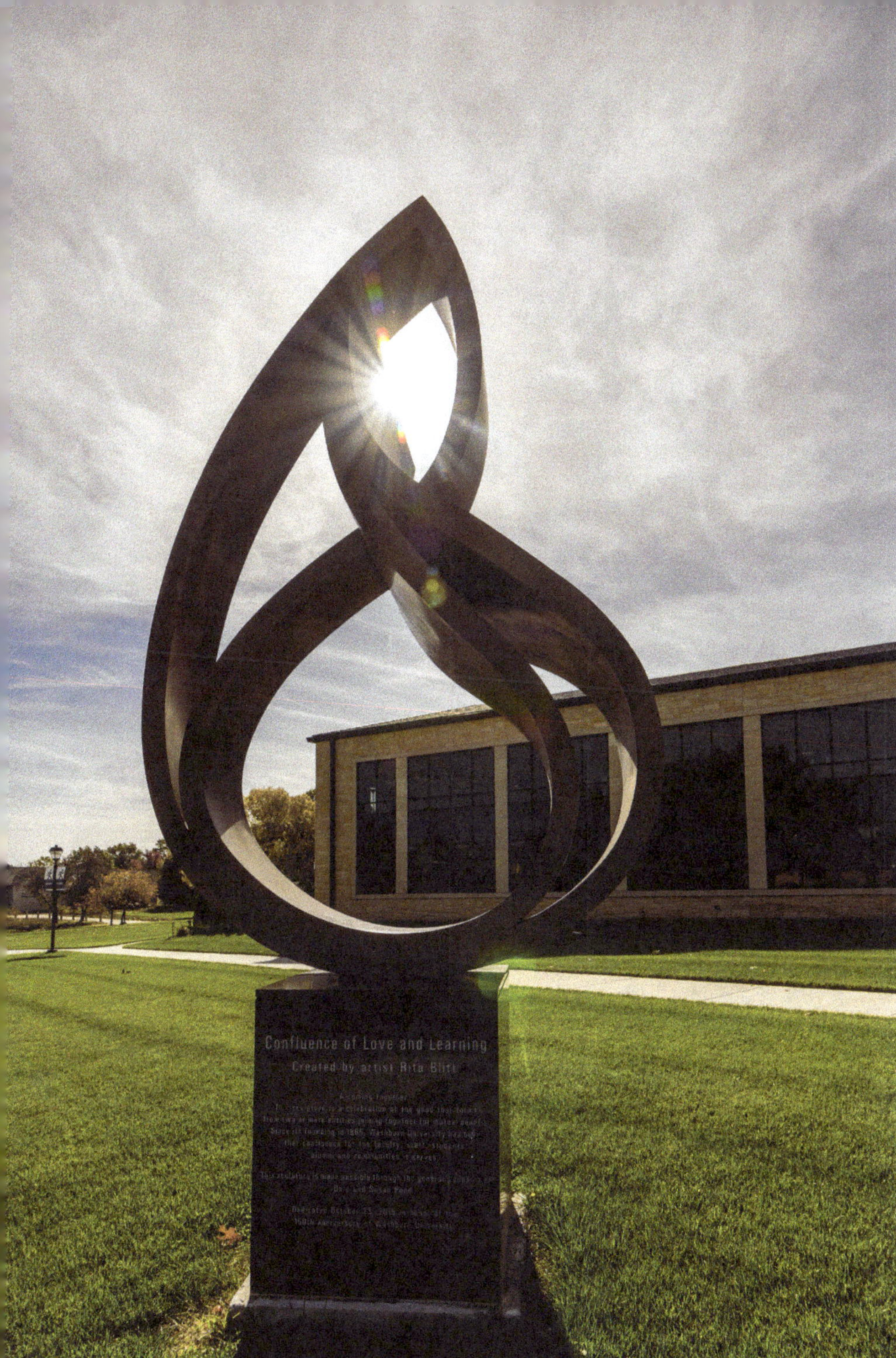

Rita Blitt, *Confluence*, located in front of the administration building at Washburn University, 16', 2017

Rita Blitt

See the interview on page 87

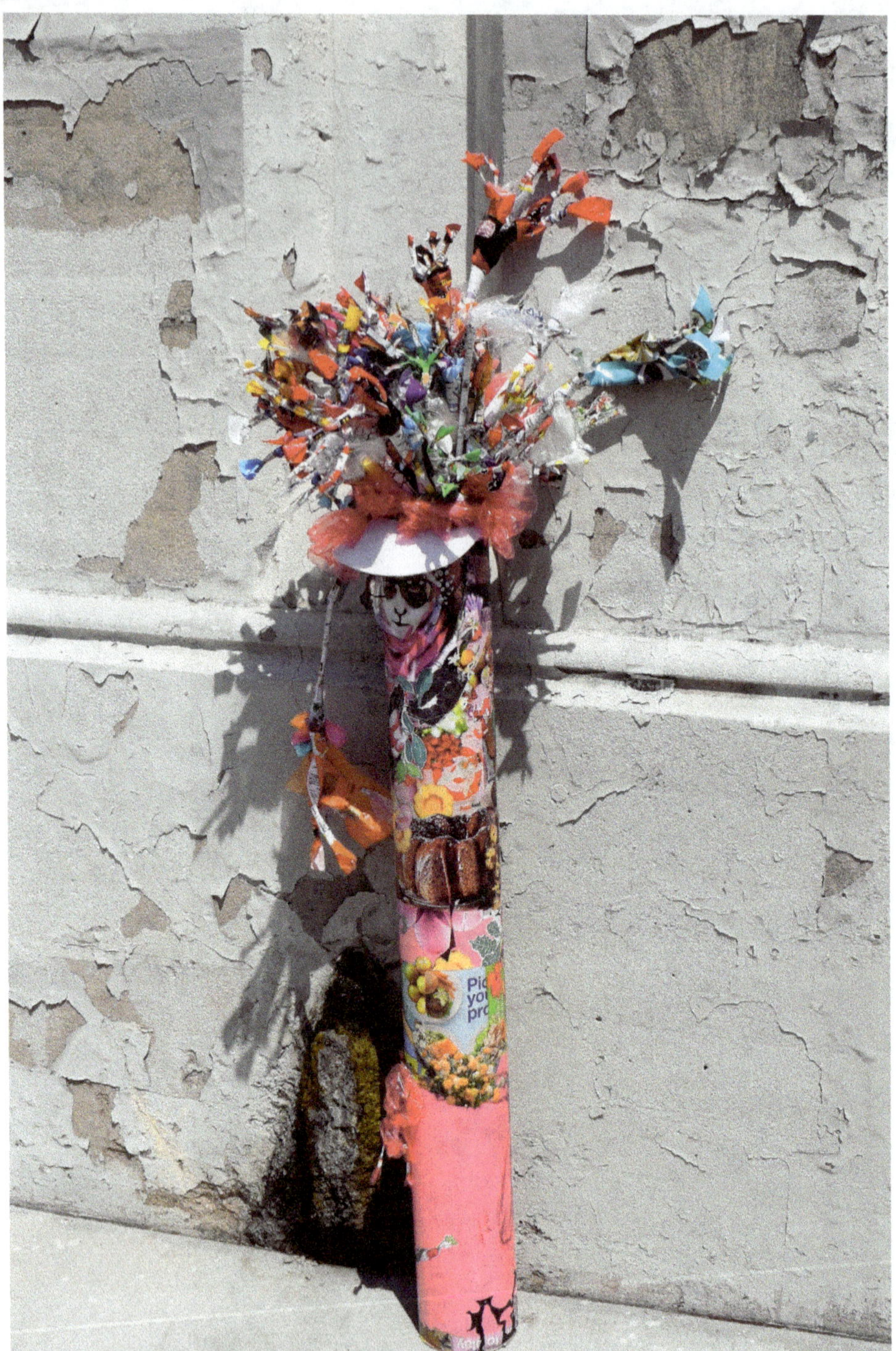

Young Yun Summers, *Flowers from Kitchen*, found objects, plastic wrappers, ads, mailers, magazine pages, and cardboard shipping tube, 30" x 65", 2020

Young Y Summers

See the interview on page 92

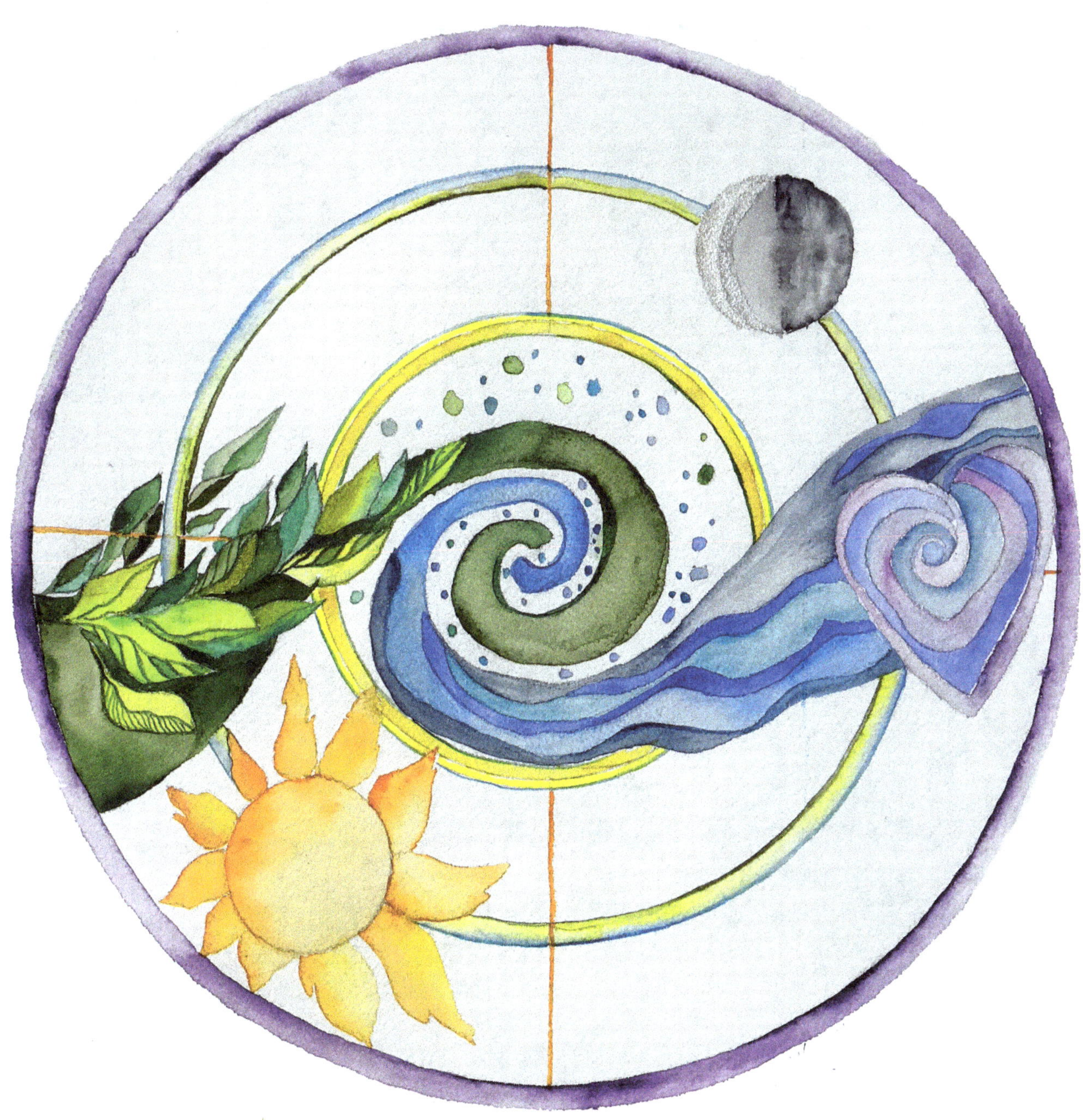

Kathleen Horne, *Beyond 70 - 2 Waves of Life*, watercolor on paper, 2021

See the interview on page 98

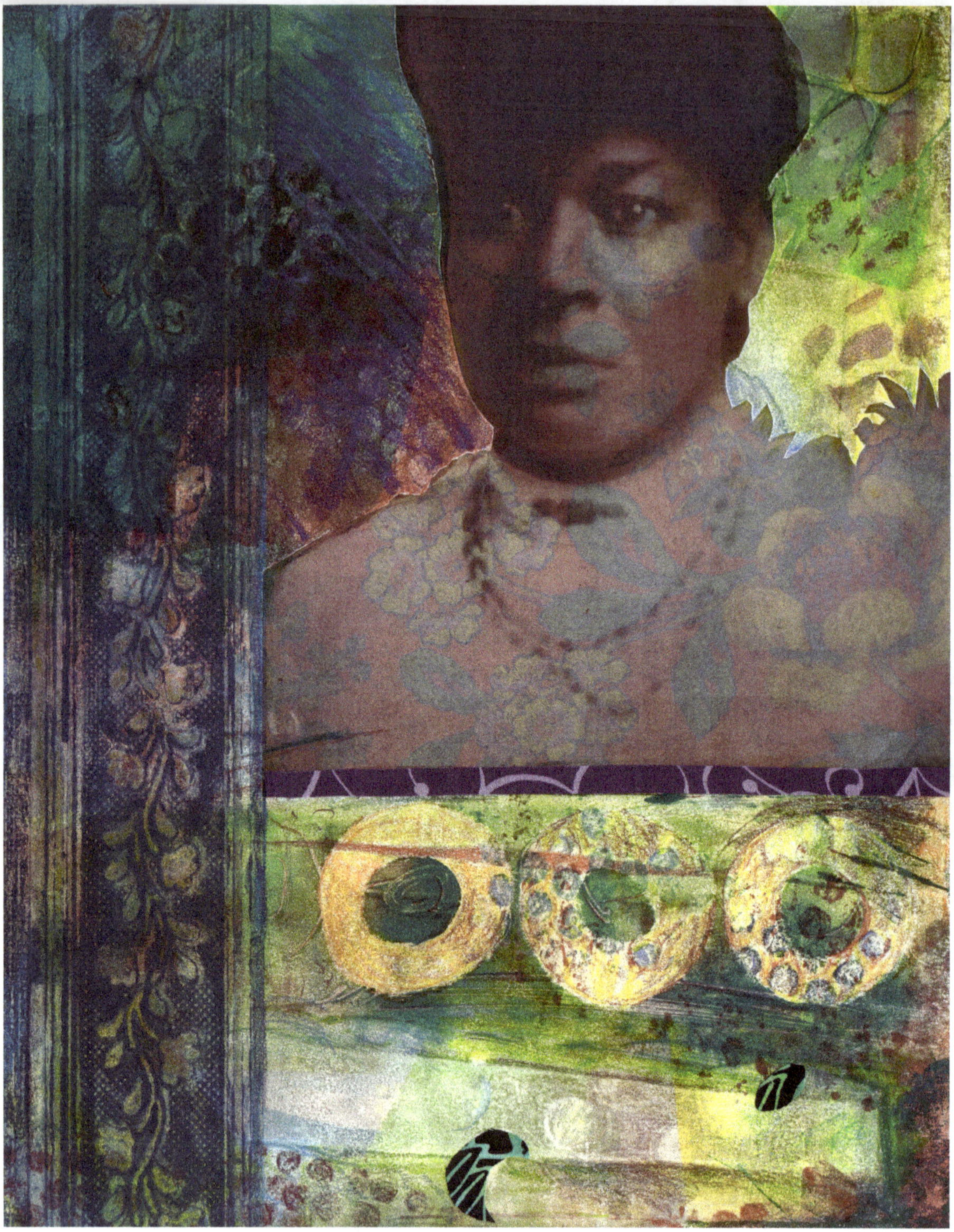

Phyllis I. Thompson, PhD., *Miss Lucy*, mixed media monotype, 17" x 14", 2018

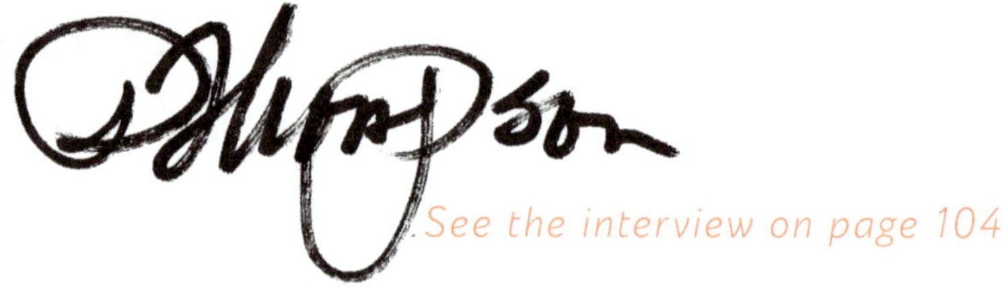

See the interview on page 104

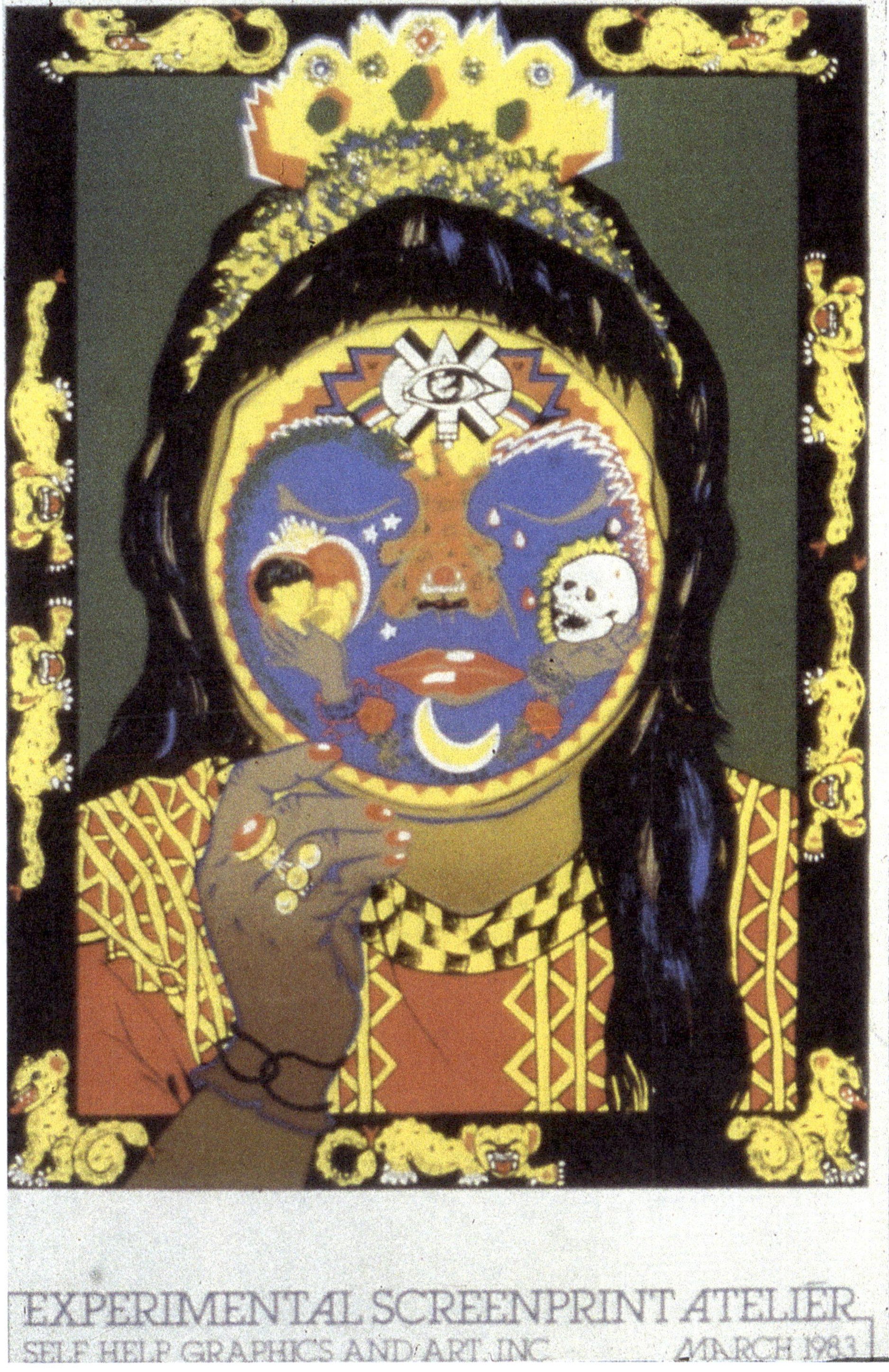

Yreina D. Cervantez, *Danza Ocelotl*, serigraph, 1983

Yreina D. Cervántez

See the interview on page 110

Nancy Wang

Nancy Wang, outtakes from *Monkey Moon*, featured on *Eyes of the Wise* DVD.

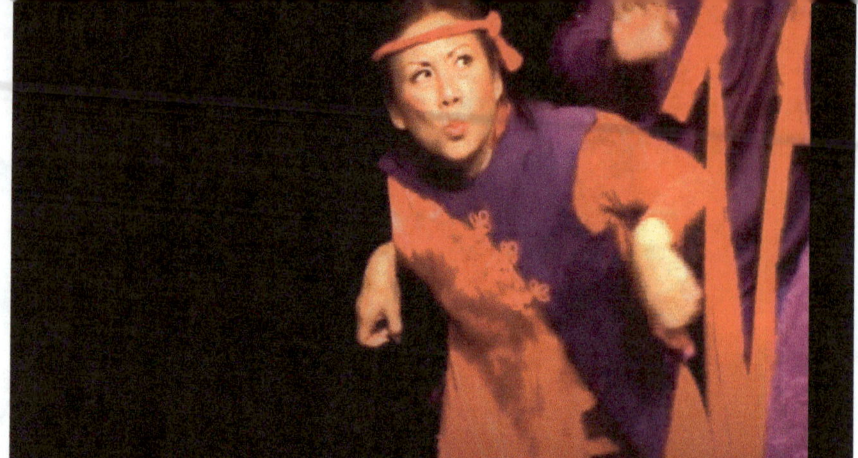

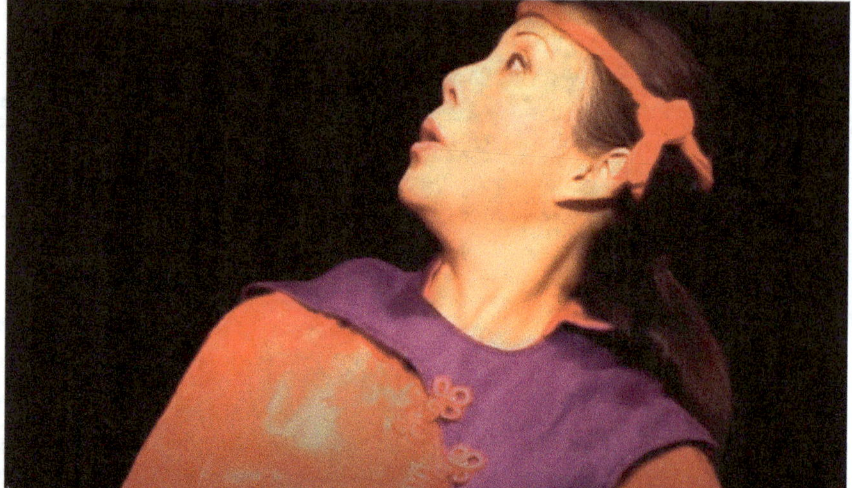

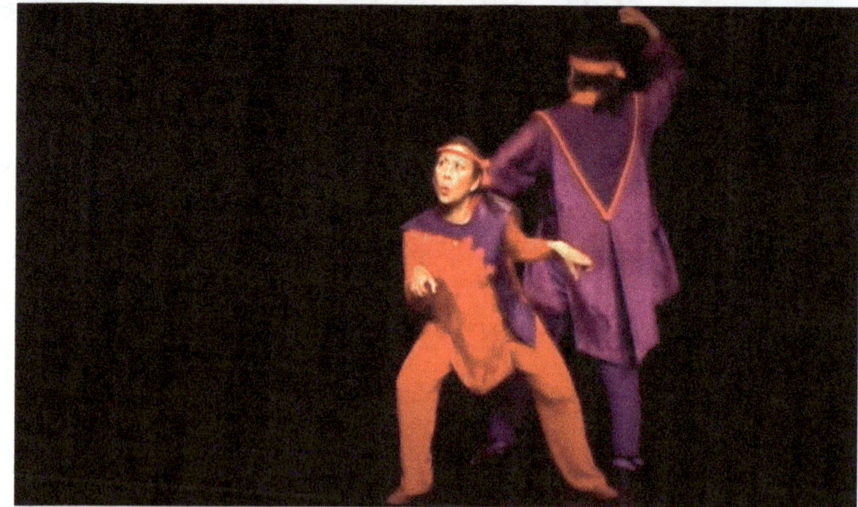

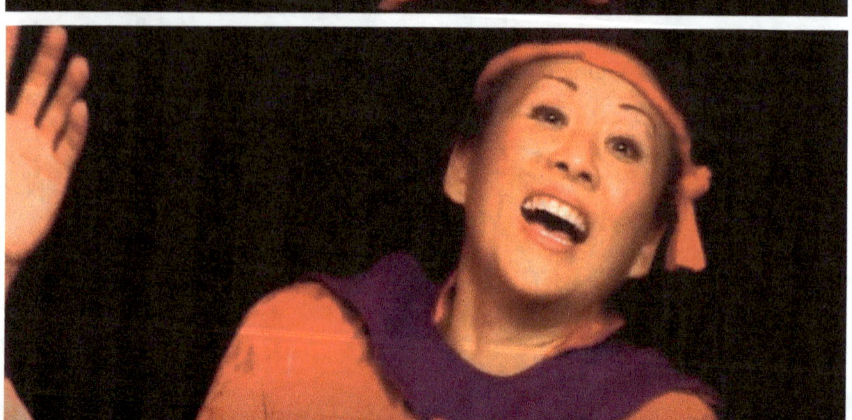

See the interview on page 119

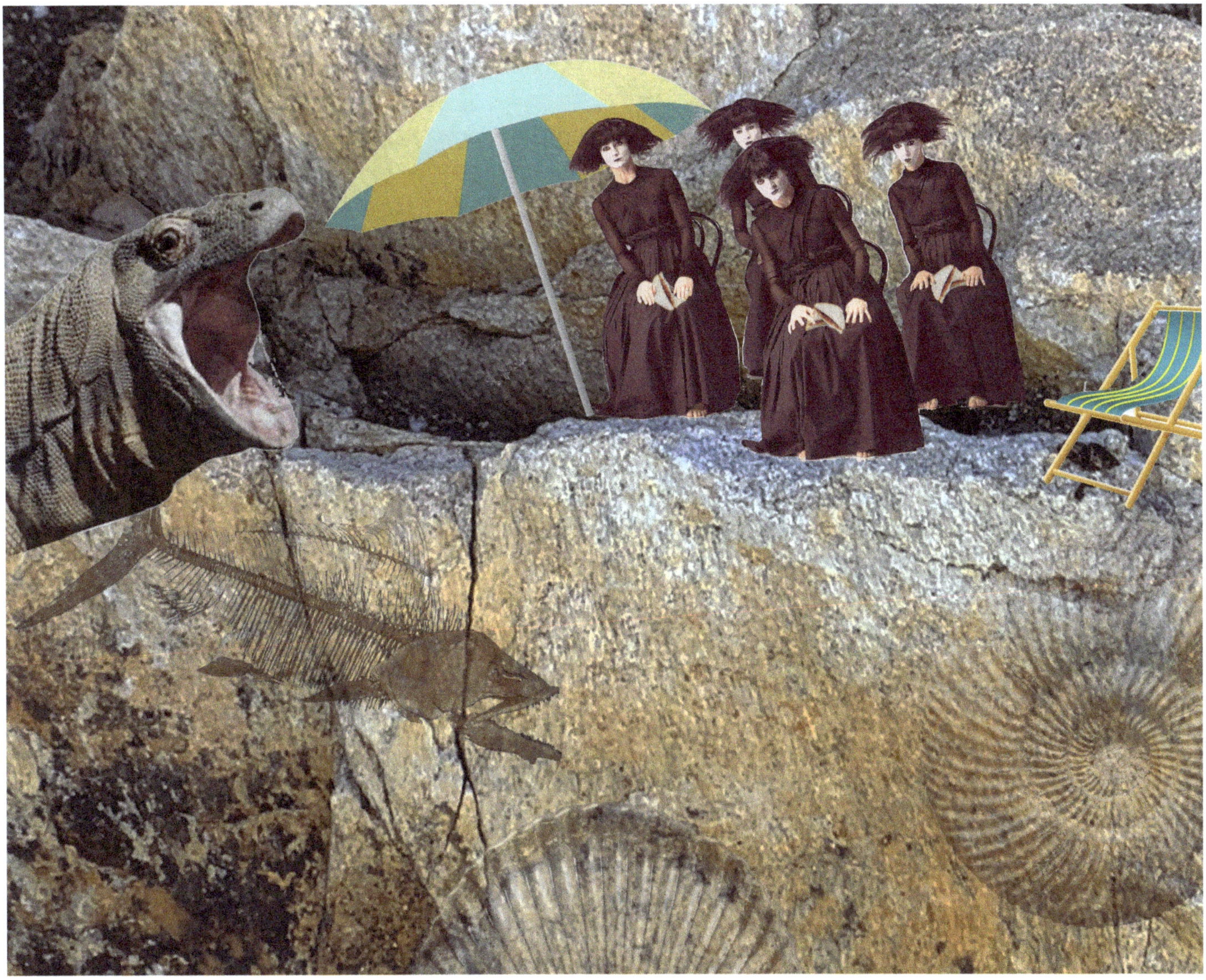

Wendy Tigerman, *Rockin' It*, 2021, digital collage

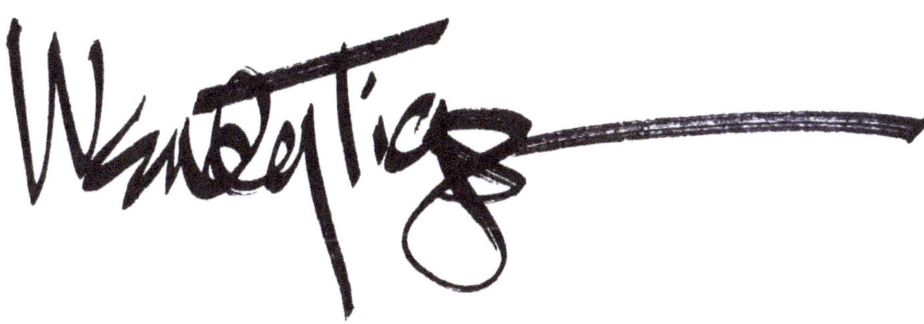

See the interview on page 125

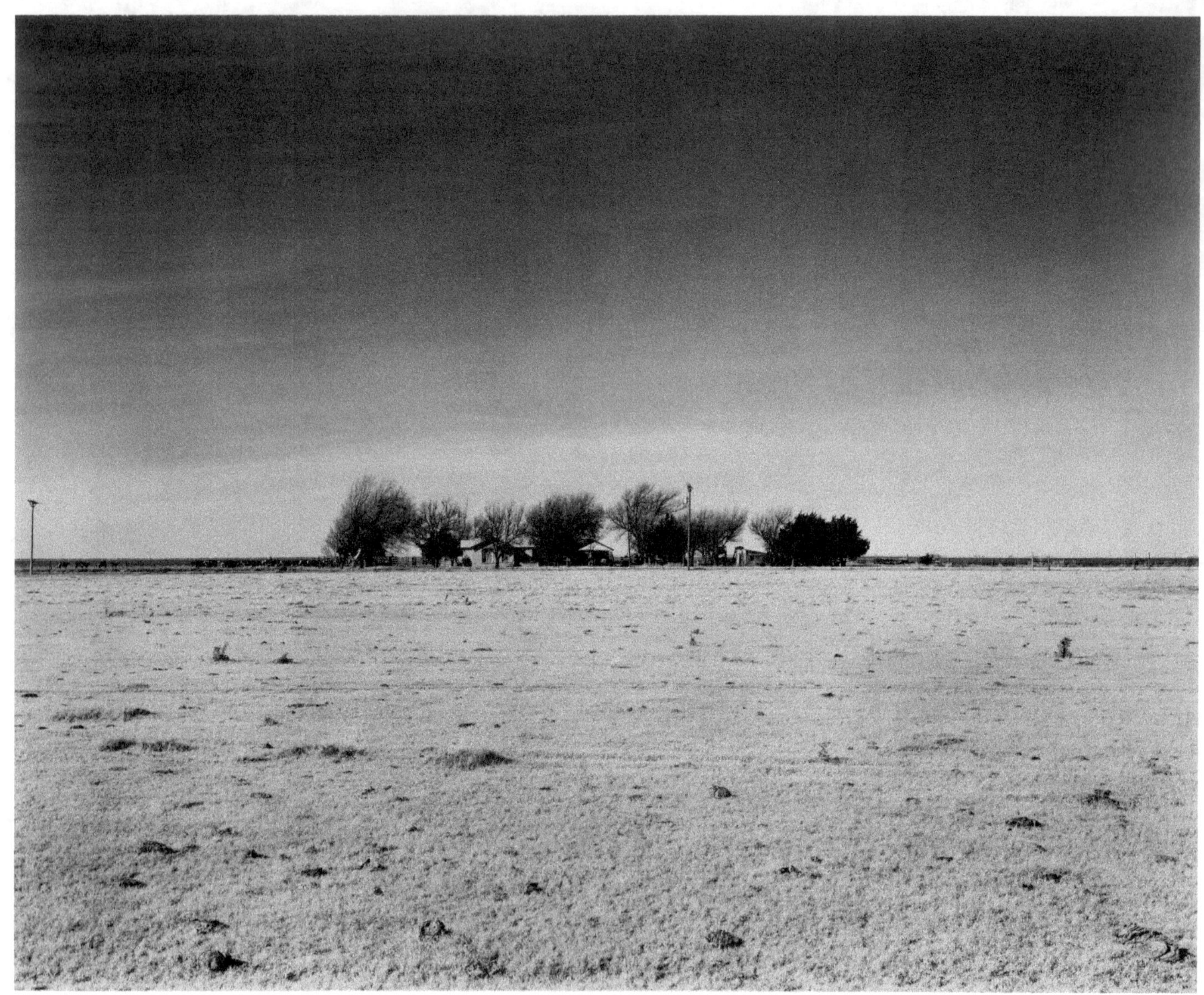

Paula Chamlee, from the series *High Plains Farm,* Adrian, Texas, 1994, 8" x 10" silver chloride contact print

Paula Chamlee

See the interview on page 130

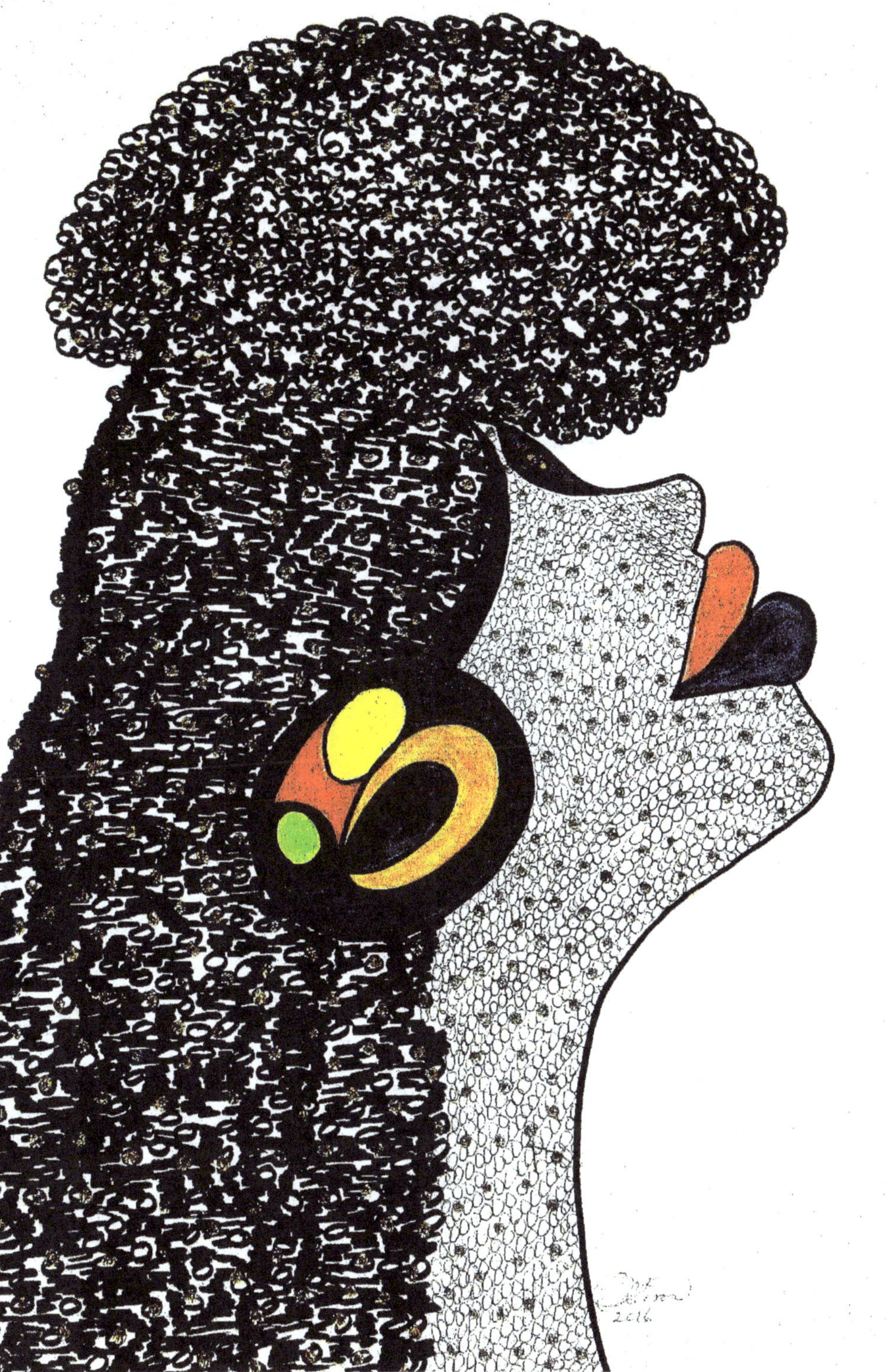

Rosemary Ollison, *Women of Color Embracing Their Individuality Proudly and Boldly, Taking Their Place in the Universe, Part A*, ink on paper, 12" x 18", 2016

Rosemary Ollison

See the interview on page 137

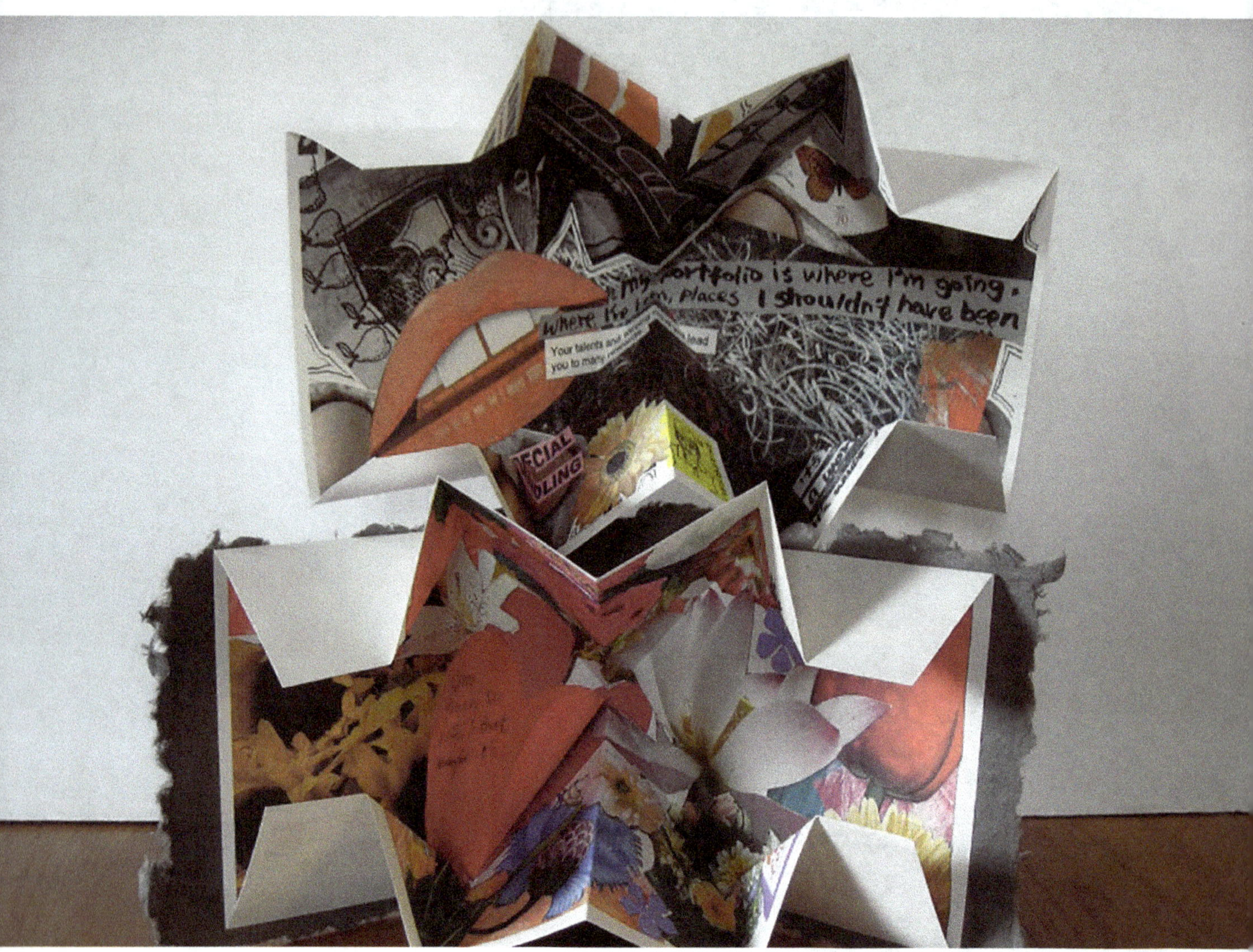

Gwyn Kirk, *Greeting Cards*, paper collage using Turkish map fold and card stock covers, 2020

Gwyn Kirk

See the interview on page 141

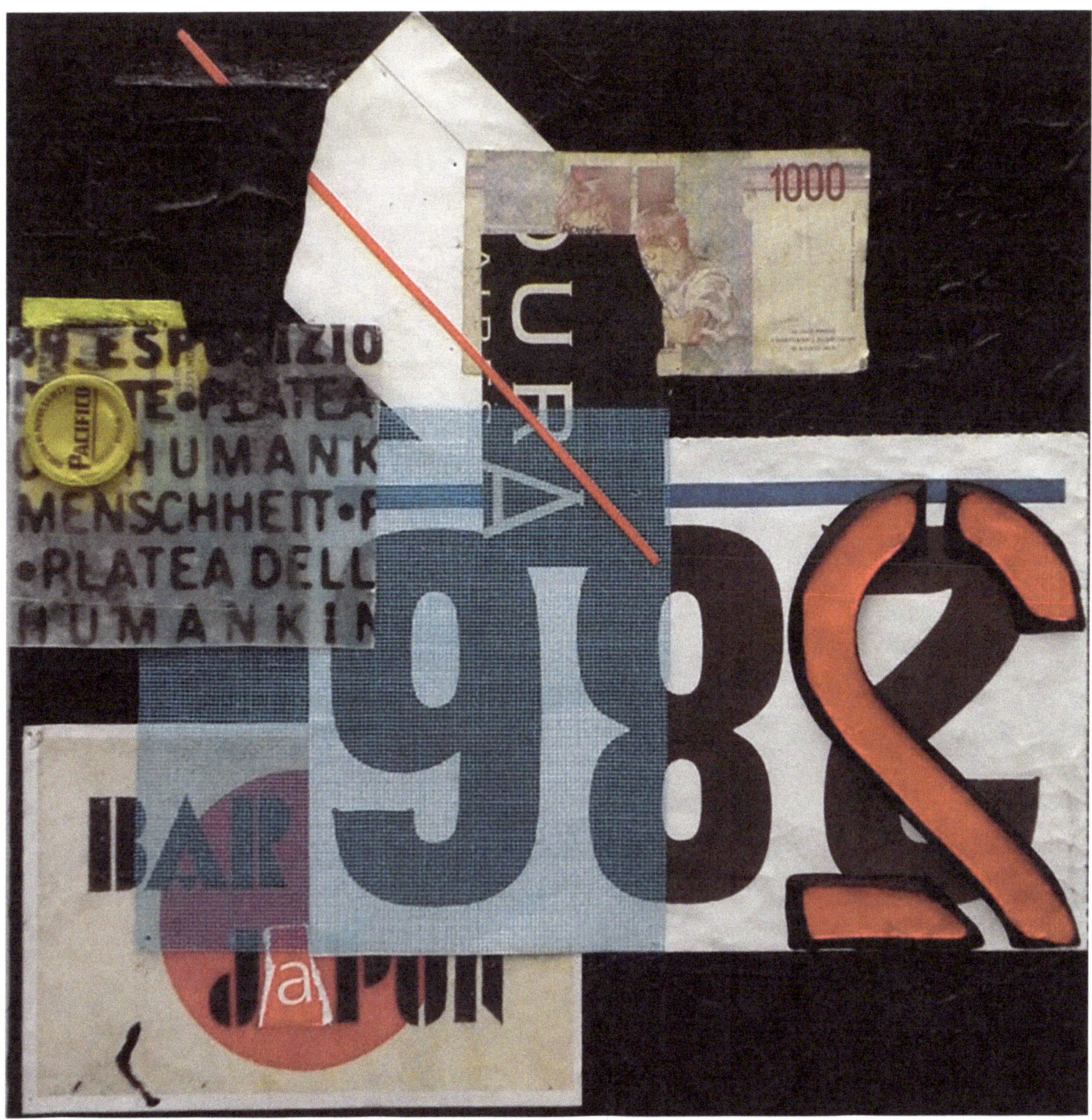

Launa D. Romoff, *Pacifico*, mixed media collage on canvas, 12" x 12", 2018

See the interview on page 146

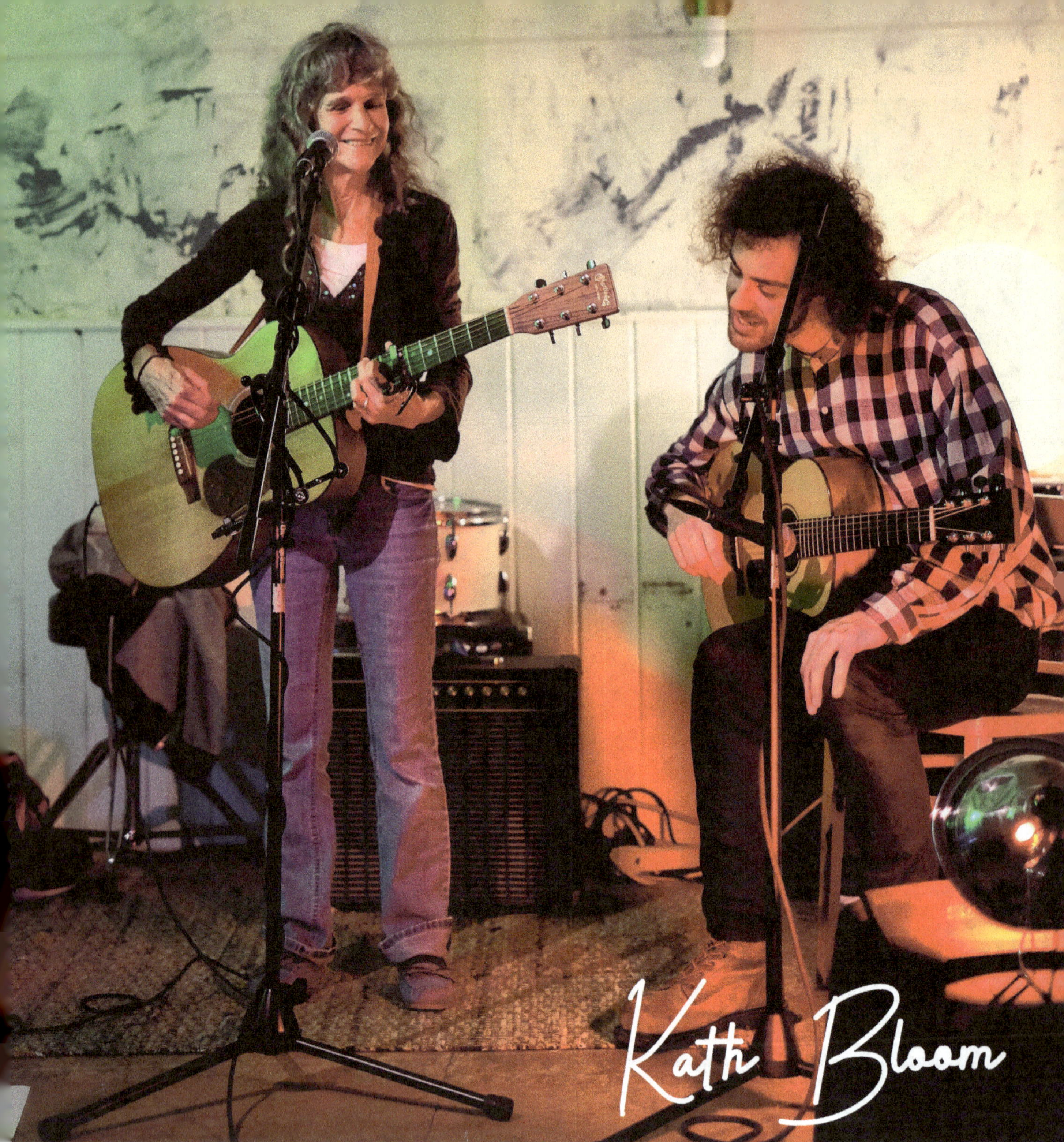

Kath Bloom, *Kath performing with guitarist David Shapiro*, 2018

See the interview on page 152

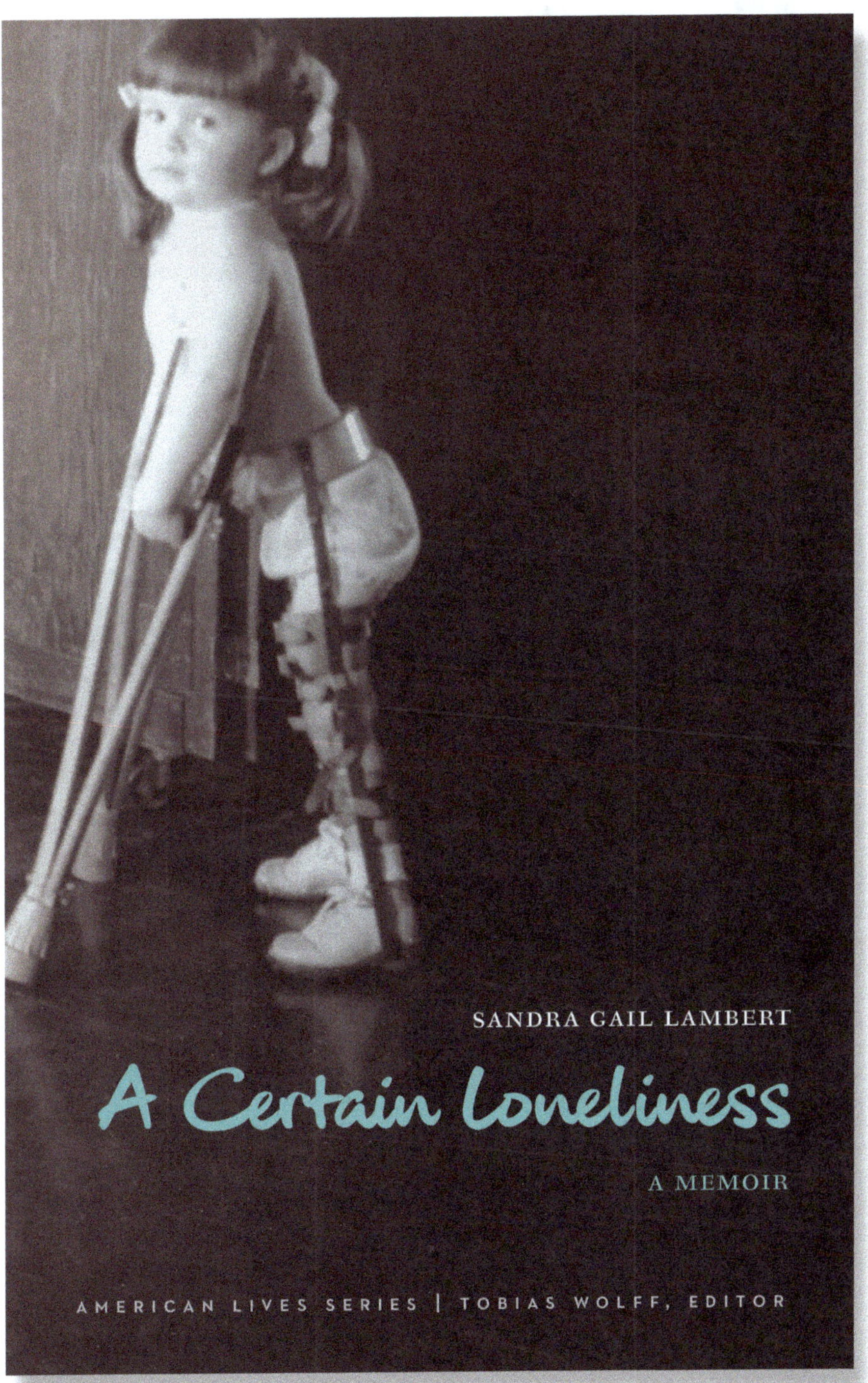

Sandra Gail Lambert, *A Certain Loneliness*, published 2018 by University of Nebraska Press

See the interview on page 157

THE INTERVIEWS

See *Mictlan Sur,* page 15

OFELIA ESPARZA

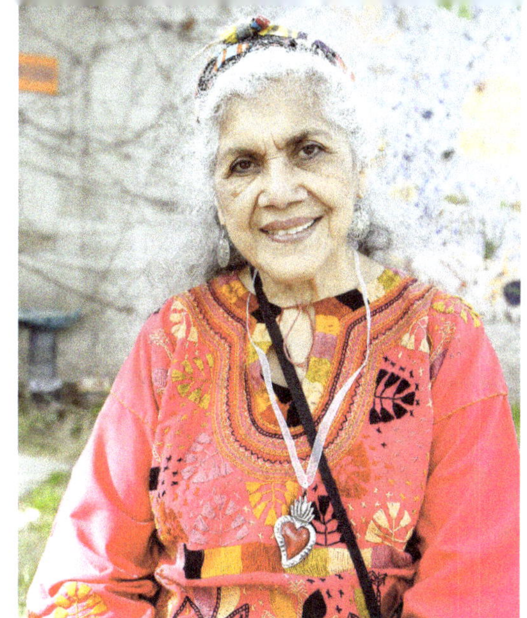

Master Altar-Maker | Printmaker
Place of Birth: Los Angeles, California
Current Location: Los Angeles, California
Age: 90
www.tonallistudio.com

ALTHOUGH I'M NINETY, I often say I see the world through seventeen-year-old eyes. I have so many visions of things I still want to do as more opportunities keep coming my way. By staying healthy, I hope I live another ten years.

I tell my children and grandchildren that I knew I was an artist since I was age six or seven because I was an observer of nature. I would make patterns on the ground as a form of meditation. We had a dirt yard with an umbrella tree that dropped long stems, almost like pick-up sticks, and I would use a rake to form them into designs.

I CREDIT MY MOTHER'S CREATIVE SPIRIT

We lived in an adobe house in East Los Angeles in an old neighborhood that was a hub of Mexican people. As a little girl, I carved a drawing of a house into the wall of the adobe. My mother called this my first drawing. She didn't scold me but explained I couldn't create art on the house like that. I started drawing on meat wrappings or whatever paper I could find.

I always credit my mother's creative spirit for influencing me and the way I see the world. She came from Huanímaro, a very small town in Mexico. It's on the Guanajuato side, on the border of Michoacán. She made altars throughout the year for Catholic observances of holy days. Most of these observances had been melded into that community's indigenous traditions and practices. It went beyond being a Catholic for my mother; it was a representation of her artistic spirit. These practices were a part of her, and she continued them later when she lived in the United States.

My mother made art out of paper, flowers, and whatever we had at home. She always had a garden. She used flowers she grew in her garden for her altars, and she made wreaths, crosses, and hearts from foliage and twigs. She was called upon by neighbors to create her handcrafts for weddings, funerals, and other celebrations. I learned these crafts, especially paper flower-making, from her. I was fascinated by the installation of her altars.

My mother's altars were humble, since she created them with what she had at hand. Her altar-making has been the biggest influence on my life, and it's the work I've been doing for many decades. Her largest projects that she was most known for in the neighborhood were creating *nacimientos*, which are Mexican nativity scenes. Her *nacimientos* were multi-tiered with hundreds of items, including toys added by me and other children. She would have ceremonies or activities and food to go along with the *nacimientos*.

I never knew I was poor growing up in East Los Angeles because we had food and so much joy. We ate homemade garden-grown food. I didn't even go to a doctor until I was thirteen. My mother used herbs or called in the neighborhood woman healer. I'm so grateful for my upbringing and all the memories.

TO MAKE LIFE INTO ART, YOU NEED TO CREATE

I was also influenced by my first beloved teachers in elementary school who acknowledged and supported me. They made me want to be a teacher. I was a strong student, and my teachers encouraged me to go to college. In high school, I took college preparation classes that we now call Advanced Placement. I also kept developing my work as an artist during this time. You could say I was self-taught, but I took some art classes along the way into my teenage years. I continued to draw what I saw around me. Once I started having children, I veered into portraiture using pencil, charcoal, and other materials I had at hand.

I did go to college after high school, since I was focused on becoming a teacher, but I didn't stay once I married and started my family. Art was still part of my life and my home. I knew that to make life into art, you need to create and hang things you make. The rain brought down some of the plaster of the home where I lived with my husband and children, so the slats of the ceiling were exposed. This bothered me, so I created paper flowers with my kids like the ones my mother

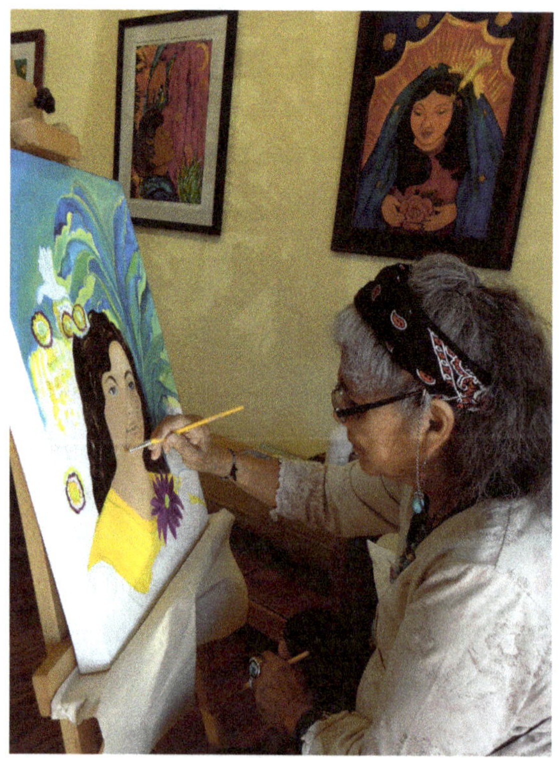

Ofelia painting *Diosa del Jaguar*, acrylic, 2015

made for her *nacimientos*. We made many of them, and I hung them with sewing thread from the exposed slats. It was like a mobile, and it went well with the exposed wood.

After I had nine children, I started taking night classes for core subjects, such as English. I also got a job as a teacher's aide at my children's school. It was a great opportunity. I was able to get into a program that supported those of us who wanted to go to college to become a teacher while working as a teacher's aide. Many others in the program had not finished high school, but I had, so I started going to college under this program to earn my degree in liberal arts. All this time, I was drawing, and I would submit my work for student exhibitions at the college. Once I graduated and became a full-time elementary school teacher in 1975, I taught art and was the art person at the school. I also had side-employment to teach other educators the art curriculum.

It was after I became a teacher that I started volunteering at Self Help Graphics in 1979. That was a significant turning point in my whole art career. Between the years of age forty-five to sixty-seven, when I was teaching, I started emerging as an artist. Self Help Graphics was just two blocks from my home. They were celebrating the Mexican Day of the Dead. At the time, it wasn't being celebrated anywhere in the United States as it is today. The director at Self Help was Sister Karen Boccalero, a Franciscan nun and artist. She studied at Immaculate Heart under the artist and designer Sister Corita Kent. Social justice was Sister Karen's mantra. This all fit into how I looked at the world.

I WAS AN ARTIST, BUT I DIDN'T THINK OF MYSELF AS AN ARTIST OUT IN THE WORLD

In my personal life, at school, and in my community, I was an artist, but I didn't think of myself as an artist out in the world. Sister Karen was the first person who acknowledged me as an artist in this way. I started doing Saturday workshops there for Day of the Dead. I worked with the artist Michael Amescua to make headdresses for the annual processions.

During the processions, we would walk to Evergreen Cemetery, which was about seven or eight blocks from Self Help Graphics. Following the processions, we would have a celebration in the Self Help parking lot. Inside the building, I also started to build altars with others. Of course, I knew about the practice from my mother. There were large community altars with several artists getting together to collectively create them. This became my art space as I developed as an artist.

In 1988, the artist Yreina Cervantez contacted me. She explained there was a call for an artist to make an altar at a gallery in the Little Tokyo neighborhood of Los Angeles. She recommended me. That was the first time I was officially hired to do something as an artist.

IT'S REALLY ABOUT CREATING SACRED SPACE

With my altar-making, I adhere to the traditional style of Mexican altars from the area where my mother came from in Huanímaro, Guanajuato, along the northern border of Michoacán. I always have the marigold tissue paper flowers formed into an arch. At times, I've created altars that look more contemporary, but with the same format and style. It's really about creating sacred space. Altars offer another dimension of aesthetics. They carry a message of a human practice that has been passed down from generation to generation for many centuries. They represent honoring, respect, and remembrance. Altars also build connections, bridging the living with the dead and bridging generations and cultures.

When Sister Karen died in 1997, I was asked to do a memorial altar for her in the upstairs salon at Self Help. This was the first monumental altar I had ever done. So many artists and people in the community brought *ofrendas*, meaning "offerings" in English, which gave me a lot of material to work with. There were fresh flowers, paintings, photos, and other mementos. The altar covered the whole stage in the salon. It even spilled down the raised stage to twelve feet around. It was phenomenal and beautiful.

During that time, I was also doing altars and workshops at Plaza de La Raza, which is a well-known art center in Lincoln Heights. After the director of Plaza de La Raza saw the Sister Karen altar, he said, "I don't want any small altars anywhere. I want a big one like you did for Sister Karen." For over twenty years, I created huge community altars there, and it has now

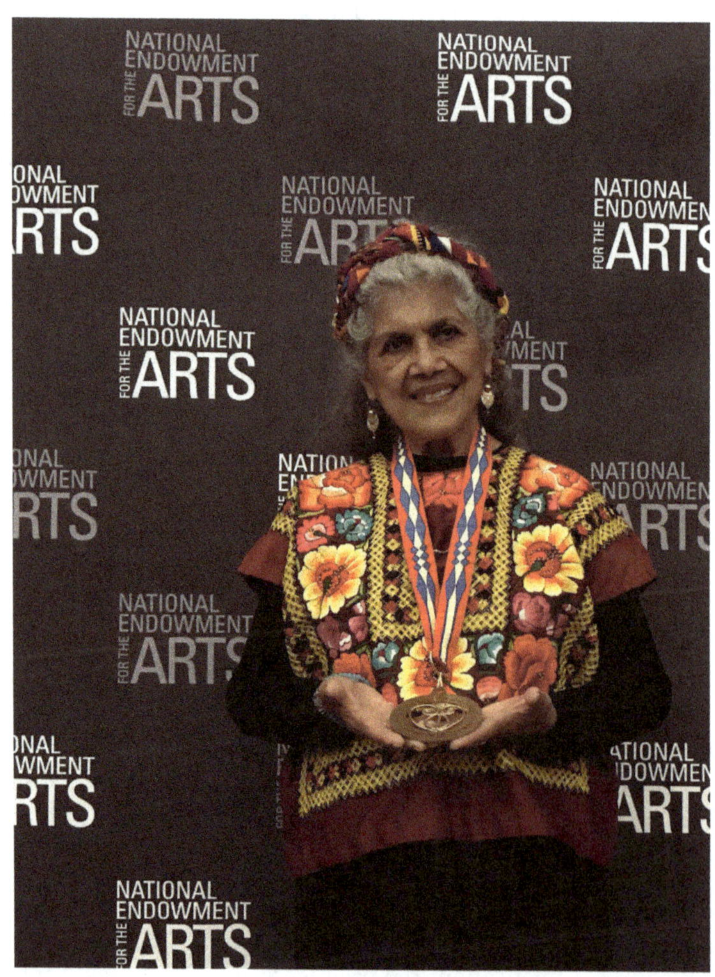

Ofelia receiving a National Endowment for the Arts, National Heritage Fellowship Medal, 2018

been forty years that I've been an altar-maker at Self Help Graphics. This work has taken me to so many places.

I have created altars internationally. In 1976, I was invited to create one for the Day of the Dead in Glasgow, Scotland. They had never celebrated the holiday there before. There was an artist exchange. Two artists came to Self Help Graphics, and I was one of three artists who went to Glasgow. It was a wonderful experience.

> THERE WAS NO DOUBT THAT I WAS GOING TO CONTINUE MY WORK AS AN ARTIST

So much has happened since the Glasgow journey. Over the past ten years, in my late seventies and eighties, along with my daughter Rosanna Esparza Ahrens, I've done huge projects and a lot of traveling. We created an altar at a folk art festival in Tucson, Arizona, two years ago. We presented our work as part of a big folklife celebration in Philadelphia. I've been in many museum shows, including in San Francisco and at the Museum of Latin American Art in Long Beach, California. I've created large altars in Southern California. I've gone twice to create altars in the National Museum of Mexican Art. A landmark project has been a permanent altar my daughter Rosanna and I installed at the Natural History Museum in Los Angeles in 2018. We also just accepted a commission for a permanent altar at the Plaza de La Cultura here in Los Angeles. The icing on the cake was the creation of an altar with Rosanna, accompanied by my children, at the Smithsonian National Museum of the American Indian in 2019. I was also honored as a National Endowment for the Arts National Heritage Fellow in 2018.

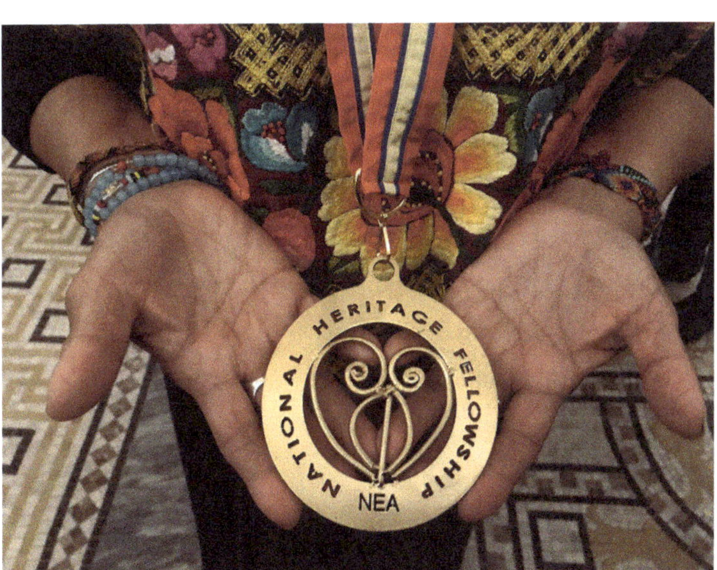

Ofelia Esparza's 2018 National Endowment for the Arts, National Heritage Fellowship Medal

When I retired from teaching at age sixty-seven or sixty-eight in 1999, after twenty-six years of service, there was no doubt that I was going to continue my work as an artist. My daughter Rosanna and I now have a small studio in East Los Angeles where we offer art workshops on painting and printmaking, but mostly, we teach paper flower-making and altar-making. We have other artists come in and present their work also. It's been a dream of mine to have such an art space here in my community. We opened the studio in 2012, and I look forward to picking things up again after the pandemic.

I also currently teach visual poetry and art at a women's prison with Rosanna. The women write poems and use mostly watercolors, but also acrylics, to create visual representations of their words. They also do portraiture. It's been life-changing for me to discover their experiences this way. The women are hungry to tell their stories.

ARTISTS NEED SUPPORT TO THRIVE

I have always had so much energy, and, of course, I've had wonderful support over the years. My mother lived next door to me. I don't know how I could have done everything without her. In my early years of motherhood, my husband and my oldest sons were also a great support. My husband passed away in 1991. And, of course, there is my daughter Rosanna. We collaborate, conduct research together, brainstorm, and create ideas. She renders our designs into a digital format, which provides my son Xavier the plans for foundation building. All my children are involved with altar-making, and they've received recognition as my apprentices from the Alliance for California Traditional Arts.

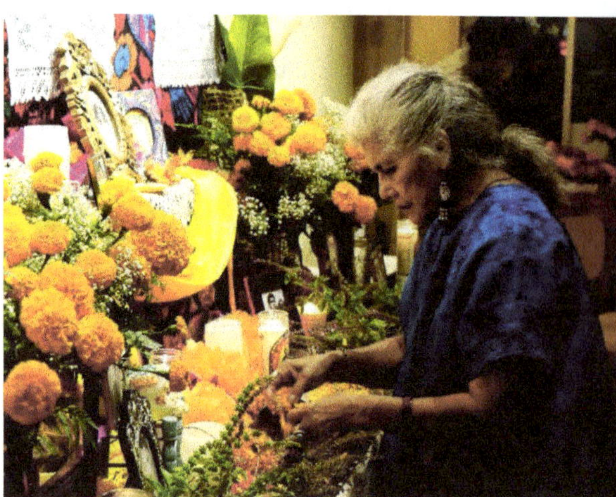
Ofelia creating a sacred space at Tonalli Studio, 2015

Artists need support to be able to thrive. To be an artist, there is the monetary element and the space element. I believe that being an artist stems from the passion to create. Some are fortunate to get an opportunity to show their work if they really want to sell it. Full-time artists need to be able to earn a living, but many cannot. They need to have another job to sustain them.

Exhibiting in a museum opens up so many doors to a wider public who might never see your work otherwise, but the museum system is very difficult to break into, especially for artists of color who may not be considered in the "mainstream." This includes Chicano artists, which is where I place myself in terms of my identity. I have been fortunate that the cultural aspect of my work has become of greater interest in recent years. One of the ways artists are sustained is by a grassroots art economy in our own communities, in addition to networking with other such communities and using neighborhood venues and shared art spaces to produce and sell art.

I WOULD MAKE ONE HUGE ALTAR

If I could do anything at this stage of my life with no restraints, including financial ones, I would love to do more printmaking. Many years ago, I learned printmaking at Self Help with John Montelongo. I created woodcuts, monotypes, and linocuts. I later traveled around to different states and Mexico to learn more. That's truly my favorite media. If I had the means, I would create a large piece. I think I've done four prints in the past eight to nine years. I'm hungry for more. I would like to create large format prints for altars.

Another one of my dreams before I die would be to have an altar at the Vincent Price Museum at East Los Angeles College, my alma mater in my neighborhood. I have tons of things in storage that I've collected over the years to use. I would make one huge altar there. It would be a statement about my life and work. ❖

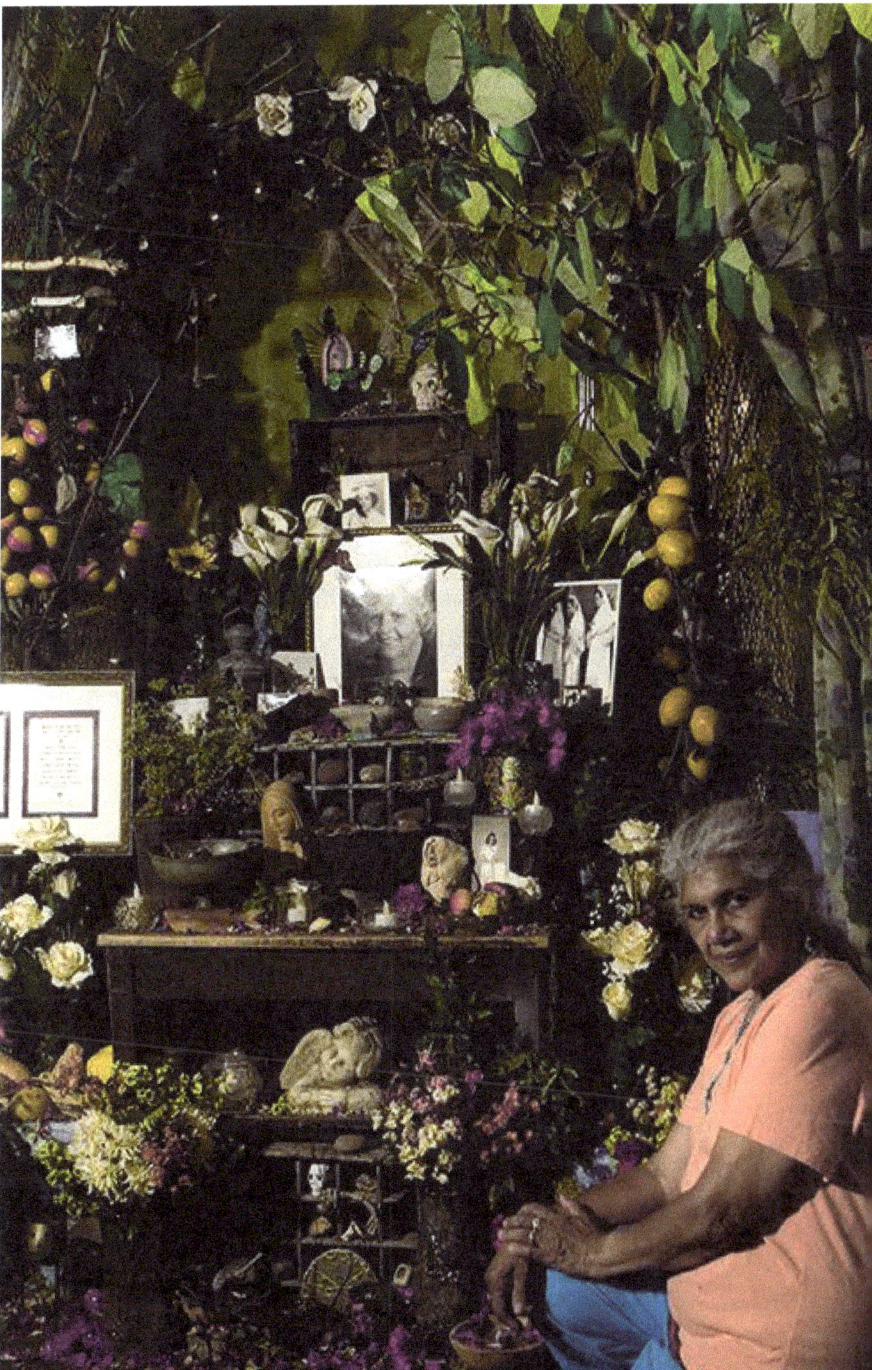

Ofelia Esparza and Rosanna Esparza, assisted by Xavier Esparza, *Self Help Graphics 10 Year Anniversary for Sister Karen Boccalero, Karen's Garden*, 2007

See *Still Life with My Father's Silver Bowl,* page 16

SUZANNE C. OUELLETTE

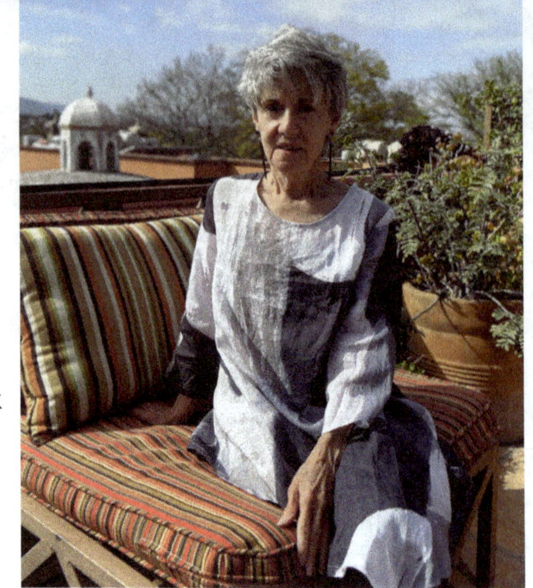

Painter
Place of Birth: Meriden, Connecticut
Current Location: New York, New York & Pine Plains, New York
Age: 74
www.souellette.com

ART PROVIDES A space where something new can happen. It also brings peace and joy that spread into other parts of life. I wish that as a society we better recognized and appreciated what art can do. It shouldn't be that a school cuts the art programs first when it encounters financial struggles. From the earliest of grades through higher education, art needs to be there and taught well. It is not enough for a teacher to be a wonderful painter or musician. She also needs to have exceptional teaching skills.

Making a sharp distinction between education in the humanities and education in the sciences is a problem. The best educated and probably happiest people are those who have been well-trained across many disciplines. Why shouldn't Leonardo da Vinci be an example to us all? I also worry about dividing the world into those who do things with their hands and those who do things with their minds. This often takes the form of the distinction between those who learn a trade such as carpentry or plumbing, and those who get a college degree. A higher value is placed on the latter. This is a mistake. Many people who work in the trades find great meaning in their work, and many people with a college degree are disappointed in their desk jobs, pushing numbers around, and being a little cog in a big incomprehensible wheel.

Perhaps the arts can free us from these distinctions. The artist is a wonderful example of a person working successfully and meaningfully across many disciplines, with both hands and mind. The artist confronts materiality while letting her imagination and creativity soar.

As a child, I loved to draw. Christmas was the best time because of the holiday cards. I drew all the images: Madonna and Child, winter scenes, holly sprigs. Putti—those chubby, frolicking child angels—were my favorite subjects. My father, who was responsible for magical holiday decorations, inspired me. As a young person, he enjoyed painting, but he came from a large family without a lot of resources. He was expected to start working early on to help support others. His interest in art was seen as frivolous. Nonetheless, he made art throughout his life, and he enjoyed working with his hands on many projects.

"YOU'RE TOO SMART TO BE AN ARTIST"

I was also a child intent on keeping everyone around me happy. Although I thought it wonderful to draw, many adults seemed worried and discouraged me. I remember being told, "You're too smart to be an artist." It was expected that I would go to college and graduate school to be trained for a career. After getting that message (going on to get graduate degrees in theology and psychology—you could say I really got it), my focus on drawing shifted to the sciences, literature, math, and so on. I continued to look at art and read about it, and enjoy friends who were artists, but I didn't have a real turning point and return to doing art until I took a Japanese ink painting class in my early forties at the Koho School of Sumi-E in the SoHo neighborhood of New York City.

The first time I completely immersed myself in art as an adult was in the Japanese ink painting class. Koho Yamamoto was a master painter and teacher. Her little studio was an amazing space. We would grind our own ink as meditation while she played Japanese music. A pigeon that she found on the street and now groomed roamed around the art materials. It was a grand, wonderful bird. Part of me wondered what I was doing in this entirely new world, but another part knew I was in exactly the right place.

[I] PAINTED ALL DAY … IT WAS HEAVEN ON EARTH

From then on, I practiced art in a more formal way. I took a very inspiring drawing class at Parsons The New School when I was around forty-five or forty-six. Once again, I found myself feeling like I was just where I needed to be. At the end of the course, riding in the elevator with the teacher, I asked her, "What do I do next?" The elevator doors opened, she stepped out, and before the doors closed, she said, "You do Parsons in Paris."

I rushed to the administrator's office to discover more about study abroad. I only had one day to decide. I was at the beginning of a sabbatical year from my academic job as Professor of Psychology at The Graduate School of The City University of New York (CUNY). My husband was going to be traveling for months for his work. It was perfect timing. I enrolled in a six-week full-time program and drew and painted all day every day. The first four weeks were in Paris, and the last two weeks were in the South of France. It was heaven on earth.

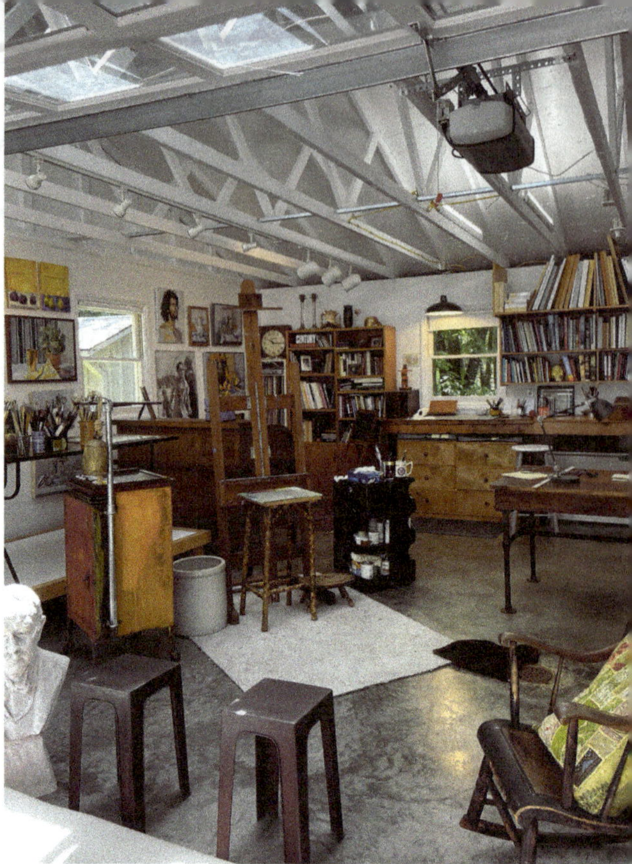

Suzanne's Pine Plains Studio, photograph of transformed garage, 2020.

I returned to New York and did fundamentals training at Parsons while completing the writing and research I needed to do for my sabbatical. I continued to take more art classes over the years, including training at the National Academy Museum and School. There, I studied with the brilliant painter Sam Adoquei, whom I consider my most important teacher.

The particular circumstances of my marriage enabled my pursuit of life as an artist. We didn't have children, and my husband worked in the theater. I attended art classes in the evenings when he was working. He typically had two shows on Saturdays and one on Sundays. That gave me more time in Sam's atelier training.

I WAS OVERCOME BY A SENSE OF CONNECTION

It was a busy dual life. As a tenured full professor, I taught a full load of classes, had research grants and publications, worked up close with many terrific students, and met administrative responsibilities. I loved many parts of my academic life. Working with the students was a real blessing; I had gifted colleagues, some of whom remain good friends, and when I joined CUNY, I had the best university president one could imagine in Harold Proshansky.

For the most part, I enjoyed a harmony between my art practice and my academic career and felt that one kind of work helped the other. Being a student again, I could better see and understand my students' challenges and aspirations. The study of art provided new, seemingly endless metaphors that improved my teaching (and living). At the easel, I could see how it mattered that I had studied psychology and religion for all those years.

Over time, parts of academic work became less appealing and engaging. I worried about the lack of jobs available to our graduating PhD students and the lack of funding for them during their training. There was not enough support from "on high" for the academic program we wanted to build. And the proverbial straw: my stint as head of the program taught me things about human behavior that I wish I had never learned!

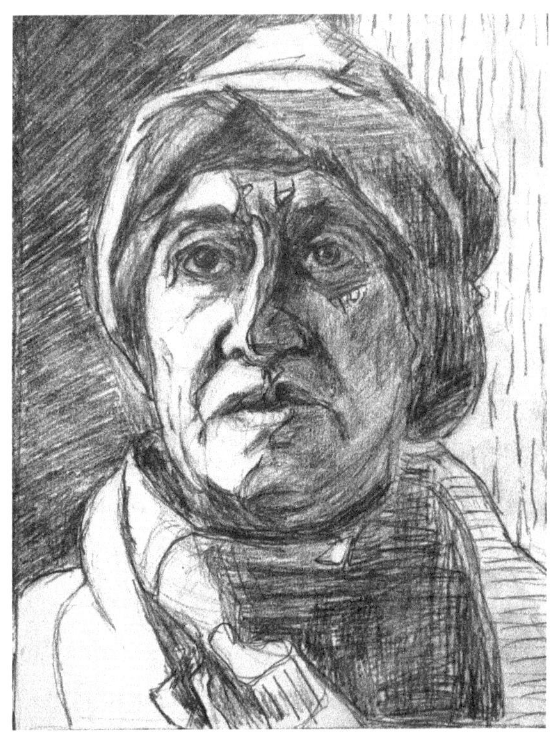

Suzanne C. Ouellette, *A Kurdish Alevi Woman*, pencil drawing, 9" x 6", 2019

The epiphany, the realization that I had to leave the academy, came in my garden in Pine Plains, New York, where we had built a retreat from city life. After an especially trying week of faculty meetings, I dove deep into garden chores. While weeding one of many perennial beds, I was overcome by a sense of connection with something much bigger than me, something very meaningful and transcendent. I knew instantly that I wanted to experience that feeling again and again in whatever I called my main work in life. I also knew that it wasn't happening at the university, but that it had happened in the painting studio. I had reached a point of not being authentic in my academic life, especially the administrative parts. I had been part of too many compromises in the university, but I experienced being as honest as I could be in front of a canvas. In my early sixties, I retired from the university.

ANOTHER AFFIRMATION CAME: "IT'S TIME FOR YOU TO HAVE A SHOW"

My retirement from academia was not what I imagined when I was a younger woman in my thirties or forties. I had envisioned reading student papers on my deathbed. It was a surprise for me and my students and colleagues when I decided to leave. Once I made the decision, there were times when I woke up in the middle of the night wondering what I was doing, but I kept receiving signs, blessings even, that I had made the right choice. For example, I needed a place to do a commissioned portrait. It had to be in the city; my studio in Pine Plains wouldn't work. A friend suggested that I contact an acquaintance, the recent widow of Saul Lambert, a well-known illustrator and painter who had worked in a marvelous studio atop their brownstone in Greenwich Village. I was a bit hesitant to ask, but Joanna agreed that I could use the studio to do my painting. The deal was sealed when a very large black cat, Saul's favorite cat not known for liking people, came by to lick my shoe. Many portraits and still life paintings later, I am still working in that city studio.

Another affirmation came when a woman who had worked in the art world and owned and ran a tea house/gallery in Northwestern Connecticut told me: "It's time for you to have a show, and I will present it." I thought, "What?!" but I went for it. I had my inaugural show and sold every painting. Best of all, the first painting was sold before the show, through an ad, to an artist working in the area and widely recognized as a painter's painter. Soon after that, there were more shows in other galleries in the Hudson Valley and Berkshires, and new homes were given to my work.

Since then, there has not always been such lively sale of my work, but I do not need that now as I did back then—and, as my teacher Sam reminds me: "You didn't leave the university and set up studios to sell paintings. You had a more important reason to paint."

I hope to continue through my seventies and beyond with painting at the heart of what I'm doing. I want to get better. I want to work harder and longer. I so love what I see in the world and then carrying that over into a dialogue with my canvas. I want to share what I see with others. This can be something as seemingly small as the handle of a teacup. I want to be more involved with other people's art: I want to look at a lot of drawing and painting, read poetry and other literature, listen to music, and attend theater and concerts again (yes, I am thinking post-pandemic).

I'M A BETTER PERSON BECAUSE OF MY PAINTING

I'm a better person because of my painting. I feel it has expanded my ability to do good things in the world. The honesty I experience in painting reaches beyond the easel into whatever else I do. I feel truer to myself when I paint. I even think I'm nicer to other people. Painting makes me feel more expansive. And there are also all these metaphors for life when we consider art. There's this pushing and pulling in painting. As you work one part of the painting, another part needs attention. Art requires that you put yourself out there, but you may find yourself needing to change the direction you are going. Sometimes, you need to pull back from a painting and then jump back in. I think that's what life is about too.

I've realized there are other parts of my life that are similar to painting. Since the pandemic began, I've been cooking a lot. I now see how cooking is like painting, including the attention to mixtures and composition and the making and giving of something new to the world. I want to hold onto this awareness after the pandemic is over. It's similar to the connection I see between gardening and painting. On the path to my painting, my gardening played a big role. In the garden, I felt that I was part of something bigger. That is how I feel with painting. There is a spirituality in it. I get lost in my gardening and experience the same with painting. Hours pass. It never feels like a waste of time. ❖

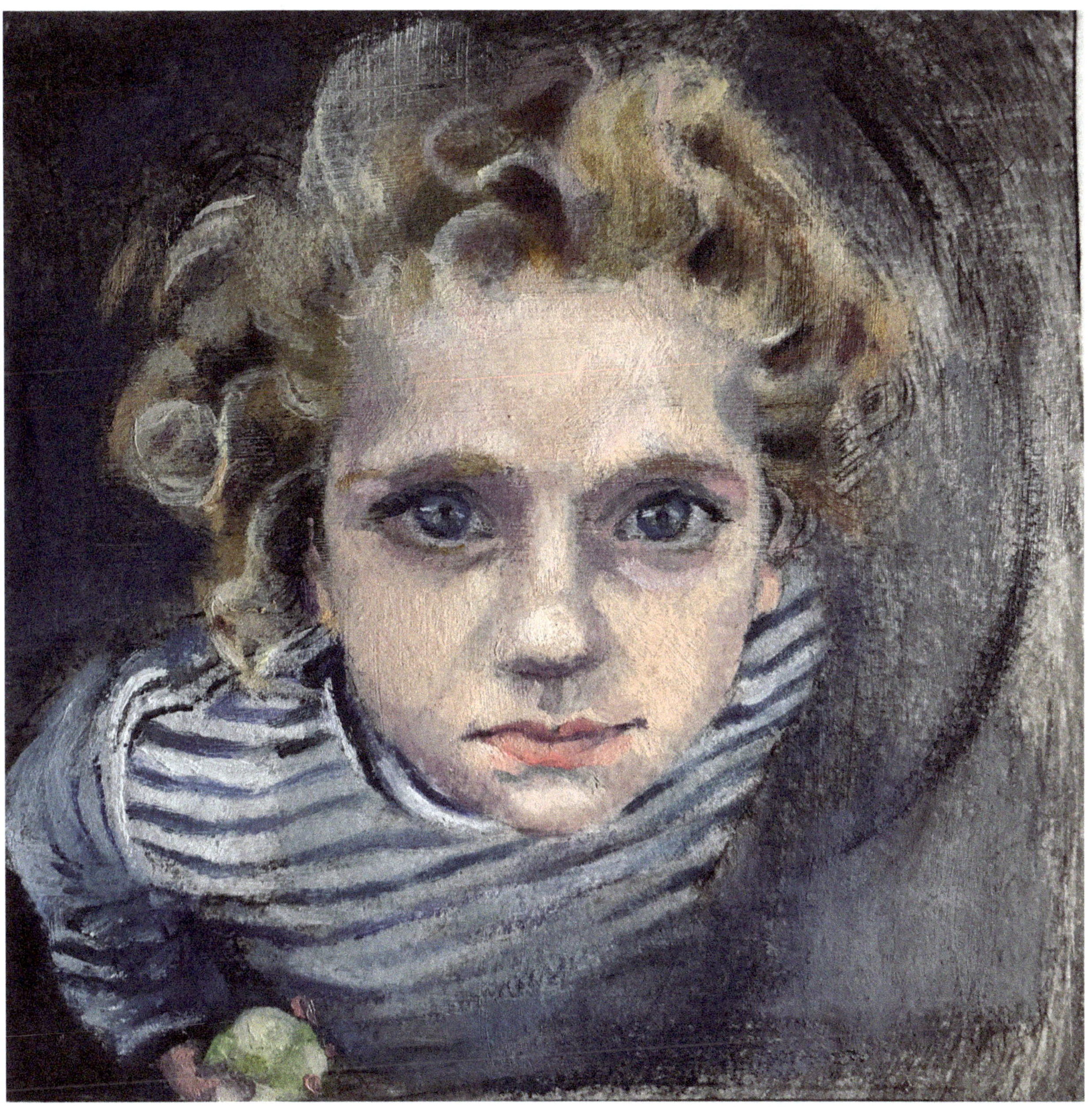

Suzanne C. Ouellette, *Yazidi Child in Community Fleeing Isis*, mixed media, oil over etching, 8" x 8", 2017

See *Frida Kahlo—Cuatro Libros,* page 17

SUELLEN COX

Collage, Assemblage & Book Artist I Poet I Gardener
Place of Birth: Grants Pass, Oregon
Current Location: Orinda, California
Age: 73
www.suellencox.com

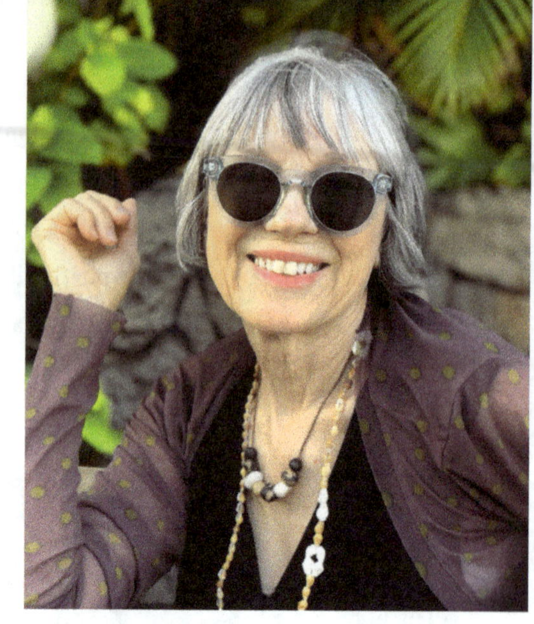

I BELIEVE I'VE always had the soul of an artist. I'm self-taught and do not have a degree in art, but since very young, I've been curious about the world and how things work and go together. Throughout my life, I've been interested in bringing a sense of order, symmetry, harmony, and beauty into an often chaotic, sometimes messy, yet always infinitely interesting life and world.

I didn't know what artists' books were until my daughter introduced me when she was getting her degree in book arts from Mills College. Book arts can be described as a form of art that is created to be interactive, portable, movable, and easily shared. A lot of artists will take an existing book and then reconstruct it and recreate it in some imaginative way. Some book artists don't begin with physical books. For example, I don't work a lot with physical books; instead, I make my own books. They may not look like your traditional book, but they have the quality or some of the intrinsic elements of a book, such as text and a cover. They can open and expand. Sometimes, they become sculptural objects. Certainly, several of the books I've created are sculptural objects. There is a famous book artist, Hedi Kyle, who refers to a lot of her creations as biblio-objects.

[MY ARTISTIC LIFE] BEGAN IN THE GARDEN

I was probably sixty-nine when I made my first artists' book. Long before this though, for most of my adult life, my artistic creativity blossomed and flourished when I started gardening around the age of thirty. I've created two gardens. The first one was at my home in Silverado Canyon in Southern California. My second garden is at my current home in Orinda in Northern California. Gardening has been one of the most enduring and significant things in my life.

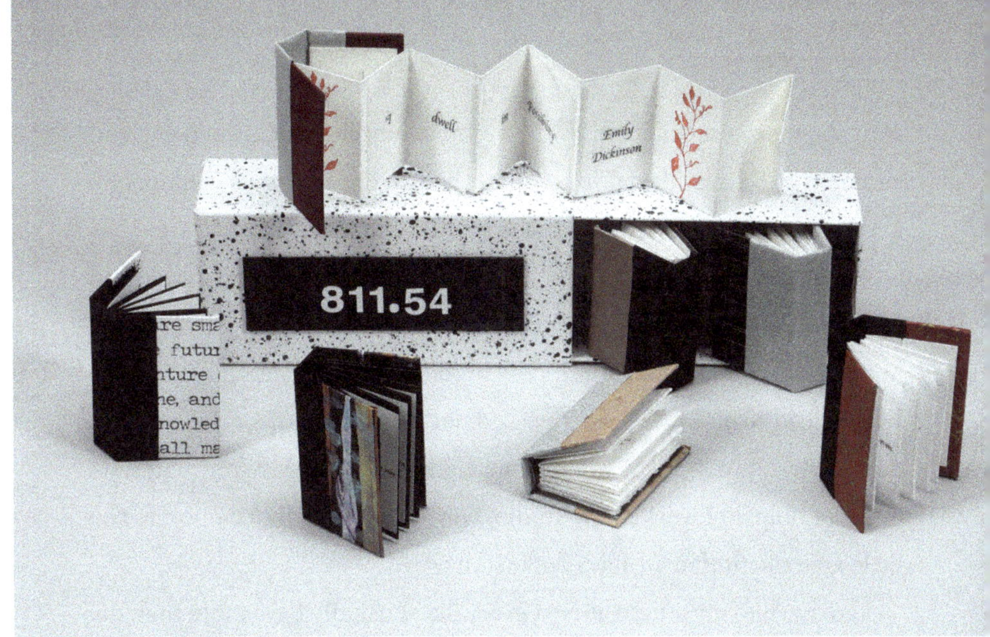

Suellen Cox, *811.54*, April 2019

Through gardening, I began to experiment with colors and textures and forms and scale. This is similar to a lot of things that you do when you're creating art. It was trial and error for me. Some successes, some failures. Early on in my gardening life, I referred to my garden as my canvas. I used California natives and colorful annuals and perennials. I considered them my paints and palette. I never thought about it until talking now about my artistic life. I know it began in the garden.

I think gardening also taught me important lessons that can be applied to my work in the art studio. It taught me a great deal about patience, especially in late fall and winter when everything dies back and you need to wait for the spring when things start to emerge again. It taught me persistence. My gardening also taught me it's okay to fail. I learned something may not work out the way you thought it would, whether it's color or the height of a plant next to several other plants.

My first garden in Silverado Canyon taught me how to deal with limitations, including a lack of sun for a certain number of months out of the year. I had to be very careful about what I planted, because some plants require much more sun for longer periods. My Orinda garden has offered different challenges. The clay soil is very hard, and I have much more sun here. I've had to utilize those learned skills of patience and persistence. Now that I'm older, I can't go out and work in the garden for ten hours a day anymore. That's been one of the hardest things for me. That also transfers to my work in the studio.

I GO DOWN TO MY STUDIO ALMOST EVERY DAY

I've developed some of the aches and pains of aging. The artistry and the rigors of gardening have naturally evolved into a more sedate form of creativity—if I can call it sedate. Working in my studio is physically more sedate, but making art is as mentally challenging and engaging as gardening. I'm still working with my hands to create order, symmetry, and beauty, but it's on a much, much smaller and more intimate scale.

About three years ago, we took part of the basement in my house and carved out a space for my studio. Before this, I was working on my art at the dining room table. I would be in the middle of something, and I would need to pick everything up and put it away if someone was coming over. Now, I have a space where I can walk away and leave my materials out. Not only do I work in my studio, but I've also expanded out into this little apartment that we have downstairs.

I go down to my studio almost every day. I usually have more than one project going at a time. This all started around 2016 when I made collages for a juried exhibition titled *Mark on the Wall* that was being held in conjunction with an international conference on Virginia Woolf. I've been obsessed with the Postimpressionist artist Vanessa Bell, who was Woolf's sister, for a long time. I've written some poetry about her paintings. I considered this a way to have a poetic dialogue with her and her art. She is not alive, so I cannot ask her questions, but the poems provided a way to connect with her on a deeper level. I created five collages using my poems and other materials that were in this dialogue with five of her paintings. These five collages set the stage for my current practice and this new phase of my creative journey. I've progressed to making more collages and doing quite a bit of assemblage.

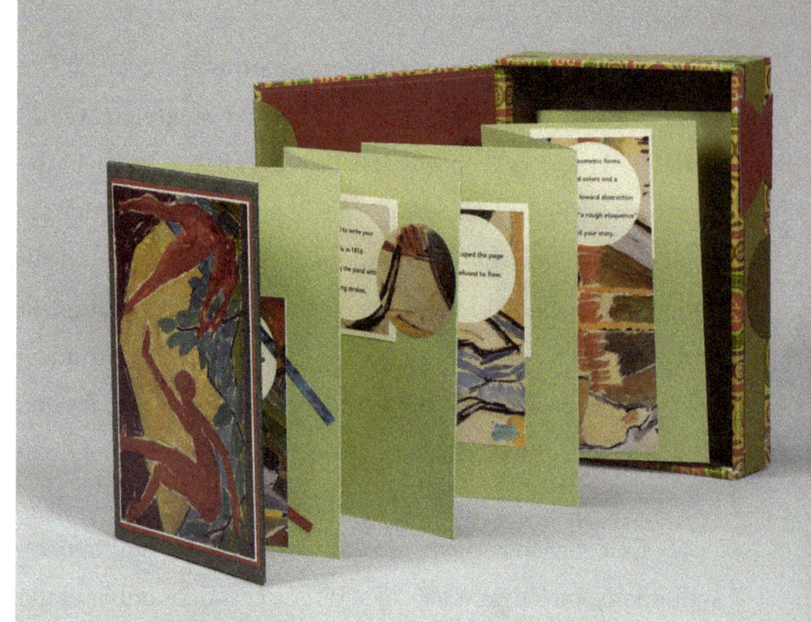

Suellen Cox, *A Rough Eloquence*, February 2020

Also in 2016, I suffered a bad back injury. Then, three months following the injury, I fell again and fractured three ribs. This put an end to my professional career as a librarian because I could not sit or stand for extended periods of time as required for teaching and working at the reference desk. At the time, I was working at St. Mary's College of California. I loved my work, the students, the faculty, and my

I HAD TO EVOLVE

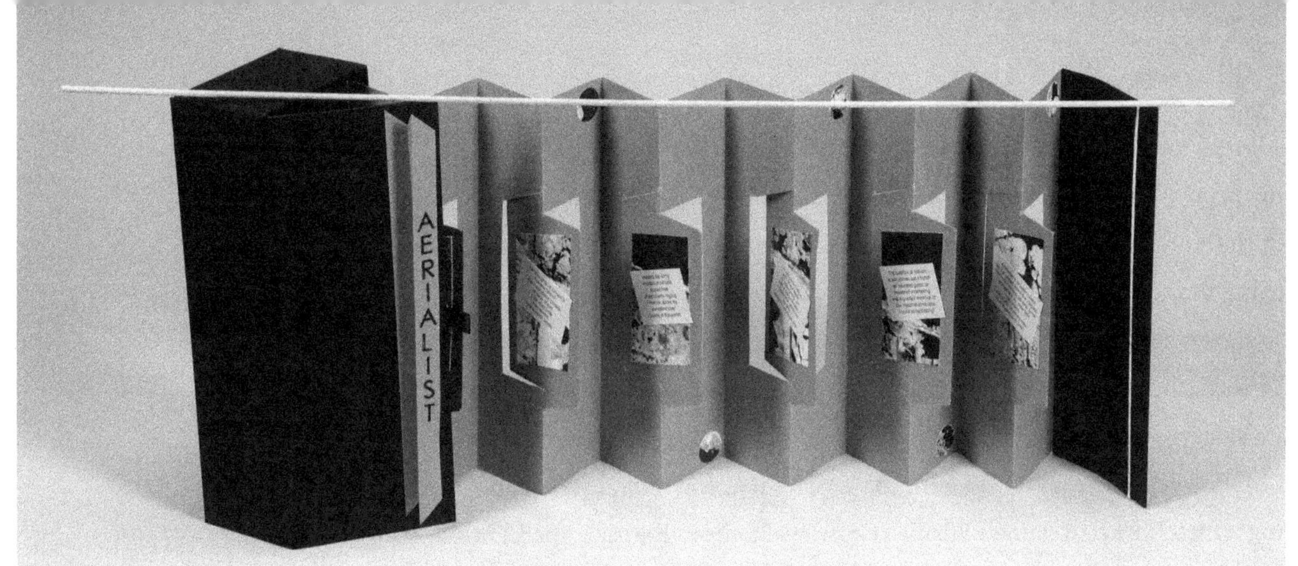

Suellen Cox, *Aerialist*, March 2020

colleagues at the library. It was just a wonderful environment. Although they wanted me back, even if it took a year, I knew within two or three months of the healing process that I wasn't going to have the physical stamina.

This reality of my professional career ending was very difficult. The assemblages I created in my studio for the next four to five months all had to do with vertebrae and broken bones. When I look back, I think I needed to address this issue. I needed to come to terms with my grief of no longer being a librarian. I had to evolve.

My love of books, libraries, poetry, and text is incorporated into almost every piece that I make. I've also always been analytical, methodical, and seeking a high degree of order and consistency, but my creative right brain has also been with me, attempting to break out. My orderly librarian brain is the first place I go, and I struggle with that, especially since I do not have a formal background in art, yet it is a strong part of me that I like things linear and nicely balanced. I'm continually striving to break out of that order and to allow some chaos and some of the unexpected to come in and surprise me. It's interesting to consider though that when I go to museums, my eyes, brain, and heart are more drawn to art that is possibly more ordered and less chaotic. There's something soothing about it.

I'M STILL LEARNING

When I was a younger woman, I imagined my life at this age. It is not at all how I imagined it. I saw myself sitting at a reference desk in a library throughout my seventies, eighties, and hopefully into my nineties. I imagined myself connecting patrons to information sources and recommending books to read. I feel fortunate that I had my professional life, since it was one that I just loved so much. Nothing in the world can compare to it. Being a librarian, I was learning something new every day.

Early in my career, I was working at Laguna Beach Public Library. This was before I was a librarian and even before I completed my bachelor's degree and went on to get a master's degree in English and then my library science degree. I was a library assistant at the time. I was working with a librarian named Bernice Crowley. I believe Bernice was in her early eighties, and she was sharp as a tack. She also had a beautiful sense of humor. She was probably one of the most well-read women I have ever met. She was immensely curious about everything. She was my role model. I wanted to be like her into my seventies, eighties, and beyond.

Anytime I thought about being older, I'd picture myself like Bernice, sitting at the reference desk. My life turned out quite differently than I expected. I'm no longer sitting at the reference desk in a library, but I'm sitting at my worktable in my studio. This is okay because I'm still learning. The materials and tools are different, but I'm still expanding my horizons and discovering things about the world and myself.

I think it would be fascinating to sit down with some of the women artists and writers that I most admire from the past and present—Artemisia Gentileschi, Hilma af Klint, Betye Saar, Shirin Neshat, Virginia Woolf, Adrienne Rich, Toni Morrison, and Louise Glück—and discuss their practices, struggles, and creative processes. At the moment, I don't know in what ways these conversations might change my creative process and journey. I do know that they would be extremely illuminating and inspiring.

I DON'T KNOW WHAT I'D DO IF I DIDN'T HAVE MY ART

Hopefully, my art will continue to evolve throughout my seventies and beyond. Perhaps this will happen in unexpected ways that I can't even imagine today. I would have never thought that those five collages I created in 2016 would lead to the work that I'm doing now. It will be interesting to see where it goes from here. Coming out of my long professional career as a librarian, I have a deep desire for learning. There is an inherent connection between libraries and lifelong learning that is within me.

I hope to still be creating pieces that challenge my mind, give me joy, and provide a space to offer others a sense of discovery and inspiration.

I think the most difficult thing I have to come to terms with is that I can't physically spend hours in my studio. This is a frustrating thing because the ideas come so fast. I can work for a while, and then I need to stop and give my back a rest, but my mind is buzzing and brimming.

My mind is willing, ready, and engaged, but my body may refuse to cooperate. This makes it hard to stay in that state of flow that is so important to the creative process. Still, I have things set up in a way where I can work on my art for a certain period of time and then, while lying flat on my back, I can work on one of my several writing projects. I alternate between art and writing. This has been a way for me to continue to feel creative.

If it wasn't for my art, I don't know if I would be here. Sometimes, I feel that my back injury and the degenerative discs I deal with have been a gift, because this experience has channeled me in a different direction. It has allowed me, through my art, to evolve and to keep my mind engaged in challenging and difficult design problems. Because I can't get out and work in the garden as much as I would like, art has given me an outlet to still work with color, texture, and form. I don't know what I'd do if I didn't have my art. ❖

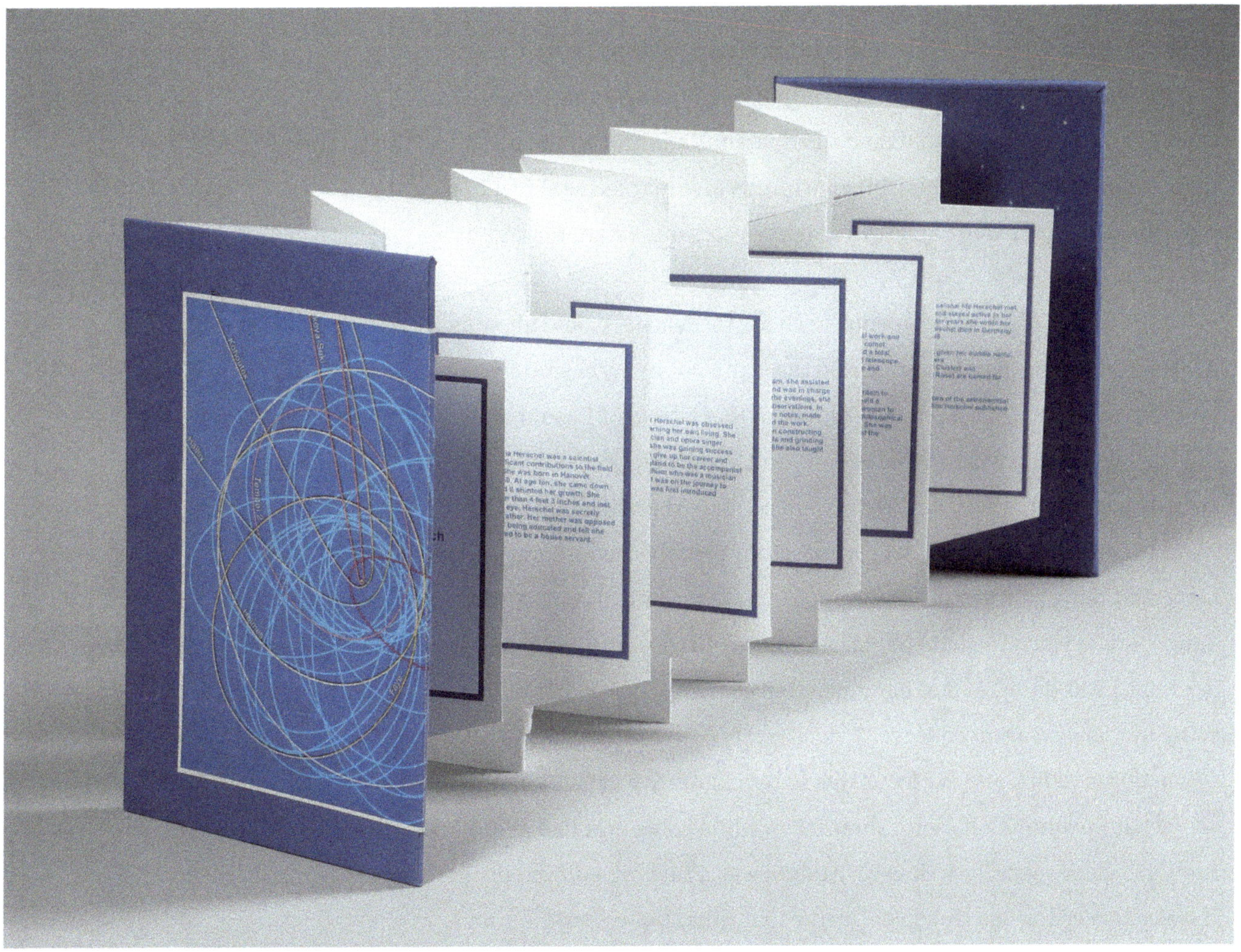

Suellen Cox, *Caroline Herschel*, April 2020

See *Waiting For My Set I,* page 18

JUDY BOWMAN

Figurative Artist I Collage & Pastel Artist
Place of Birth: Detroit, Michigan
Current Location: Romulus, Michigan
Age: 70
www.judybowman.com

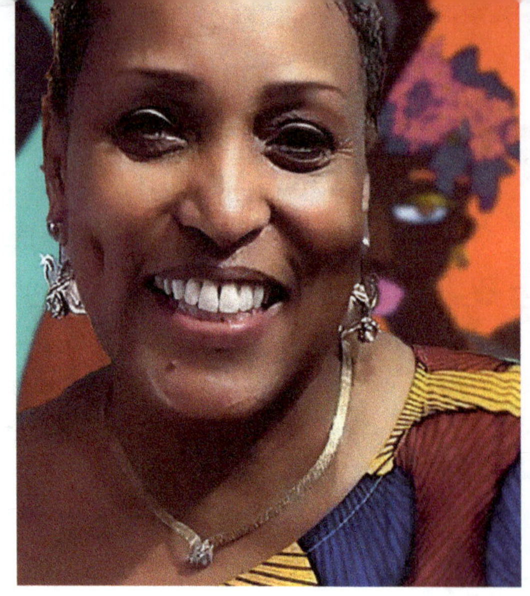

I AM SATISFIED with my art practice at this time; however, if I had no constraints and could do anything, I would love to have a large studio space with good lighting and high ceilings. This would allow me to create larger pieces of art and installations. I think being able to experiment in a larger space could possibly change or improve my current art practices. As I imagine what else I could do if I had no limitations, I would also have a team to help with publishing, printing, and marketing. I feel I am exploring the world of art and trying to navigate where I am now. I am still taking baby steps.

In the first grade at my elementary school, the teacher would allow us to draw on the blackboard. I loved the way a girl in my class drew, and I wanted to do what she did. I didn't know at that time that I could draw, so I started copying what she was doing, and I realized, "Hey, I'm an artist. I can draw as well as she can." That is when I started getting into art.

HEY, I'M AN ARTIST

As I grew older, I went to art classes at our neighborhood library. Then I started taking summer classes at the Detroit Institute of Art on Saturdays. I would catch the bus there from where I lived. I was really enjoying what I was doing. When I graduated from high school, I knew I was going to major in art at college.

I majored in art, and my focus was to be a figurative artist. I studied art at Spelman College for three years while being enrolled at Morris Brown College then Clark College. Atlanta was a turning point in my life. It was a mecca for Black people. During that time, I saw the power and beauty of art. I saw Black people of all kinds, and Black leadership was

I SAW THE POWER AND BEAUTY OF ART

prominent. It was quite common to see civil rights leaders in everyday situations and to speak to them.

Artist Benny Andrews was one of my teachers. I did not know Benny was a renowned artist at the time until I later came across his name in art books. Another experience I had was working with Coretta Scott King and Alberta King. They wanted an artist to take Dr. King's quotes and put them into an art form. They selected me. I was nineteen years old! These early moments showed me the beauty of art and how it introduces you to so many people that you would not run into in your ordinary life.

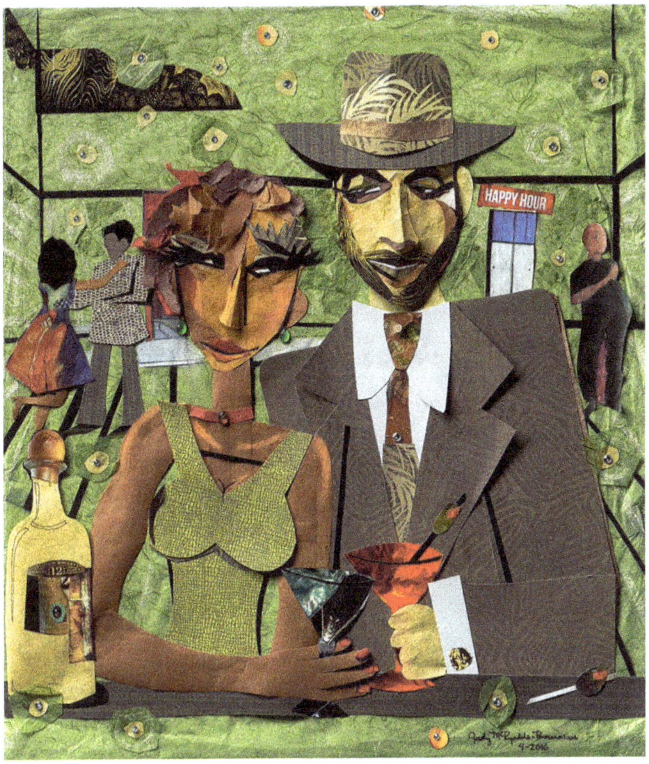

Judy Bowman, *Happy Hour*, mixed media collage, 2016

My college experience was different from most other people because I was married at the age of eighteen. I did not live in a dorm. I lived in married student housing. I also had a baby when I was nineteen. I was going to college, but I did not quite feel like I was in college. Instead of going to my classes and going back to my dorm, I would go home to married life, but that was cool too!

In my senior year, I moved to Flint, Michigan. There, I enrolled in the University of Michigan-Flint. It was only a small satellite school and, at that time, without an art department. By the time I was twenty-five, I had four children. It took me ten years to finally complete my degree in general studies, and then I returned to school for a teacher's certification.

While in Flint, I met a group of artists. I would make art with them, and it felt so good to do my art again. Over the next few years, we added six more children to our family. We had a full household with ten children. That basically put an end to me doing any art. I had to get a "real job" to help pay the bills. I was so busy with my children, my teaching career that led to me becoming a principal of the Detroit Academy of Arts for grades K-2, and being a wife that there was no time to create art. When I retired from education, after a gap of thirty-five years of doing no art at all, I said to myself, "I wonder if I can still do my art."

I WANTED TO BE WHAT I FELT I WAS CREATED TO BE

It was not anything that happened that made me think of my art. I went back to it because I wanted to be who I was supposed to be. I wanted to be what I felt I was created to be. There is something special about being an artist. I believed I was given a gift and I was ordained to use it.

In my late fifties, I started where I had stopped. I returned to making portraits. I would create images of faces in pastels. I wanted to create larger work but didn't know how to make large pastels. I believe the largest pastel I created was about twenty-six by thirty. However, I found some bright and colorful papers at a store. I said, "Well, I'll use these and start doing collages." That is how my collage art started. I self-taught myself. It was a big change from my pastels. Most people now identify me as a collage artist.

When I started making the collages, a whole different audience appeared that appreciated my collages. My collages seem to resonate with people. Most of the ideas in my collages come from my community and my family. I was strongly influenced by the works of Charles White and how he depicted images of Black people as strong, soulful, and dignified. Even in a cotton field or a similar situation, they still have a presence about them in his work. I was motivated to make Black people look the way I see and feel us. The narrative that is often depicted is that we are such a downtrodden people. That is not how I was raised, and that is not at all what I saw in my community. I wanted to create a narrative of us as a mighty people, so that is what I did and what I continue to do.

I WANTED TO CREATE A NARRATIVE OF US AS A MIGHTY PEOPLE

Some people say that the east side of Detroit, where I was raised, is such a horrible, terrible place, but in my community, everybody had a mother and a father. The fathers went to work, and the mothers stayed home to raise their families. There was dinner on the table every day. As a child, I would set the table. It was so different from the books that I read and the way I saw things depicted on TV. Some artwork always shows us as sad. We weren't sad at all. We had parties and celebrations. We took trips together. The people in my family had a thing about dressing up and being dignified. Even though my father was a factory worker, his goal was for us to graduate from college. All of this is what I portray in my art.

Judy Bowman, *Lafayette and McDougall, Black Bottom Series*, mixed media collage, 2020

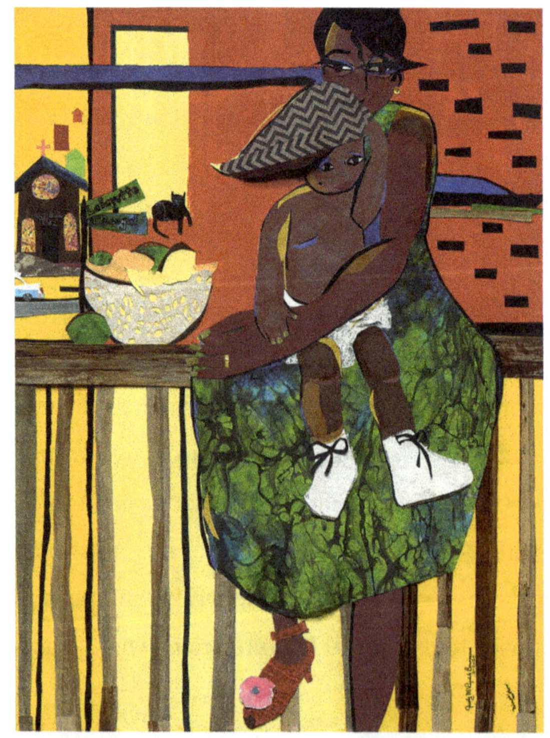

Sometimes, at art shows, I do not identify myself as the artist so I can listen to the different comments made about my work. I feel so good when people get it. I will hear them say that what I portray in my art was also their experience. It is as if my art transports people back to a time of proud and happy memories.

If I could help others become artists in the United States through legislation, I would make changes to the K–12 grade curriculum to make fine arts a mandatory requirement. As a former principal of a school that placed high emphasis on fine arts, students who were not always book smart had an avenue to shine when they received affirmation from their dancing, drawing, or singing. We found that these students became more engaged in school when their skills in the fine arts were acknowledged and celebrated. This curriculum I'm imagining would also include learning the business of art, curating, and marketing. I believe this change would increase students and parents seeing art as a viable career choice.

MY GOAL WITH MY ART IS TO LEAVE A LEGACY

My goal with my art is to leave a legacy. I don't want to come to this earth, die, and that's it. I want to leave something behind that people can feel, see, touch, and know that I was making a statement. I am visually telling a story of what I've seen during my time on earth. I see my art as a narrative for others to show we are powerful, beautiful, and can do and be who we are meant to be. I know this to be true.

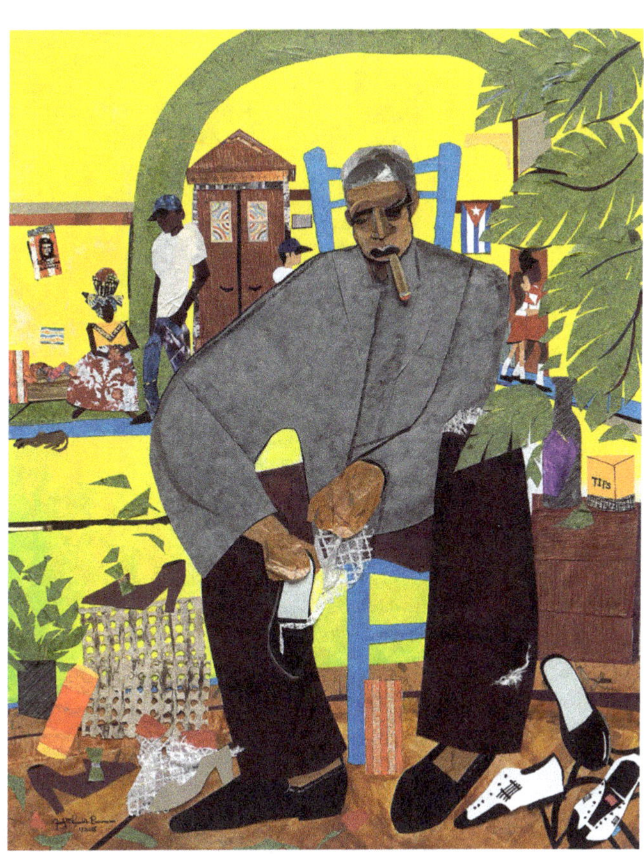

Judy Bowman, *Havana Shoeshine Man*, mixed media collage, 2018

When I think of the future, I want to be like Samella Lewis and Artis Lane who are viable artists working in their nineties. They are still making a difference. I feel like I was given a gift, and I do not want to waste it. I want to make an impact and document that I was here. I want my art to tell the story.

I want to be in museums across the world so my family and future relatives can come and say, "That's my great-great-great-grandma." I want them to know that I am in them. I want them to look inside of themselves and know that they can be what they are created to be, because I did it. But even more than that, I want to change the narrative of how Black culture is portrayed in America. I want to share the Black culture I see and live—one of pride, family, and community.

I am a walking statistic. I married at eighteen. I am Black. I am a woman. I had ten children. These were all strikes against me, but I still became an artist. I am who I knew was in me, my true self, even when obstacles got in my way and life brought its challenges. I kept moving forward. I kept being what I am supposed to be. So, I am saying to you, keep putting in the work, and when you do what you are supposed to be doing, doors will open. You WILL get there! ❖

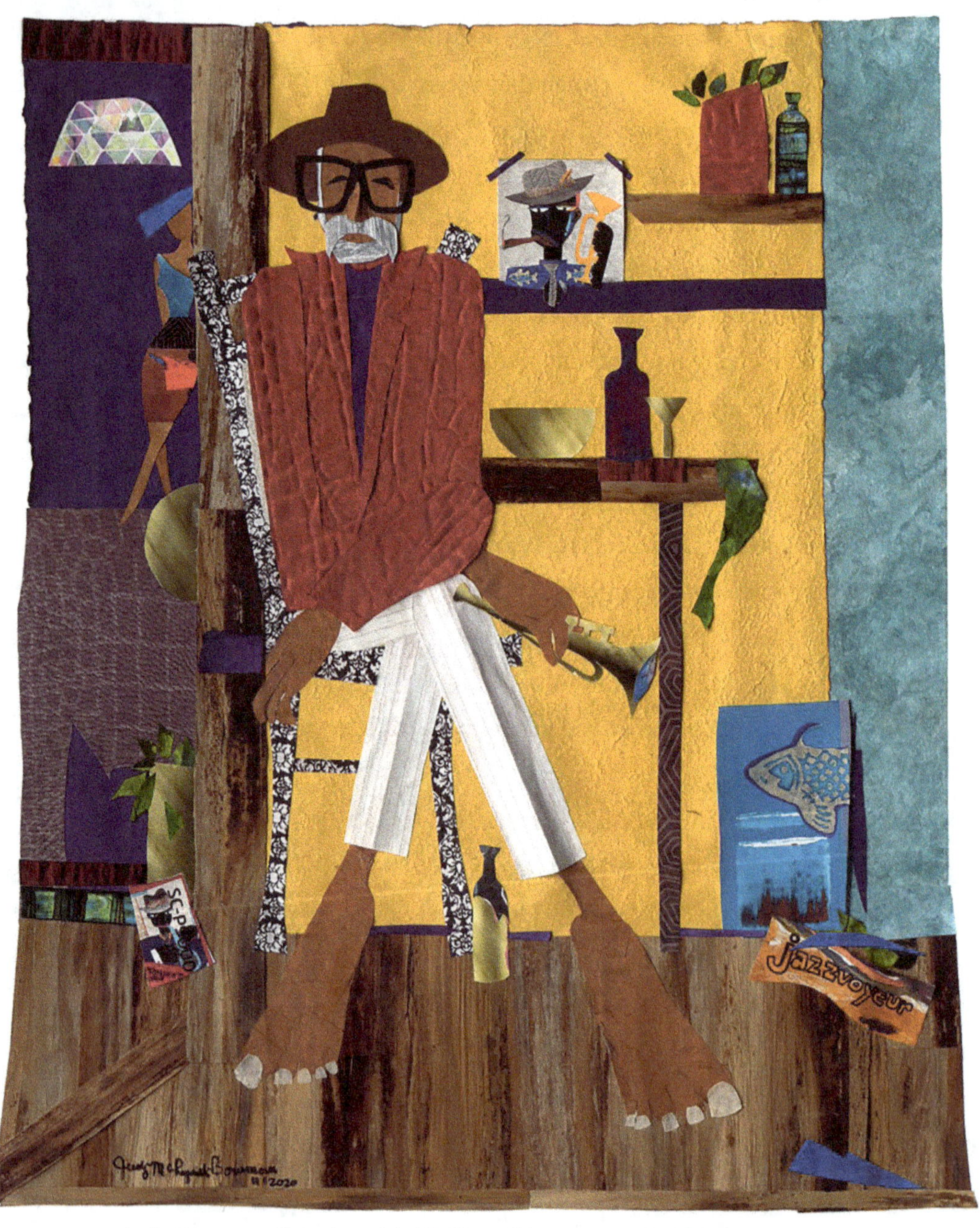

Judy Bowman, *Relaxing with My Blues IV*, mixed media collage, 2020

See *Is Graffiti Art?*, page 19

FRANCES PORTER

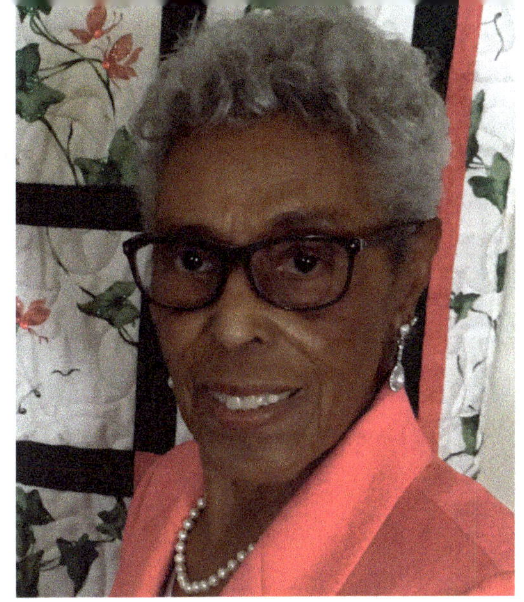

Quilter | Fiber Artist | Member of the African American Quilt Guild of Oakland
Place of Birth: Houston, Texas
Current Location: Oakland, California
Age: 98
www.aaqgo.org

THERE HAVE BEEN many firsts in my life. I was the first person of color to earn a Bachelor of Arts Degree in Dramatic Arts from the University of California, Berkeley. I was the first and only African American clerical supervisor with Oakland's Naval Supply Center for nine years. While staying connected to the arts, I had a long career in social work that culminated in my being the first African American woman in the state of California to hold a Director of Social Services position. These accomplishments are part of my life story as well as my journey as a fiber artist and quilter.

Having lived a long life, I have witnessed many historical events. I was a child when President Roosevelt's Works Project Administration (WPA) was created and funding was made available for artists. That was a time like today where people struggled with housing, hunger, and unemployment. The WPA funding was for all types of art: music, theater, dance, photography, writing, fine arts, murals, carpentry, and so on. Funding was also used for training. I would support similar legislation today to help working artists. Ideally, this would include funding for arts in the schools. Art has been taken out of most public schools. There is one very competitive high school with a focus on the arts in my area's school district. I wonder what happens to the kids who can't get in. I was fortunate to receive support and inspiration for my

Frances Porter, *Summer Dance, quilt*, 2018

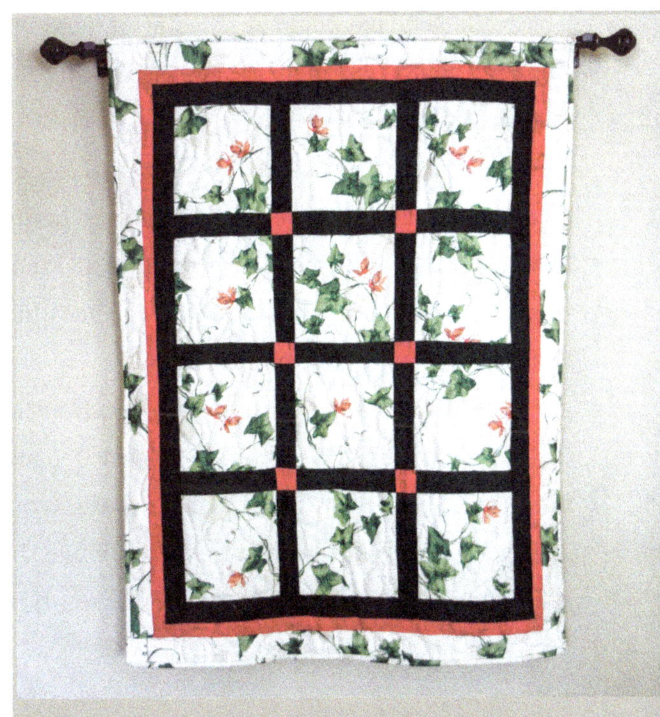

creativity from a young age, and to have studied the arts from grade school through college.

BY AGE SIX, I MADE MY FIRST DRESS

Since I was the only young girl in my neighborhood, my playmates were all boys. When I tired of playing with them, I visited a close family friend who I thought of as an aunt. She owned a clothing business. I enjoyed visiting my aunt and watching her work. With a needle and thread, I began to do simple things for her. This was during the Great Depression when money was very limited.

By age six, I made my first dress with fabric I purchased at five cents per yard at Kress, a five-and-ten department store. This was the beginning of my interest in textiles, fibers, textures, and threads. From that point on, I made my own clothing. When I was around nine, my dad purchased my first electric sewing machine. I also learned to knit, crochet, and make lace. As you can imagine, making lace is very intricate. You use a single piece of thread to make detailed patterns. It's a method called tatting. I used to think of my work as handicrafts, but now, I understand that these are all forms of art.

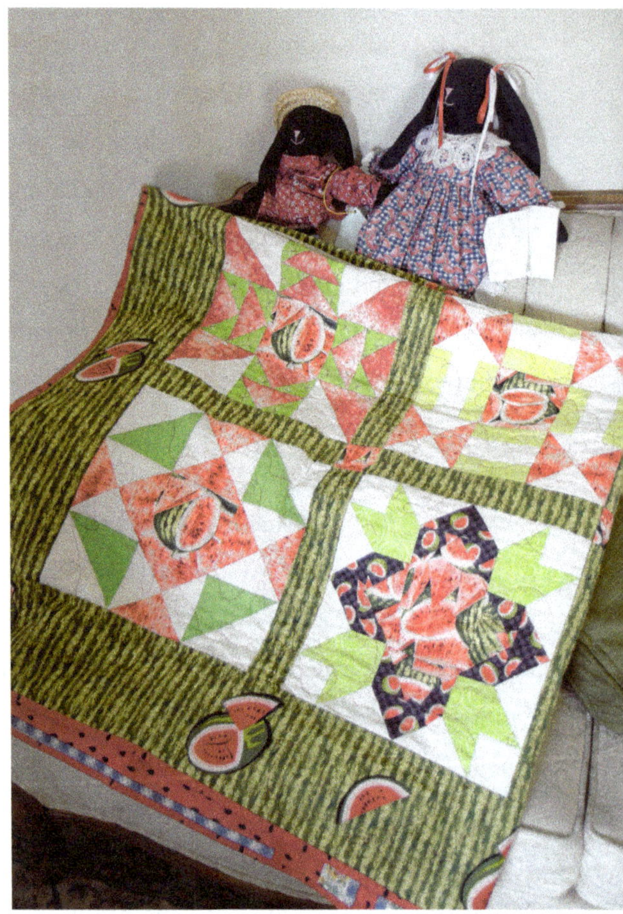

Frances Porter, *Watermelons Galore*, quilt, 2006 (detail).

I was born and raised in Houston, Texas, which was very segregated. This didn't bother me as a child since it was all that I knew. In high school, I studied drama. In the South at that time, even as a college-educated woman, I knew the only jobs available to me would be teaching or nursing. I ended up going to Dillard University in New Orleans. It is one of the historically black colleges and universities (HBCU). I attended Dillard for three years during World War II, experiencing my second introduction to the arts as I majored in dramatic arts. I worked at a little theater and performed all kinds of tasks, from building sets and acting to wardrobe/costume design. You name it, I was involved with it.

In the meantime, my sister moved from Houston to Washington, DC, and then to California. I decided to move to California with her. In my fourth year of college, I transferred from an all-Black Dillard University to the mostly white University of California at Berkeley. This was in 1945 when World War II had just ended. Being a student at UC Berkeley was really my first exposure to interacting with white people on a large scale. I saw a few white people before moving to California since my dad worked for a Jewish auctioneer and my mom worked in the homes of white families. In high school, I worked as a seamstress at Battelstein's, a small, upscale department store in downtown Houston that catered to white families.

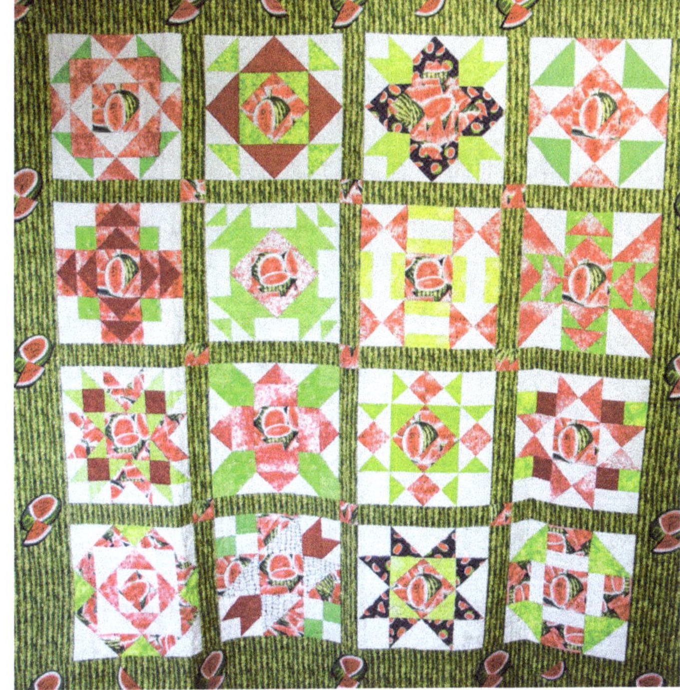

Frances Porter, *Watermelons Galore*, quilt, 2006

I was so overwhelmed when I stepped on the huge Berkeley campus of twenty-three thousand students that I didn't even realize I was one of only six Black students in my graduation class of five thousand. My experience was very different than what I was accustomed to in the segregated South. What impressed me most was that I was accepted by my professors and classmates. I was allowed to sit at the same lunch counters and use the same bathrooms and water fountains as white students.

I graduated with a bachelor's degree in dramatic arts from UC Berkeley. My goal was to teach, but I was unable to take the required classes to get a teaching credential due to lack of money for tuition. I tried to find clerical work, but I had no practical experience. Typing was essential. Back then, typing was only taught in white high schools. The expectation in the South was that African Americans would be doing some kind of manual labor with our hands to earn a living. I still didn't know how to type when I graduated from college.

I BROKE THE GLASS CEILING

Throughout college, I continued sewing and always carried a needle and thread with me. I earned an income the first year after graduating from Berkeley by sewing at home. I could do any kind of altering someone may need, and I made dresses and other clothing. Eventually, I gained the skills I needed for employment in an office job, and I was hired by the Naval Supply Center in Oakland as a clerk.

In less than one year, I was promoted to a supervisory position. For nine years, I was the Naval Supply Center's only African American female supervisor. I started to experience a lack of opportunity to advance beyond that. My skin color absolutely played a role in my being stuck.

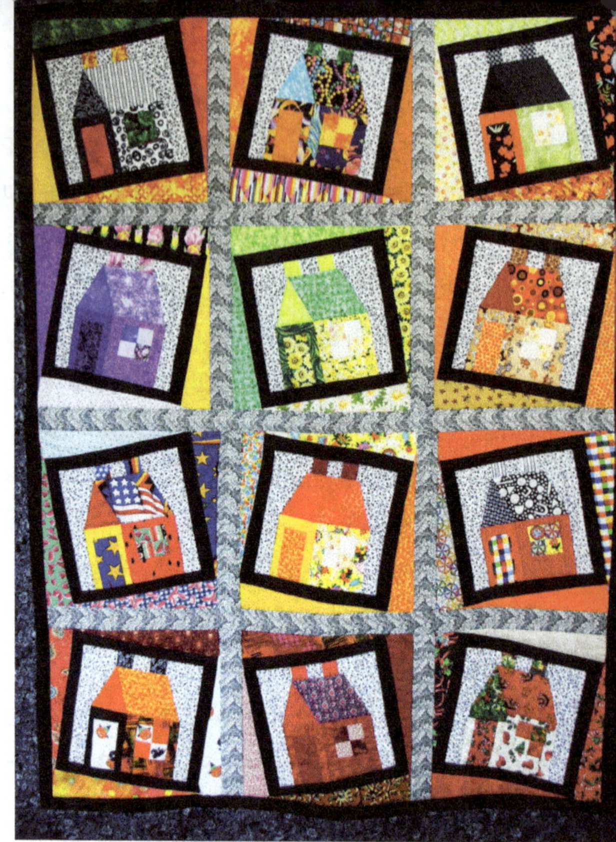

Frances Porter, *After the Levees Broke*, quilt,2005

After being passed over for a position that I was overqualified for by a white warehouseman without a college degree, I said, "It's time to leave." There was an opening for a social work position with Alameda County. I applied and took the test, but I didn't pass.

I had no idea what a social worker did. I got books and studied for three weeks. When the test was offered again, I passed it. I was hired as a first-line social worker for three years. Then I became a supervisor, but I didn't really know the theory of social work. I applied to UC Berkeley and was accepted in the master's program for social work. I knew I was going to be pigeonholed without an advanced degree. Once I earned my master's degree, I became a second level supervisor and kept going up the ladder until I broke the glass ceiling and became the first Black female Director of Social Services for Alameda County. I ultimately retired from this position in 1978 at age fifty-three. All this time, I was making my own clothing, knitting, crocheting, and staying involved with the arts.

Throughout my career, I made all of the dresses I wore. Even today, I rarely wear purchased clothing. Years ago, I also experimented with fabric sculpture. I learned how to use crocheting techniques to create an elaborate curved bowl. I made place mats, collars, doilies, scarves, runners, and decorated pillowcases to make them more elaborate. I learned how to repair holes in socks with the same stitch used for tatting. As you weave with thread to make repairs, you are literally making fabric by hand. Quilting, however, came very late in life.

"LET'S START QUILTING"

I was at my church for a Black History Month event when Joy Johnson, a master quilter from the African American Quilt Guild, had a showing of her quilts. They were beautiful. She offered to teach a class in quilting. When Joy turned to me to see what I thought about a quilting class, I said, "I'm not old enough." I was eighty-two at the time. I thought that quilting was for old ladies, and I did not consider myself old.

Two years later, Joy returned to my church with more beautiful quilts to share during our Black History activities. I guess at eighty-four, I considered myself old enough. This time, I said to Joy, "Let's start quilting."

Joy was an excellent mentor and teacher. She carried me along in my quilting journey and challenged me. She encouraged me to enter one of my quilts in the Alameda County Fair. This was a juried competition with a group of master quilters serving as jurors. There were around five hundred quilts in the competition. The jurors wrote a detailed critique of my quilt. Although the intent was to serve as a constructive critique, I felt like I had stickpins in my side. I told my husband I was going to enter again, and I guaranteed that the jurors would never have negative comments about my quilt ever again.

A couple of years later, I made a quilt for my daughter with a watermelon theme. I created it using watermelon fabrics collected from several different quilt shops. I titled my quilt "Watermelons Galore." It won first place at the fair that year. I couldn't believe it. My son-in-law took a photo of me that day. I was wearing a sun hat and holding a hot dog and a drink next to my quilt with a blue ribbon on it. It's hilarious that this photo appeared on the front page of one of our local newspapers.

I was not a member of a quilting guild during my early adventures with quilting. Although I've been a member of Alpha Kappa Alpha Sorority, Inc. for seventy-seven years, I never considered myself much of a joiner. After quilting for two or three years, I decided to join the African American Quilt Guild in Oakland, California. It's one of the best things that has ever happened to me. I thoroughly enjoy interacting with other quilters.

I HAVE BEEN AN ARTIST FOR A LONG TIME AND DIDN'T KNOW IT

I met my next mentor and teacher, Marion Coleman, through the Guild. Marion and my previous mentor, Joy, have both passed away. Marion's motto was, "Each one, teach one." It is through Marion that I became nationally recognized as a quilter and fiber artist. She was also responsible for my beginning to think of myself as an artist. Prior to Marion's encouragement, the thought of my being an artist never occurred to me because I cannot draw. I now understand that I have been an artist for a long time and didn't know it.

Once I became more involved with quilting and the Guild, my definition of art and being an artist expanded. I have worked alongside Guild members and participated with them

Frances Porter, *After the Levees Broke*, quilt, 2005 (detail)

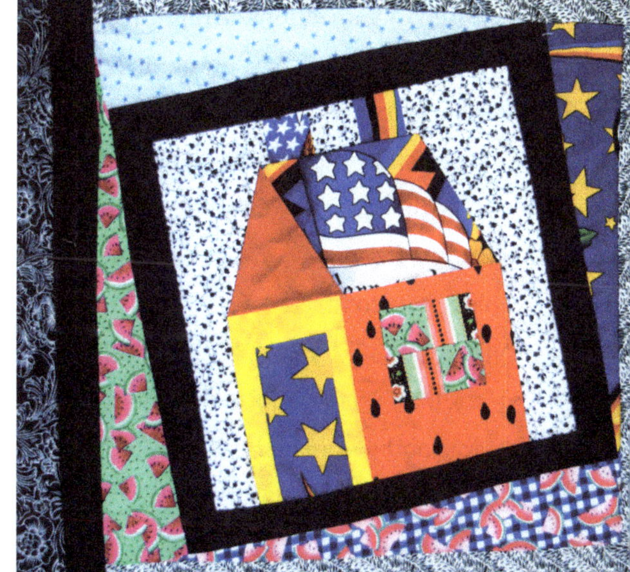

in many projects and exhibits throughout Oakland. Marion secured a grant for a year-long project, "Neighborhoods Coming Together: Quilts Around Oakland." Three of my quilts were in that exhibit, including one that hung outside of the mayor's office and another in a gallery at Laney College. Marion also received a grant to publish a book featuring some of our quilts. After reviewing the book, the curator at the National Quilt Museum in Paducah, Kentucky, requested that some of my quilts and others from the Guild be included in a special exhibit. I traveled to view the exhibit, and every single staff member who was working that day came to see me. They wanted to see an individual who didn't look or act like they thought someone who is ninety-two would look and act. Since I was familiar with all of the quilts in the exhibit, I gave the staff members a guided tour.

I never imagined that I would live this long. My sister passed away at ninety-two. When we were in our eighties, I said to her, "Somebody better tell us we're old," because we never thought of ourselves as old people.

I HAVE MADE OVER ONE HUNDRED QUILTS

I have some weeks where I quilt every day, but sometimes, I will not quilt for weeks. Since starting quilting at age eighty-four, I have made over one hundred quilts. I make quilts for my family and friends, providing them with something to remember me by. Some of my quilts have been donated to churches, schools, my sorority, and other nonprofit organizations as fundraising auction items. At auctions, my quilts bring in hundreds of dollars for charities. One quilt for an elementary school fundraiser sold for $1,700. Although many members of the Guild make quilts for money on commission, I have elected not to do that.

Of the quilts I've made, the one I titled *Is Graffiti Art?* [See page 19] is my pride and joy. I was both fascinated and yet abhorred

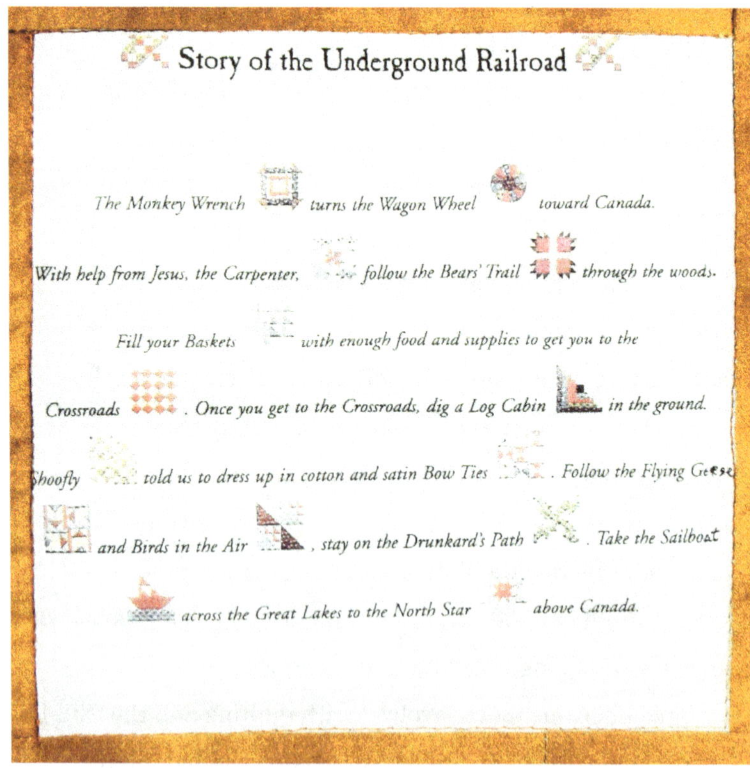

Overleaf and this page: Frances Porter, *Underground Railroad*, quilt, 2004 (detail this page)

graffiti because I saw it as an art form, but something that also damages real estate. I used the Internet to research graffiti all over the United States and Europe. When I started to pay closer attention to graffiti, I noticed similarities in the shapes of the letters around the world. I discovered the type of lettering called graffiti alphabet. I chose one form of the alphabet and used the lettering for my quilt. I purchased two sets of stencils, but I also made my own stencils out of newspaper. Every letter I created was then stitched on the quilt. Although I used to abhor graffiti, now I look for graffiti and appreciate its artistic value.

It's rewarding, flattering, and humbling to receive national recognition for my art. Over the past several years, my graffiti art quilt was featured in the *New York Times* and the PBS series *Sewing with Nancy*. I was on a three-person "Why I Quilt" panel at the Berkeley Art Museum and was a featured guest on a radio talk show in San Francisco.

It's really something. Here I am in my nineties. I've been artistic my whole life without recognizing it in myself until Marion Coleman made me aware of my identity as an artist in my eighties. I have so much gratitude for the people who recognize my talents and bring my gifts forth to share. ❖

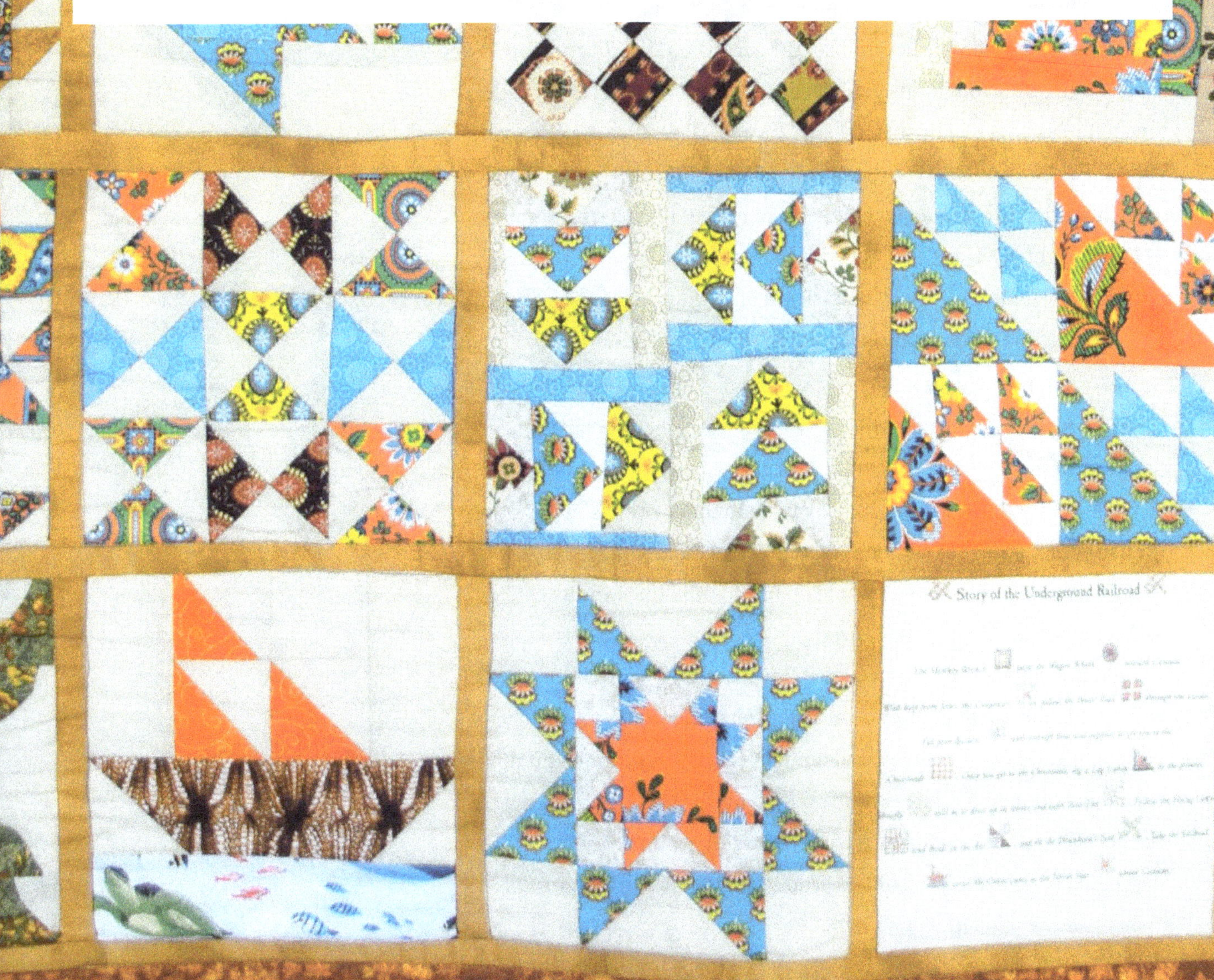

See *Fool with His Shield,* page 20

PAT B. ALLEN

Visual Artist | Writer
Place of Birth: West Orange, New Jersey
Current Location: Berkeley, California
Age: 70
www.patballen.com | www.cronation.org

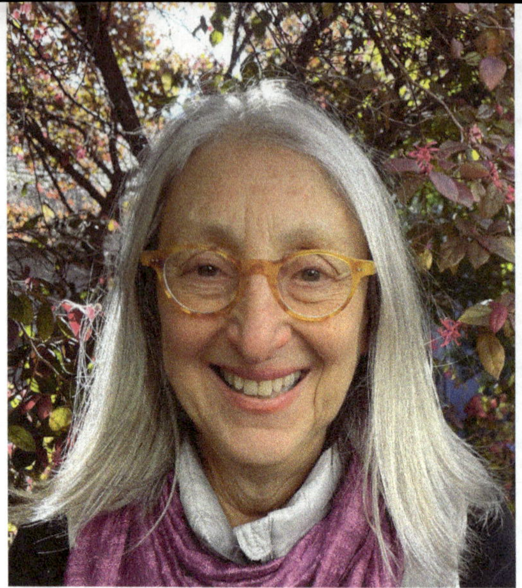

BERKELEY IS A funny place. I'm really happy here. I live in a little house in a neighborhood called Poet's Corner where many of the streets are named after poets. Behind my house is a small cottage I use as my studio.

I'm currently learning how to play the accordion. I'm discovering how to access music through this non-linear and non-Western way. I've done this before as part of a drum circle in Chicago. I need to practice and build my skills, and I don't expect to ever be very proficient, but slowly, it is my intention to learn enough to enjoy playing with others.

I also selected the accordion because I wanted an instrument that would be portable. One of my fantasies is of me later in life hanging out in a park playing the accordion. I want to sit in Strawberry Creek Park in Berkeley and play music while children and dogs run around.

> [STUDYING ART WAS] BOTH AN ATTRACTION AND A TERROR AT THE SAME TIME

With all the art and writing I've done throughout my life, I'm presenting an idea that there is a world beyond the world that we see. The creative process allows us entry into that world as much or as little as we're willing to go there. When I was a child, I played in a way that I now consider artistic. I would connect with other worlds by gathering stones, sticks, and flowers.

I did not call myself an artist until I transferred to an art program in college. My father thought I was out of my mind for studying art because I had a full scholarship in an academic setting and my family did not have much money. My father didn't talk to me for a while after I made the decision to study art. Any advice I received was to get my "regular degree" first, and later, I could do art on the side. This made me not entirely capable of owning my identity like other people I saw in art school, even though art was clearly where I was pulled and where my energy lived.

I studied art at the School of the Museum of Fine Arts, Boston in the mid-1970s. Around age twenty, when I was beginning to claim my identity as an artist, it was terrifying. The role models of success were mostly hard-drinking males with a heroic self-conception. It definitely wasn't a simple thing since I didn't feel I had support. It made me feel like a fraud, so it was both an attraction and a terror at the same time. I was also not doing what was considered magnificent work. People weren't saying, "Oh, you're amazing."

At the time I was in art school in the 1970s, the traditional way of teaching—drawing from plaster casts of the human figure, for example—was falling apart following huge shifts that came out of the 1960s counterculture and the free speech and civil rights movements. Still, there wasn't anything terribly robust to replace the old curriculum with, and there wasn't a lot of direction in school, just sex, drugs, and rock and roll. In the midst of this, I discovered the field of art therapy.

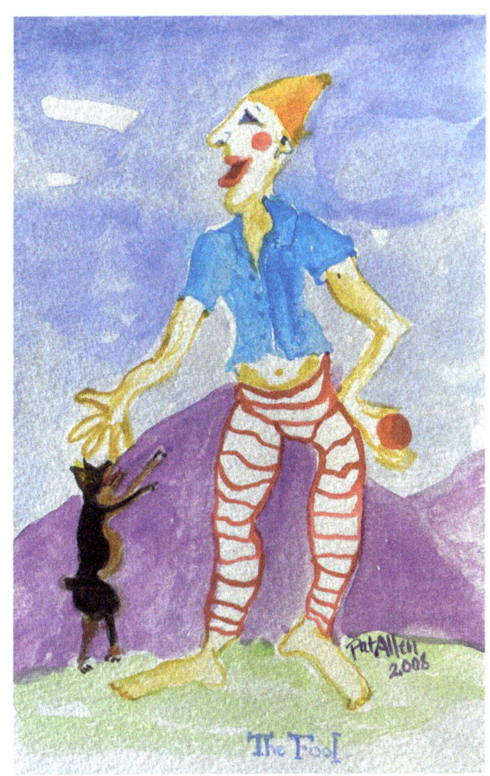

Pat B. Allen, *Fool and Friend*, watercolor on paper, 5.5" x 8.5", 2008

MY PRIMARY ARTIST IDENTITY IS THE HOLY FOOL

I often say that my primary artist identity is the Holy Fool. I experience bizarre coincidences and bump into things that seem completely insane on some level.

In the Boston Public Library, I came across some old and out-of-print books by a psychologist and early practitioner of art therapy named Margaret Naumburg. They blew me away because they had something to do with art and the inner life, which was what I was blindly groping toward, but I was not able to put a name to it. Since the books were old, I assumed the author was long dead.

I was in the hallway at art school one day, and I overheard a woman talking about a seminar she's taking at Margaret Naumburg's house. I literally grabbed her by the shoulders and said, "What are you talking about?" It turned out that Naumburg was in her eighties and had been forcibly retired. She had just moved to Boston! Realizing Naumburg was not only alive, but she was living in the same city as I was, I wrote to her and said, "I want to meet you."

Naumburg wrote me back and told me to come see her and bring some of my artwork, which I did. When I showed her my art, Naumburg told me, “This isn’t the real you.” She gave me specific directions to go home and soak heavy watercolor paper in the bathtub and then use big brushes to paint with, “from a dream, if you have one,” which I did. She was giving me something that was far clearer than what was going on in art school, but there were definitely problematic issues. She was very wedded to the psychoanalytic idea of transference, for example, so she wanted to interpret my art as about her and about her relationship with me, which was not what it was about for the most part.

Still, I started following the methods that Naumburg suggested. It was a form of spontaneous painting that tapped into the unconscious and released a tremendous amount of energy. None of the faculty at my school knew what to do with what I was creating. To them, it looked like shit and just weird marks on paper. I believe they ended up graduating me with the idea that I didn’t really want to be an artist anyway. It was all pretty nutty.

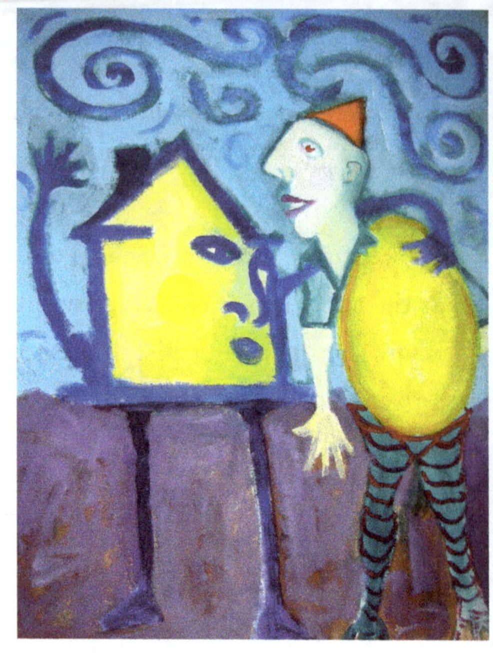

Pat B. Allen, *Fool and House*, tempera on paper, 20" x 26" 2006

WE ARE ALL FELLOW TRAVELERS MAKING ART TOGETHER

Another thing that happened while I was in art school was that I went into the work-study office one day after I discovered art therapy and said, “Hey, I’d like a job as an art therapist.” I experienced another coincidence: someone had just called that day looking for a person to provide art therapy in a program for adults who were being kicked out of state mental hospitals. “Deinstitutionalization” was the goal in those days.

I ended up getting hired to work with people struggling with mental illness. I really knew nothing, but I was very comfortable hanging out with people that were not all there or had serious problems. I was just nineteen at the time and was given incredible training and supervision by the psychiatrists and social workers on staff. Other people could not tolerate being in the room with people who had been deeply institutionalized, very damaged, and often medicated up the wazoo. I liked these people, and I was happy to hang with them.

I ended up going to graduate school at Goddard College in Vermont to become an art therapist. I officially became a registered art therapist in 1977. During my training, I learned the whole interpretive framework of how to approach other people's work. It was quite seductive, but I came to see it as bullshit. I ultimately ended up leaving an academic job where I was teaching art therapy and founded the Open Studio Project in Chicago in the early 1990s with two of my former students.

The same year the studio was founded, my book *Art is a Way of Knowing* came out from Shambhala Publications. The studio provided me a way to deeply explore the ideas in the book. I got to experiment with the ideas that guided my own art practice and see if they worked for others. We completely moved away from the traditional art therapy process of having people make drawings about things you think they should and then you make up a story and tell them what their art means. I had come to believe that was a violation of the creative process.

The process that emerged at the Open Studio Project involves making an intention for the type of experience you want to have. You use art materials to create something, and then you write about what you create. Participants read the writing to each other, but no one acts as a therapist or interprets anyone's writing or visual art. There is a no-comment rule, so no one else says anything about your work, and you do not segue into explanations. We believe we are all fellow travelers making art together, and we do our own authentic process side by side with the participants as participant-facilitators. The process flattens hierarchies; each person is in charge of their own creative process. The Open Studio Project continues to function to this day in Evanston, Illinois.

I've traveled all over to teach the Open Studio Process and mentor others. I also taught the process to undergraduate art students for fifteen years at the School of the Art Institute of Chicago, which feels like one of the most important things I've done as an artist. My daughter, who is a rabbi where I now live in Berkeley, also founded a project based on my work that she calls the Jewish Studio Project. It feels incredibly meaningful to pass my work on as a lineage to my daughter as well as to others I've mentored in Mexico, India, Taiwan, and Korea. I continue to embrace my creative identity as the Holy Fool and the possibilities that come my way.

Beyond my work with the Open Studio Project and teaching, over the years I've continued to create in different art media for my personal art practice. Mask-making has been a constant part of my practice. Even though I've done a ton of paper-mache, painting, and object-making, masks have definitely been a through line. In my book *Art is a Way of Knowing*, I detail some of my mask-making, including masks I made of my father and mother that are two of my most profound art experiences. Both were created to deal with the grief of losing a parent.

TWO OF MY MOST PROFOUND ART EXPERIENCES WERE MAKING MY PARENT'S DEATH MASKS

To make my masks, I form a plasticine mold and then use paper-mache over the mold. It's a lengthy process that I discovered in a book in the art school library. It feels like an art practice that is directly connected to soul, spirit, and the other world. Perhaps this is because there is a long history of masks being used in death rituals and as a way of remembrance.

The masks of my father and mother were made more than thirty years ago, about ten years apart. I have carried them around with me all these years. It was maybe around 2015 when my husband and I bought a house in Ojai, California, and I embarked on an inner retreat. I'd been living in Chicago for thirty years at the time. I would go out to the California house for weeks at a time by myself. I put these two masks in the room I was using as my study. Although they had hung on a wall silently for years, the mask of my father started to emanate all this energy, asking to be witnessed again. I wrote spontaneously in response to the mask, which has now been part of my practice for close to fifty years and something I do with almost every piece of art I make. So, here I was, by myself in the California house, and I started having a dialogue with this mask of my father that I made more than thirty years ago.

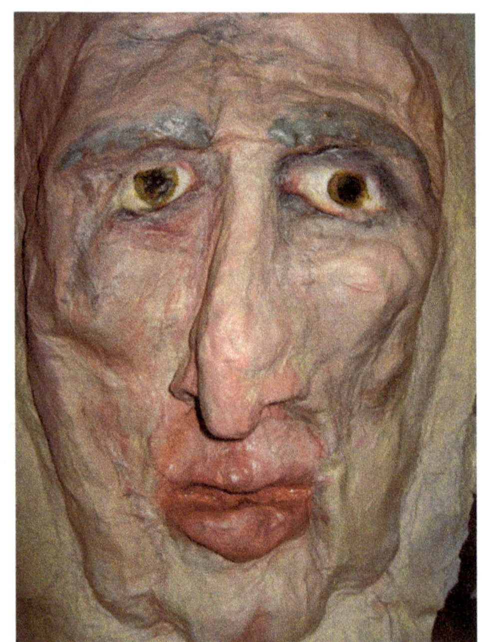

Pat B. Allen, *Mask of My Father*, paper-mache, acrylic paint. Initial date of creation 1984, date of process transformation 2013

The mask had resembled my grandfather, my father's father, and it was actually my grandfather who was asking for contact. He had molested my older sister and a cousin, both of whom were much older than me, and he was basically asking for help in moving on in his soul's journey. The witness process is very similar to the process of Active Imagination described by Carl Jung. I told him I could not help him and that he needed to come to terms with his actions. After several more encounters, he acknowledged his responsibility. I repainted the mask, which had closed eyes that were now open.

The experience of dialoguing with those who have passed on is something that happens to artists who work in this way, whether personal relations or more distant ancestors. Immersion in deep creative process is a way to make these connections.

When I was around age forty, a good friend asked me, "So, how's your cronation going?" In some people's rubric, age forty is when you start turning into a crone. At the time, I rejected it, but the word "cronation" stuck with me and continued to percolate over the years. It ended up becoming the title of my novel that was published in 2016. *Cronation* has an underlying premise that we're at a point in history where the reemergence of the divine feminine is happening. It's speculative fiction with various fantasy elements. In the book, there are very old women, wise crones, who are mentoring and guiding the world into a transition where the male principle is waning.

THE REEMERGENCE OF THE DIVINE FEMININE IS HAPPENING

For many years, I did not think about getting older. My mother died of cancer when she was fifty-two, so I felt that I'd better hurry up and do everything in case I don't make it past fifty. This caused me to be a relentless producer who jammed an entire lifetime into a certain number of designated years. At some point, I thought, "Oh, I guess I'm not going to die when I'm fifty." Once this thought came, I started imagining how I want my later stages to be.

If I could change my current art practice as I approach age seventy, I'd have access to a bigger space to do large-scale fabric pieces that I could leave in place while I work. I would also like to teach an online Alternative Art as Medicine course without the constraints that come in academic training programs. I'm currently in discussions with a colleague about possibly actualizing this.

I want to also do more activist work. I've had different chunks of time in my life where I felt like the work I was doing was activism. One example is my work with Art Hives, which is a network of art studios that uses art as a way to build community. I've also had some level of participation with The U.S. Department of Arts and Culture's grassroots action network that offers initiatives rooted in empathy, equity, and belonging. This work ties into what I would put into motion if I had the ability to make major changes for artists.

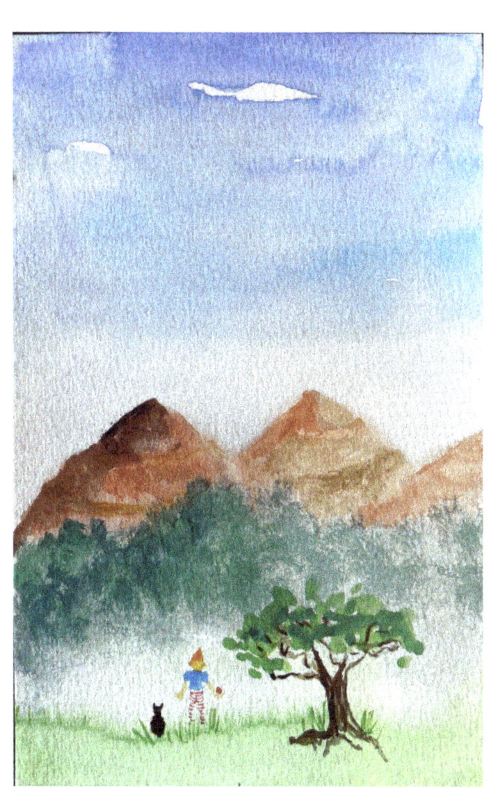

Pat B. Allen, *Fool at the Mountain*, watercolor on paper, 6" x 9", 2008

I WOULD LIKE ... A SOCIETAL SHIFT WHERE IDEAS FROM ARTISTS ARE DISCUSSED AND VALUED MORE

The overarching legislation I would create would be the *Community Well-Being Act.* Its intention would be to establish an ethic of care to build community, break down silos in community government, and deconstruct the segregation that upholds white supremacy. I would create departments of art and culture on a municipal level that would employ artists in a range of job titles. Some would be expressive arts/arts therapists who would consult and help plan community interventions through traveling and in-home support services. They would work with police and others who interface with the public to provide social and emotional support for their jobs through art. I would also have artists be a part of city planning, including the construction of buildings to bring an aesthetic lens to projects. Artists with a social justice focus in their work would be hired to create exhibitions in vacant storefronts. The voices of youth, the unhoused, immigrants, and other populations would be amplified through the exhibitions. I would add artists to library and public school staff. Kids would have an open studio to safely explore feelings and life challenges on a regular basis as part of the work/school day.

I would like there to be a societal shift in mindset where ideas from artists are discussed and valued more. I feel like there's a whole other world around us that could open up and be possible. I have been very fortunate in being able to pursue my artistic practice throughout my life. Still, it would have been helpful to me—and I'm certain other artists—if creating art was held up as a worthy way to spend one's life that, by its very nature, is an act of service. ❖

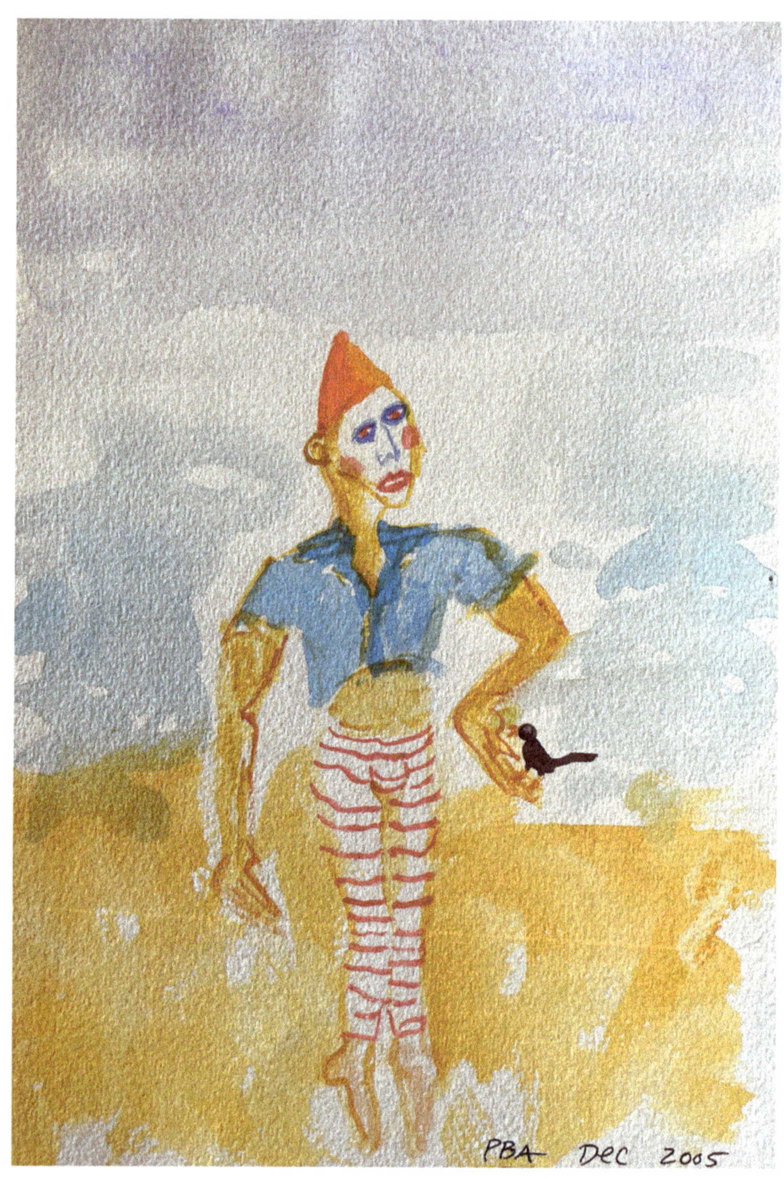

Pat B. Allen, *Fool and Bird,* watercolor on paper, 7" x 10", 2005

See *Who Me, Chicken,* page 21

DELLA WELLS

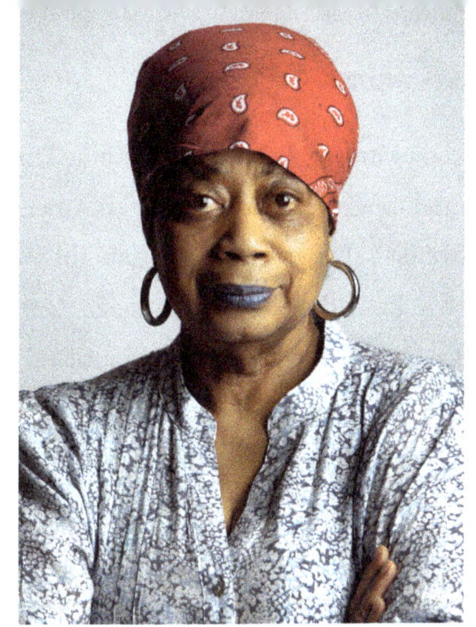

Self-Taught Visual Artist | Collage Artist | Dollmaker
Place of Birth: Milwaukee, Wisconsin
Current Location: Milwaukee, Wisconsin
Age: 71
www.portraitsocietygallery.com/dellawells

I WOULDN'T CHANGE anything about my life and art. My life experiences are what drive my creativity. I don't know if I would have created art or if I would have anything to say as an artist without my life experiences. My artmaking is more than me making it. Just knowing how to do something has never been enough. It is important for me to see a vision and have a purpose to make art. Art was not at the top of my list of things to do when I was younger. The vision and purpose were not there yet.

My story with art goes back several decades. In my middle to late thirties, I was injured on the job. I was working in data entry and computer operations. I was in intense pain for about two years. The doctors suggested that I quit my work with computers and find another job. I decided to go back to school and become a psychologist. I started going to Milwaukee Technical College.

SHE TOLD ME THAT SHE THOUGHT I WAS AN ARTIST

My advisor at the college, who was also my history teacher, said I needed to take some humanities. She recommended an art survey course. I thought this was good since I knew a little about art. When I was younger, around age eighteen, nineteen, and twenty, I was involved with a place called The Gallery Toward the Black Aesthetic, but I wasn't an artist then. My father also had books on a whole host of subjects when I was growing up, including art. I always liked art, but I never thought about me doing art.

In this art survey course, we had to write a paper. I was in my forties at the time. I knew people were probably going to write about Andy

Warhol, Van Gogh, and Rembrandt. That's what most people did. I wanted to write about an African American artist who was local to Milwaukee. I remembered artists that were part of The Gallery Toward the Black Aesthetic from years ago. One was the artist Evelyn Patricia Terry. Over the years, I read about Evelyn in the paper. I called her up and asked if she remembered me. I said I wanted to do a paper on her. When I interviewed her, she told me that she thought I was an artist. I looked at her and thought she was crazy. After writing my paper, she tried to get me to do art for two years. In my mind, I thought, "That's crazy. I'm not wasting my time. Artists do not make any money." I wasn't interested.

A VOICE TOLD ME TO GO MAKE ART

I ended up transferring to the University of Wisconsin, Milwaukee. I was majoring in sociology while doing a minor in African American studies and getting a certificate in women's studies. At this particular time, I was taking a course on African religion with Dr. Patrick Bellegarde-Smith. It was really fascinating to me. Evelyn invited me to an exhibition at this gallery called Peltz Gallery that was run by Cissie Peltz. Evelyn's prints of her Haitian dolls were part of the exhibit. You may not believe this, but when I was at the show, a voice told me to go make art. At that moment, I told Evelyn, "Okay, I'm ready to make art."

Two weeks later, I was at her studio. I made two pastels that first time, and they actually turned out. I was shocked. It was very therapeutic for me since I was going through a lot of pain and suffered psychological damage. The art-making was soothing and relaxing. I was forty-two when I seriously started making art.

At the time I became an artist, I was working for Milwaukee County Department of Social Services, going to school, and volunteering at a helpline. I was busy. I would work on my art on Friday nights and from six to eight after work. A lot of the time, I would stay longer, and sometimes I spent the night and worked at the studio until the morning. Evelyn said if I created fifty pieces, she would give me a show. It turned out that she didn't need to give me a show. Within six months,

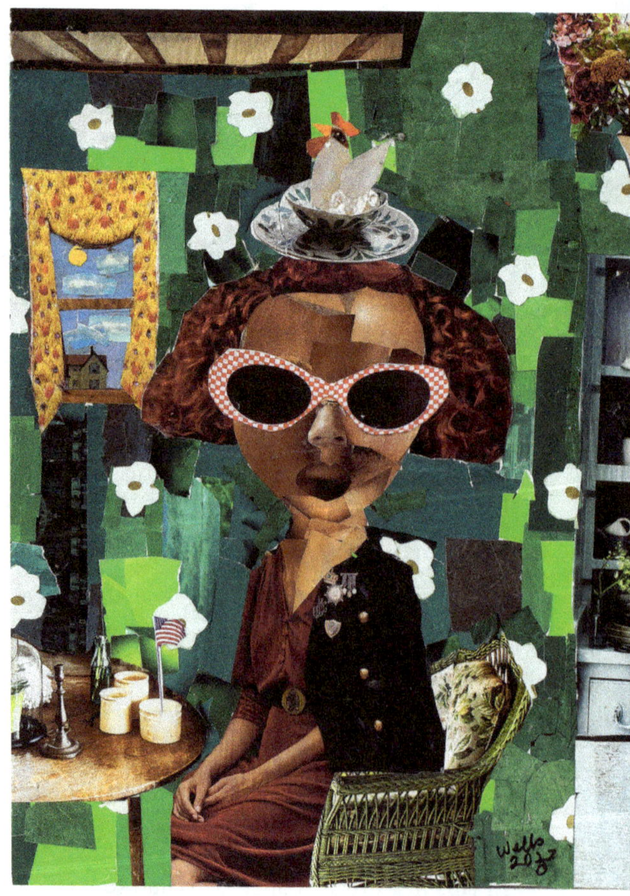

Della Wells, *Toni Valentine,* collage, 14" x 18", 2022

I got my own two first solo shows. One was at a local place, Cafe Melange, where a lot of artists get their start, and the other one was at the University of Wisconsin Women's Center. I'm now represented by the Portrait Society Gallery in Milwaukee. As a self-taught artist, I have exhibited all over the country and also British Columbia and Italy.

I didn't start out making collages, although two of my favorite artists, Romare Bearden and Matisse, worked with collage. I first thought of collages after seeing ones that were like paper sculptures created by another artist, Beverly Nunes Ramsey. At the time, I was preparing for a solo show at the David Barnett Gallery in Milwaukee in the mid-nineties. I was the first African American artist to have a solo show there. I created two collages for the show. What is funny about this is that one of my collectors who saw them said my collages were not my strongest work. I've always been told what I can't or shouldn't do. Sometimes, I'll do something despite what others say. It turned out the collage that was on the exhibition card sold before my exhibition opened. In fact, six people wanted to buy the collage on the exhibition card. Later, David told me that the collector was wrong. After this experience, I started to work with collage.

I LET MY ARTWORK TELL ME THE STORY

I'm fascinated with taking old stuff and making something different with it. Sometimes, I think about my mother. She had schizophrenia and went nineteen years untreated. It was very difficult for me as a child. I couldn't understand why my father didn't do anything about her schizophrenia. I was a very angry young woman since I imagined everybody's life was better than mine. I thought everyone else's parents and lives were like *Leave It to Beaver* or *Father Knows Best*. Then, as an adult, I started meeting other people and discovered mental illness was a part of many families and that a lot of people did not

Della Wells, *Maya's Day*, collage, 11" x 14", 2022

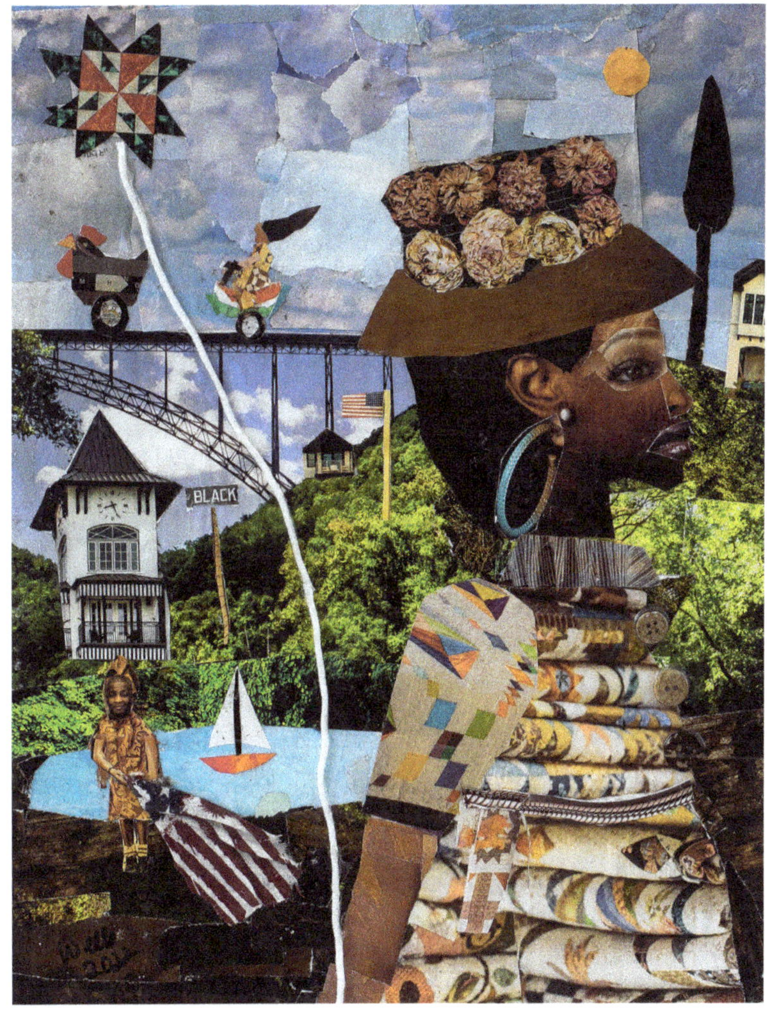

have an ideal childhood and family life. This gave me a different perspective. When I'm making a collage, I like the act of tearing pieces and looking at things that are broken or in parts and imagining other stories and visions. It's much harder to make a collage than to draw or paint for me. You have to find the right stuff to assemble it.

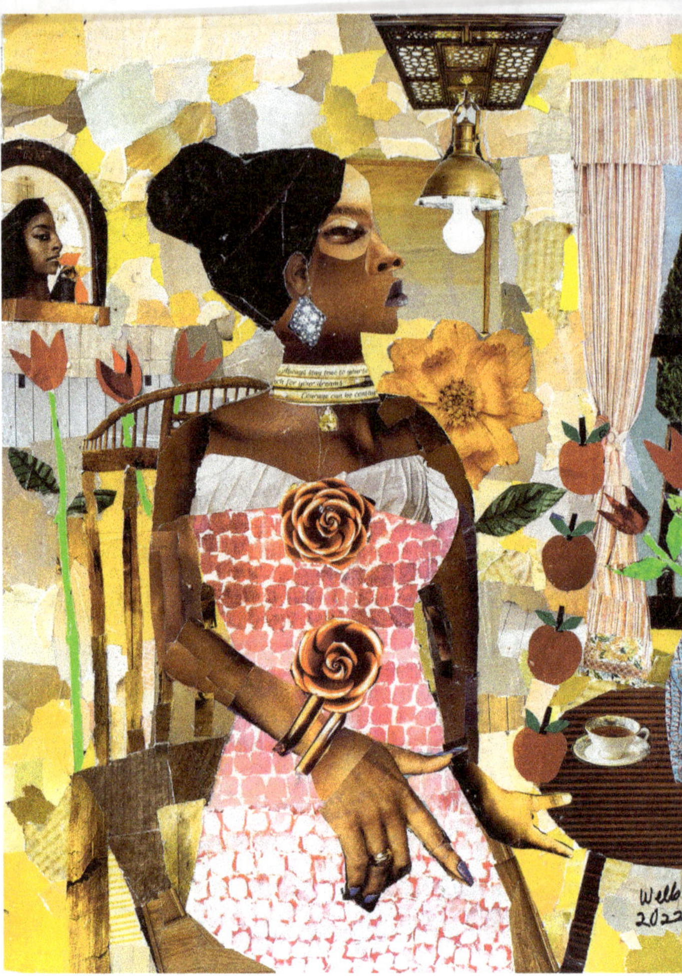

Della Wells, *There I Be*, collage, 16" x 20", 2022

It was a bit later, in the late 1990s or early 2000s, when I started to make dolls. I wanted to connect more with my childhood. When I was growing up in the fifties and sixties as an African American girl, all of my dolls were white. It never occurred to me until later. My mother gave me a blonde pillow doll from collecting cereal box tops. I wanted to tap back into my childhood and imagine what the dolls would be if I was making them. I would give them all a name, and I'd write a very short little ditty or poem about the dolls. One of the good memories I have of my mother is getting that doll. I wanted to make my Black version.

I don't name my artwork until I'm finished. I let my artwork tell me the story. It's the same with my dolls. I let each doll tell me who she is once I'm finished. My dolls are sold in galleries and also through the National Museum of African American History and Culture, a Smithsonian Institution museum in Washington, DC.

There are things I didn't expect to happen. A theater group called First Stage Children's Theater commissioned a playwright, Y York, to create a play inspired by my life titled *Don't Tell Me I Can't Fly*. 2016 MacArthur Fellow Anne Basting, who teaches theater at the University of Wisconsin, Milwaukee and runs a theater program for seniors with dementia and Alzheimer's, along with a friend from the theater, saw my exhibition at the Charles Allis Museum with the same title. After seeing my work, they thought it would be good theater. My play was the first of a series based on people who lived in Milwaukee. The play was also read at the Kennedy Center in Washington, DC, and it was performed at the Nashville Children's Theater and the Chil-

> [A THEATER GROUP CREATED] A PLAY INSPIRED BY MY LIFE

dren's Theater of Charlotte in North Carolina. This meant a lot to me because my late aunt and relatives on my mother's side got to see the play. My aunt said the playwright really captured my mother.

The reason I titled my exhibition *Don't Tell Me I Can't Fly*—that became the play's title—is because my work is mainly about African American women and how racism and sexism often promotes the pseudo notion that we Black women are doomed not to succeed. My collages take place in this land I created called Mambo Land where Black women rule. This imaginary land is inspired by fables, cartoons, and fairy tales I read as a young child. And too often in these fables, cartoons, and fairy tales, the heroines and/or heroes have to go through a lot of mess in order to live happily ever after. The women in my artwork are based on women from my life, such as my godmother Mrs. Frances Larson, my Aunt Doretha, teachers I had in junior high and high school such as Mrs. Jefferson, Mrs. Miller, Mrs. Scott, and Mrs. Forester, and women in church when I attended as a child and teenager such as Mrs. Turner and Mrs. Anderson, as well as African American women I learned and read about through my studies in African American history, including Harriet Tubman, Vel Phillips, bell hooks, Audre Lorde, Whoopi Goldberg, Fannie Lou Hamer, Ella Baker, Ella Walker, Maya Angelou, and others. My artwork is based on Black women empowerment.

As I get older, throughout my seventies and later, I will keep creating art. And I know I want to spend time with my grandchildren and great-grandchildren. They are one of my greatest motivators. Sometimes, they make art with me. But ultimately, I will keep working and keep discovering myself.

YOU'VE GOT TO KEEP WORKING WITH IT

I'm more comfortable with my creativity now. I'm at the age where you think about your mortality. I just want to enjoy life, and I want to create the work that I want to create. I don't think I could have done what I'm doing now when I was younger; I worried too much about what other people thought. Now, I don't care. I did a show last year, and this man came up to me and asked about my art: "Don't you do any with men?" I said I didn't and I don't want to. I told him he should do men. I don't think someone would come up to a male artist and tell him, "You should paint women." I may not have been comfortable saying that in my twenties, but now, I'll stand my ground.

When I think back to when I was making art for the first time at age forty-two, I remember something that Evelyn Patricia Terry told me. She told me to keep working with it. You may draw a line or something else and think it doesn't look right. She said, "Keep working with it." Now, I realize that's the same thing with life. You've got to keep working with it. ❖

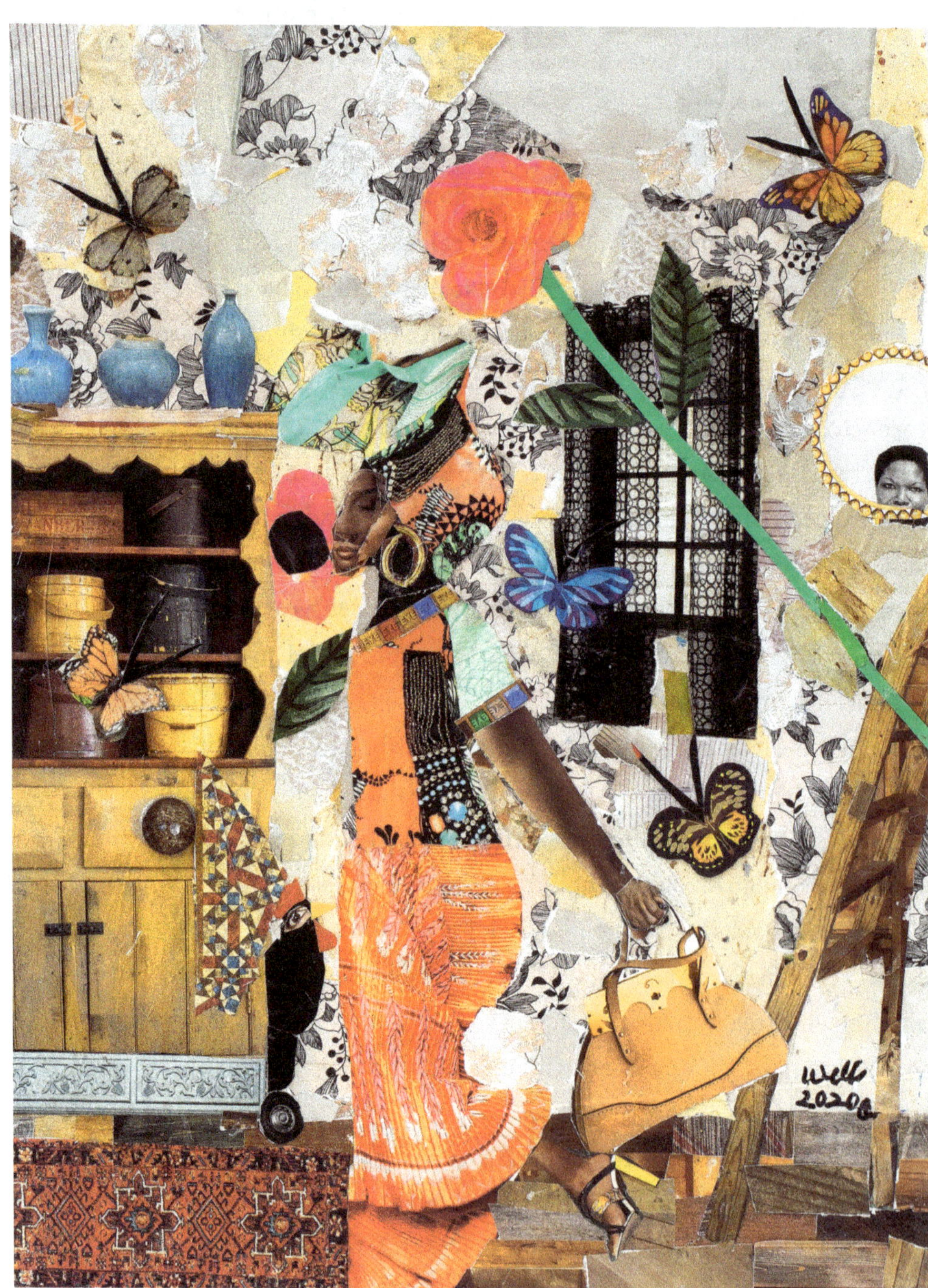

Della Wells, *My House, I Can Dance if I Want To*, collage, 16" x 12", 2022

See *Covered with a Blanket,* page 22

MALKA NEDIVI

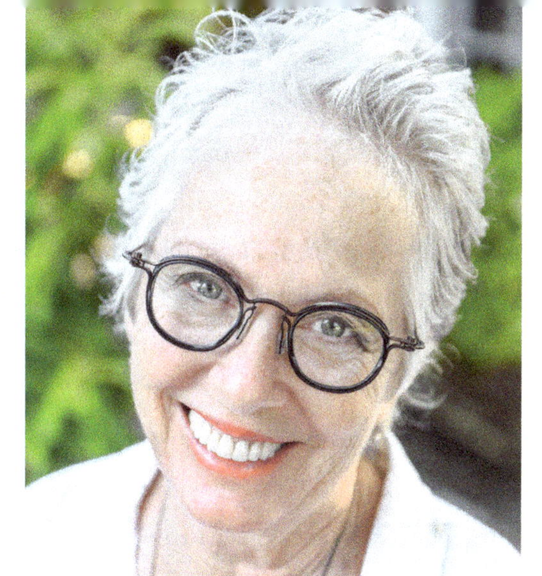

Sculptor, Painter & Mixed Media Artist | Documentary Filmmaker | Writer
Place of Birth: Israel
Current Location: Los Angeles, California
Age: 70
www.malkanedivi.com

I LEARNED ONE thing perhaps a bit late, but I'm glad I finally learned it. What I learned is to not plan. This is how I do my art and writing now. I write every day, but I don't plan. You can start to write wherever you are. You just sit and write and let what is inside you, your imagination, come out. It is the same with making art. I have my art up on the walls and throughout my house. It is not to show off, but to see my creations, because they inspire me to be courageous and continue to create new pieces without planning. All you need to do is begin.

I've been an artist all my life. When I was little, my first love was the theater. Then it was painting and drawing. My parents were Holocaust survivors, and I was their only daughter. They sent me to painting and drama classes. In those times though, when I was a child in Israel, being an artist was not considered a serious profession.

I HAD A WILD IMAGINATION AS A CHILD

I had a wild imagination as a child, and I wanted to capture this wildness in my drawings and paintings, but something stopped me from going full-speed into my art. Now that I am older, I understand what it was. My mother was different from other mothers, and our home was different than every other home. Our house was full of stuff. My mother couldn't get rid of anything. My childhood home was filled with color from my mother painting everywhere. When I went to other houses, they were beige, white, and very quiet. I wanted to escape from my mother's home. I'm sure it was a subconscious thought, but when I looked at my parents, especially my mother, I thought, "I cannot be like her. She's strange." I wanted to be different. I wanted to escape from her.

My work as a mature woman artist began after my kids got older and I had more time. I started with a ceramics class in Burbank. When I was working with the clay, I remember the teacher saying to me, "That's not you. What do you want to do?" I told him, "I want to make a sculpture. In my imagination, it's a big one." He gave me a space and said, "Do whatever is in your imagination."

I began by making a very large sculpture of a pregnant woman. I didn't plan it. It happened from the clay. While making this sculpture, I started to cry. I have three kids, and the third one is thirty years old, but before her, I was pregnant and lost the baby eight months into the pregnancy. When I lost the baby, I came home and said to myself that I was fine. I didn't want to mourn since I had two healthy kids. When I made the sculpture and I started to cry, I understood that this was the time. Many years later, I mourned the baby that I lost. From this point, my art was unstoppable.

I STARTED TO FLY

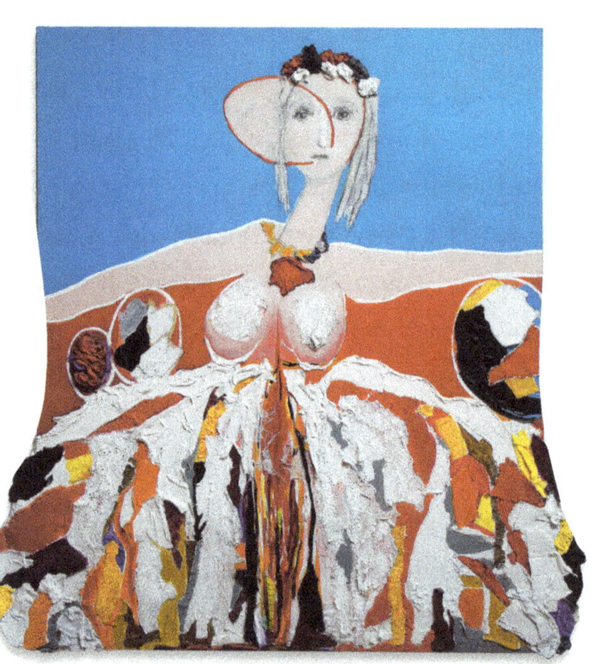

Malka Nedivi, *The Bride,*
mixed media on canvas, 5' x 4' x 6", circa 2000

My ceramics teacher also told me about an older woman artist. She was eighty-eight at the time. I was in my fifties. He said, "Go to her. I think she will inspire you." I found myself in her place with some other older women. I remember painting something really big and her touching my back and telling me to continue. I said, "I don't know what I'm doing." She told me, "It's good. It's good what you are doing. Don't explain. Don't try to understand." She was an influence in my life. She was such a good artist and so full of life at almost age ninety. I took it from there. Since my kids were older and didn't need me as much, I started to fly.

SHE IS STITCHING THE HOLES IN HER LIFE

It was around this time or a bit later that I returned to Israel to take care of my mother. She had been very attached to my father, but he had moved into a retirement home. She did not want to leave her house with all of her stuff. I cared for her for almost five years. It was a healing process.

One of my passions that I have a background in is documentaries. I worked for at least ten years as an assistant film editor. I then realized that I didn't want to edit somebody else's story; I wanted to tell my own. I took my camera to Israel. My husband has worked in the film industry for many years. He told me, "Follow your mother with your camera." That is what I did. I cared for her, filmed her, and also made art. I was making sculptures, and my mother was the inspiration.

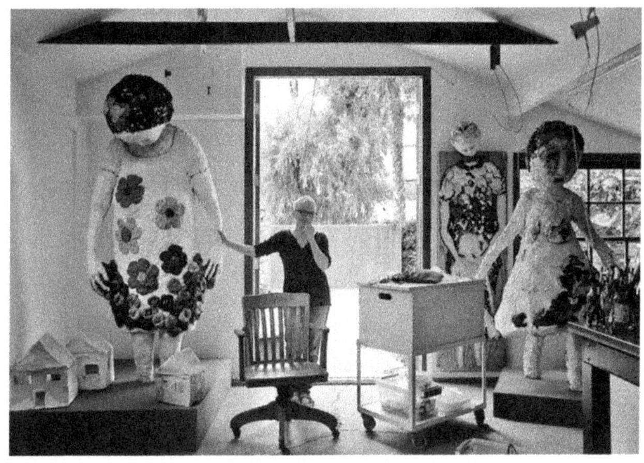
Malka in her studio, *2015*

The story of the time I spent with my mother is captured in my documentary *Tzipora's Nest*. The film is about many things: surviving the Holocaust and the psychological toll, immigration, aging, and my mother's hoarding. It is also about returning home to Israel and accepting, loving, and understanding my mother.

My mother had been a seamstress. All of my life, besides seeing her collect stuff, I saw that she could not stand holes in clothes or fabric. She could not even stand a hole in an apron. But she also could not throw anything away. She was always stitching the holes. Only when I got older and I watched her doing this did I realize, "Wow, she is stitching the holes in her life."

So many memories came back to me during my time there. I wanted to be creative with my own clothes. Something new started with me in Israel while my mother was still alive. I would take old clothes, tear them, and make something using glue and paint. I made this big lady, a sculpture, that I call a doll. I think I made a good decision to move back and be with my mother. I not only healed, but it led to a new form of my art: creating sculptures from fabric and old clothes.

I AM GIVING THE MATERIALS NEW LIFE

When I moved back to Los Angeles after the years in Israel, I brought my creations with me in a large container. The big doll sculpture from Israel was then standing here in my studio. She was made with very colorful clothes. She was almost screaming at me every morning! One day, I painted her all white. I remember my friend knocked on the door of my studio and asked, "What's going on with you?" I cried and told her my life story. For many years, I wondered if my mom was crazy. I wondered if I was crazy. I questioned if her hoarding was because of the Holocaust or if she was born that way.

I am doing what my mother did in my own way through my art. I understand now that she was an artist, but in a different time and with a very different background. I'm so much like her, and maybe I'm continuing what she wanted to do. My sculptures remain a form of paper-mache. I use paper, glue, fabric, and wood. Everything that I use is old. I am giving the materials new life.

I had this other experience when my father passed away. He passed before my mother. I was at a hotel, and I asked my husband and children to go away for a moment so I could be alone. I came across an article in the newspaper. It was an interview with an author. He said that human beings are like buildings. If the foundation of the building is not strong enough, the building will always tremble. I read that, and I cried so hard. I believe I rediscovered myself in that moment. I knew I had to get close to my mother. I'm now so thankful for her.

Since returning to the United States from Israel, I feel she is with me all the time. Through my art, a wall I built finally broke. I think when my parents passed away, especially my mother, they jumped into my soul and became part of me. They are always with me in the studio.

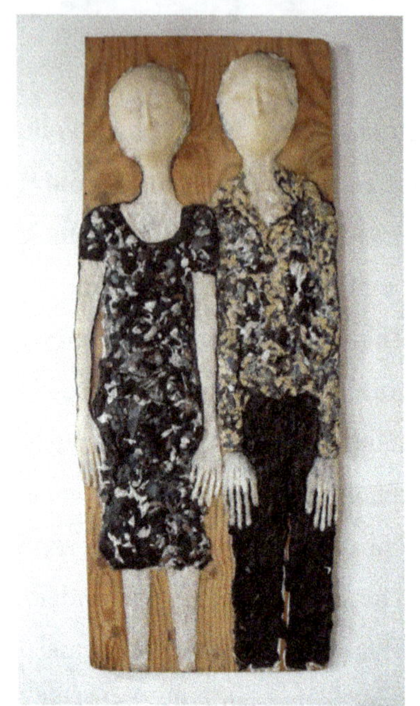

Malka Nedivi, *Couple,* mixed media on wood, 2012

IT'S LIKE I'M GOING BACK TO MY FIRST LOVE

Being immigrants was not just part of my parents' story; it was part of my story also. My husband and I came to the United States as students. Then we had a child. Life went by, and we found ourselves rooted. We built a life here. I love it here, but part of me will always stay Israeli. There is another part of me that continues to grow as an American. I try to not make those two parts fight. My immigration story is connected to the idea of home and making a home.

I've been making sculptures of houses. They are mostly created with paper. I shape them out of thin metal and chicken wire. They are not meant to be perfect. I put my feelings into them. Again, in my art, I see my mother. My mother was stuck at home. When I got to Israel to care for her, it's difficult to even describe how she was. She wasn't taking showers. She was eating moldy bread. I wanted her to be in a good place where she would eat well and everything would be better. She talked about her home like it was a human being that she could not leave. My home is part of the inspiration in my house sculptures also. I have a very nice home, but it will never be perfect. I feel that I have a need to build my home, from the inside, and I'm still building it.

I also make figures that attach to the walls of the homes. There is one woman figure, made from paper, who is almost growing from the home.

She is hugging it and also putting herself in the home. I wanted to build furniture and little figures to put inside the homes. I was starting to work on that when a curator came by. I was getting ready for a three-woman show, and the subject was being second-generation Holocaust survivors. All three of us artists had mothers who were in the Holocaust. When the curator came and I explained I needed more time to finish the homes and add the inside pieces, he said, "No, I like the homes empty. The emptiness of those homes tells a bigger story for you."

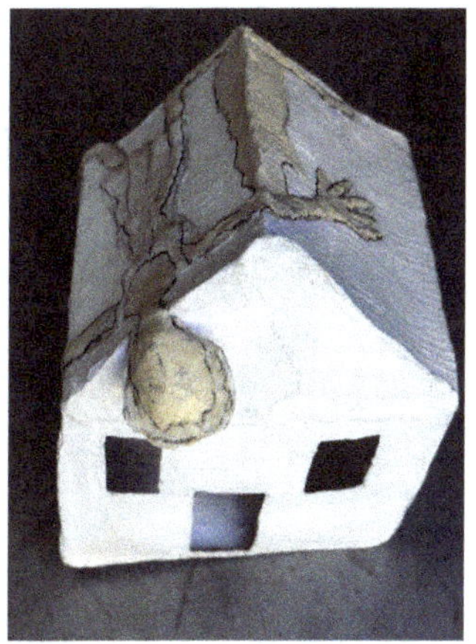

Malka Nedivi, *Home*, mixed media, 12" x 6", circa 2019

I am ambitious and want to do more with the home sculptures. I have ideas about stories and puppetry to go with the homes. I'm writing like crazy all the time. Part of this is to create and share my story in this way, which is an immigrant story. When I told my childhood friend from Israel about my idea of stories and puppetry, she said to me, "Malka, how wonderful. You first loved the theater. Now that you are starting to combine your art, sculptures, drawings, and paintings, it feels like you are starting to come full circle." It's like I'm going back to my first love: theater.

I AM STEPPING FORWARD THROUGH MY FEAR

As I get older, a lot of wonderful things are happening. I love this age. I am not afraid to be seventy. I am lucky with my health. I am able to be free. My life is only becoming better. Yesterday, I told my writing group of much younger people, "Don't be afraid to get older. A lot

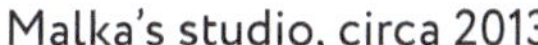

Malka's studio, circa 2013

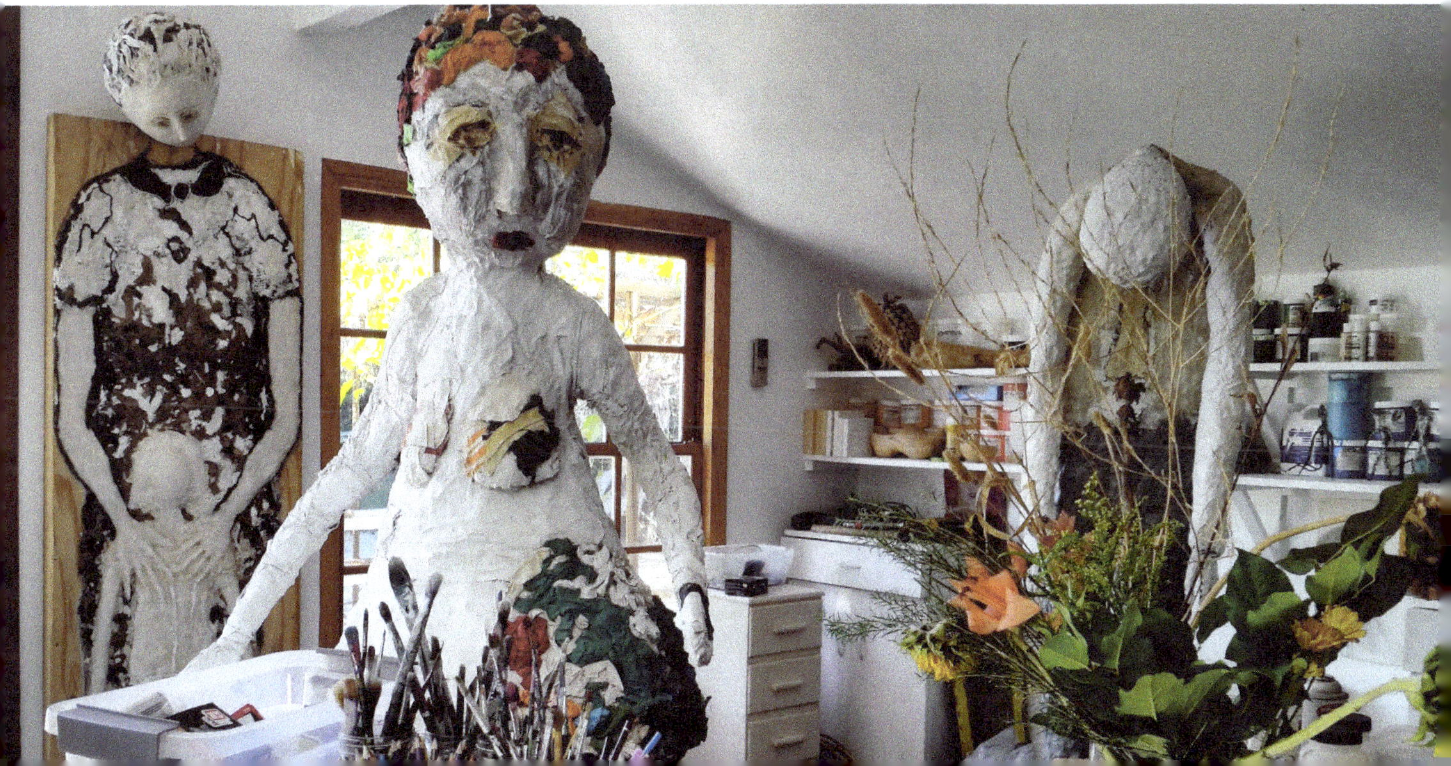

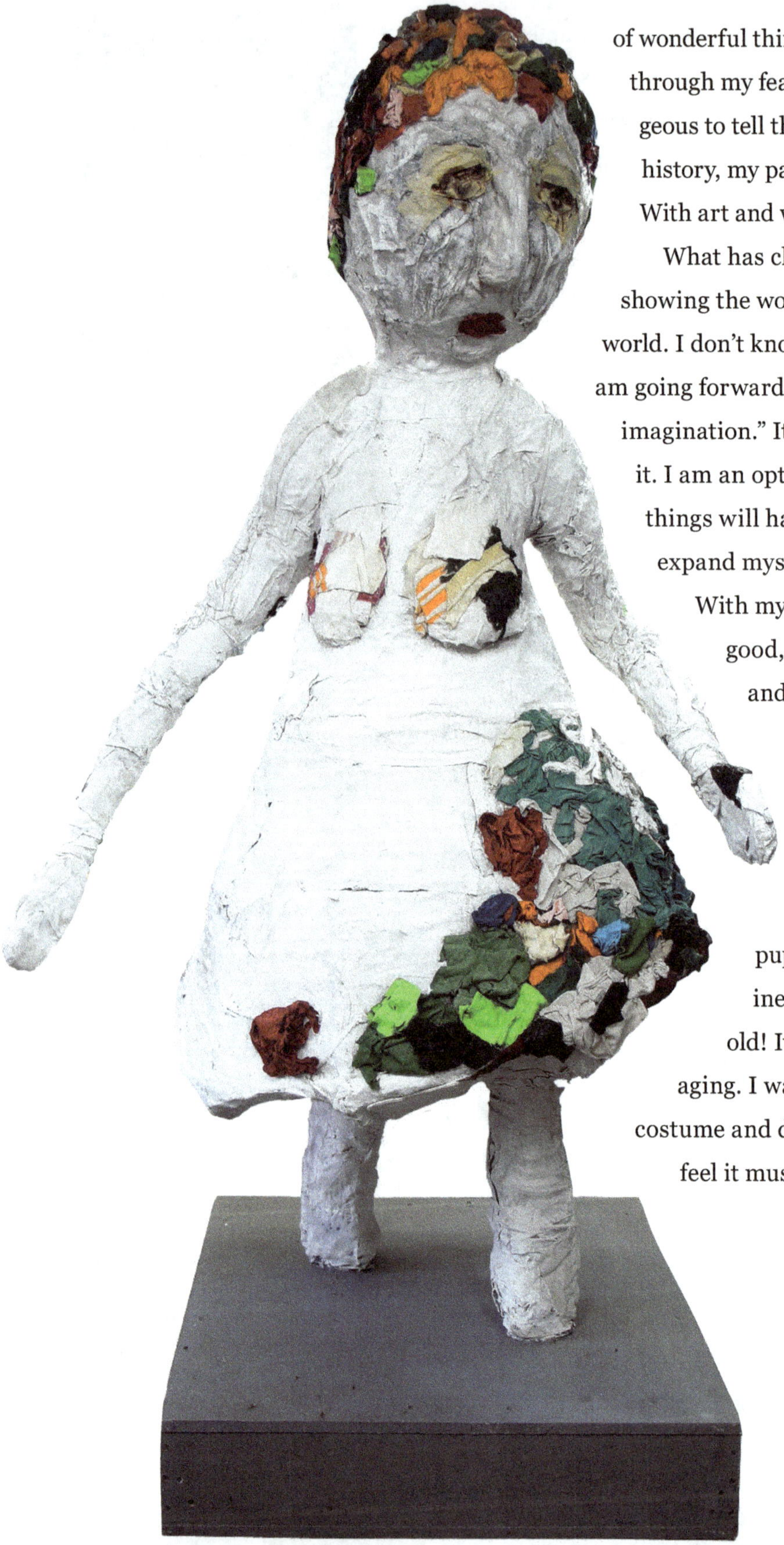

of wonderful things happen." I am stepping forward through my fear. I remain afraid, but I am courageous to tell the truth and to be connected with my history, my parents, and especially my mother. With art and writing, I can tell the truth.

What has changed with my age is less fear of showing the world who I am. It feels like, "Okay, world. I don't know what you expect from me, but I am going forward with my dreams. I am following my imagination." It's okay if the world does not accept it. I am an optimistic person, and I believe good things will happen. I'm continuing to grow, to expand myself and push myself to not be afraid. With my art, I cannot be a judge and say it is good, but I can show the truth to myself and the world.

It's amazing that I've been writing for the past three years. I found a writers group that supports me. The idea of writing my immigrant story to go with a puppet show for adults is fun to imagine. There is a humorous side to getting old! It's one of the beautiful things about aging. I want to even stand on the stage with a costume and do this show. I am still fearful, but I feel it must happen. ❖

Malka Nedivi, *My Big Doll,* mixed media sculpture, circa 2011

See *Confluence,* page 23

RITA BLITT

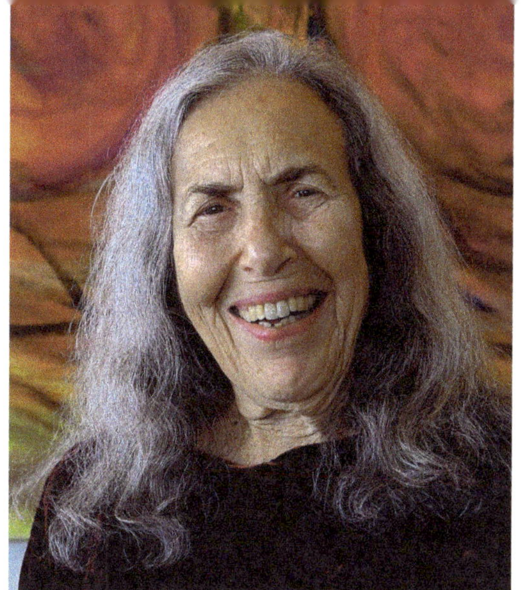

Visual Artist I Painter I Sculptor I Film Collaborator
Place of Birth: Kansas City, Missouri
Current Location: Leawood, Kansas & San Francisco Bay Area
Age: 91
www.ritablitt.com

I WOULD LOVE to see the arts and artists supported as much as possible. Art feeds the soul.

One of the most significant developments in my life as an artist occurred in the 1970s, when I was in my forties. I began drawing continuously every morning, realizing that my spontaneous lines were the essence of me, letting the works flow as long as there was still paper in the house. On this particular morning, I was drawing and probably had music in the background. All of a sudden, I picked up two Conté crayons instead of one. I was feeling so free. I drew with both hands at once. I was terribly shocked. I wrote in the lower right-hand corner of several drawings, "Two hands." I remember being startled and feeling like a circus act.

I REMEMBER BEING STARTLED AND FEELING LIKE A CIRCUS ACT

Shortly after this experience, my drawings were on hold during an installation of one of my sculptures. When I went back to drawing, which I vividly remember, I drew with one hand, and I felt awful. I felt awkward. I needed to draw with both hands to feel honest and whole.

I proceeded to work exclusively with two hands.

In 1981, I was drawing with two hands, starting at the bottom with my hands together in the center and then reaching outwards to the sides and up to the top. The shape created from this movement was an oval. After adding pastel colors and sharing the work with a friend, I shocked myself by saying, "This is what I have been searching for all these years. Why have I been dancing all over the page?" My *Oval* thus was born.

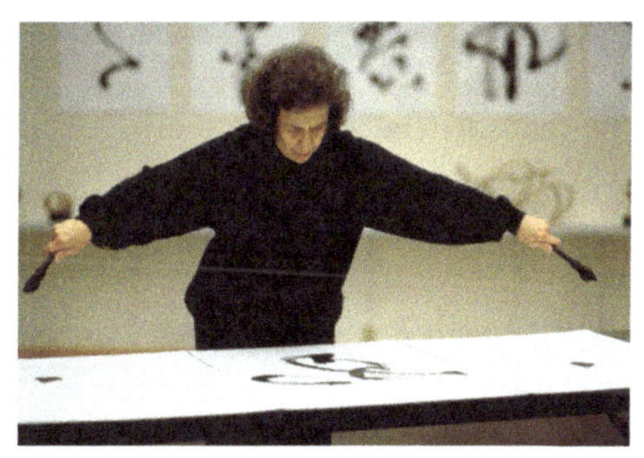

Rita painting with two hands in the late 1990s

This series contained some of my most important creations. Those works are very spiritual. After a few years, I realized that working with two hands was making me a more centered human being. This was an amazing and thrilling revelation.

After many years devoted to the oval, I returned to working with one hand, using either one hand or two as desired. In recent years, when beginning a new painting, I sometimes wonder if I have an obligation to pass on to the viewer the feeling of calm that comes from my own centering when creating with two hands at once.

Another important moment was in 1988 when I was close to age sixty. I was painting with two hands, and all of a sudden, I realized my eyes were closing as I worked. At first, I was startled. But then I decided to accept this new development in my process and not fight it like I did when I began working with two hands at once eleven years earlier. I realized that, like a musician performing at a concert, my eyes closed because my emotion is so deep while I'm painting.

MY WHOLE BODY IS INVOLVED

My body is very much part of my creative experience. When I create, it's movement. It's dance. My whole body is involved. I've become more and more aware of how important music is in my life.

Thinking about music and dance makes me want to talk about the 1990s, a very creative period, when I was in my sixties and seventies. Those years were so important for me. I was drawing every morning and "letting my hands dance on paper," until 1996, when my granddaughter Dorianna was born. During her first two months, my husband and I devoted ourselves to assisting our daughter Chela with her baby and loving every moment of it. I became so obsessed with Dorianna that it should have been no surprise when I returned to painting, wanting to dance across the eleven-foot-wide canvas with joy, that I made a painting that shocked me by its subtle reference to birth. This ushered in a new period of large, unusually strong paintings.

I WANT[ED] TO DANCE ACROSS THE ELEVEN-FOOT-WIDE CANVAS WITH JOY

In 2000, following the publishing of the book *Rita Blitt: The Passionate Gesture*, while still drawing and painting, I became very involved with films that were an organic extension of my art. The films I collaborated on provide an integration of my art with music and dance. The collection *Rita Blitt: Visions of My World* includes nine of my films of creative inspiration. The film *Caught in Paint*, which was invited to over one hundred and thirty film festivals internationally and received sixteen awards, features David Parsons and the Parsons Dance Company. During filming. I painted on four-by-eight-foot transparent surfaces while the dancers are seen through the painting making movements along with my paint strokes. The photographer Lois Greenfield captured this creative and magical energy. It has been said that to understand the art of Rita Blitt, one should view the film *Caught in Paint*.

KINDNESS IS CONTAGIOUS. CATCH IT!

Another significant part of my career is the Kindness Program. In the early 1980s, my friend and Kansas City activist Beth Smith stopped me as I was crossing a bridge in Aspen and said, "I wish you could create something we could send all over the world to make the world a better place." I was quite flattered that she thought I could do such a thing, but it seemed impossible; how could I send something all over the world, and what could it be? Five years later, these words came into my mind: "Kindness is Contagious. Catch it!"

It may seem unbelievable now, but at the time, it took a lot of courage to talk about kindness. I was afraid to embarrass myself. What would people think? Still, I felt it so deeply and cared so much that I pursued it. Now, everybody talks about kindness, and I'm thrilled.

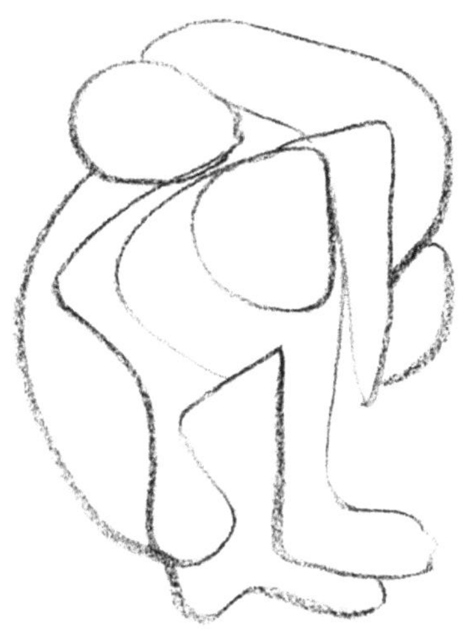

Rita Blitt, *Inner Torment*, drawing with Conté crayon, 22" x 30", 2016

In 1990, the Kindness Program was created to encourage kind and compassionate acts of humanity all over the world. The program is now managed by Synergy Services and is more localized to the Kansas City area. There is an annual essay contest with thousands of students submitting an essay nominating their favorite person for the annual Kindest Kansas Citian Award. There is also the Rita Blitt Kindest School Award. I created small sculptures to give to the three kindest Kansas Citians and a large sculpture to give to the recipient of the Kindest School Award.

It's a wonderful thing that has resulted! I witnessed how so much creativity goes into making a school a kind place. I feel that everybody who enters the competition becomes more conscious of kindness, which means a great deal to me.

I STILL HAVE A LOT OF CREATIVE ENERGY

I'm continuing to grow, following my deepest inspirations, and enjoying what I'm doing. It takes total concentration, practice, and devotion. I've always had a push within to grow and be the best artist I can become. This is not about being famous, but rather owing this to myself.

I'm currently working on a film related to drawings I made in the 1990s. I drew during a concert of Kodo drummers from Japan. I filled two drawing notebooks in response to the music. Ever since then, I've been wanting to create something more with those drawings. I love them. I didn't want them to just go into my Legacy Collection at the Mulvane Museum as closed books. Right now, I'm doing a film using about forty of those drawings. The film should be finished soon if all goes well. It's a short film, but it has filled me with the satisfaction of doing something that for a long time I have really wanted to do. The finished film will be called *The Sun Still Shines*.

While making the film, I was also very busy trying to place my remaining work, which meant I did not have as much time to create as I wanted. You can imagine how much I've created over my lifetime from drawing every morning until there was no more paper in the house! In recent years, because I am so prolific, at moments, I hesitated painting, thinking, "Oh my God. What am I going to do with it all?" But now, I realize that I must not have those futile thoughts. I should allow myself the joy of creating.

When I was younger, in my forties, fifties, or later, I never thought about what life would be like at the age I am now. I just lived in the moment and did what I loved.

As I enter my nineties, I realize I must continue to create, or I would be denying myself the pleasure of being alive. And I must continue giving and inspiring others. I just hope that I will be blessed with the energy I need. I don't move as fast as I used to, but I'm very lucky. I still have a lot of creative energy.

I'm happy to create smaller works now, but if I had no physical limitations from aging, and no constraints with space, I would be painting huge canvases. I used to dance across the canvas with great freedom and abandon. At my age, I must be cautious not to fall.

An important thing for me to share about my life as an artist is that I have always put my family first. I'm lucky to have spent my life with a

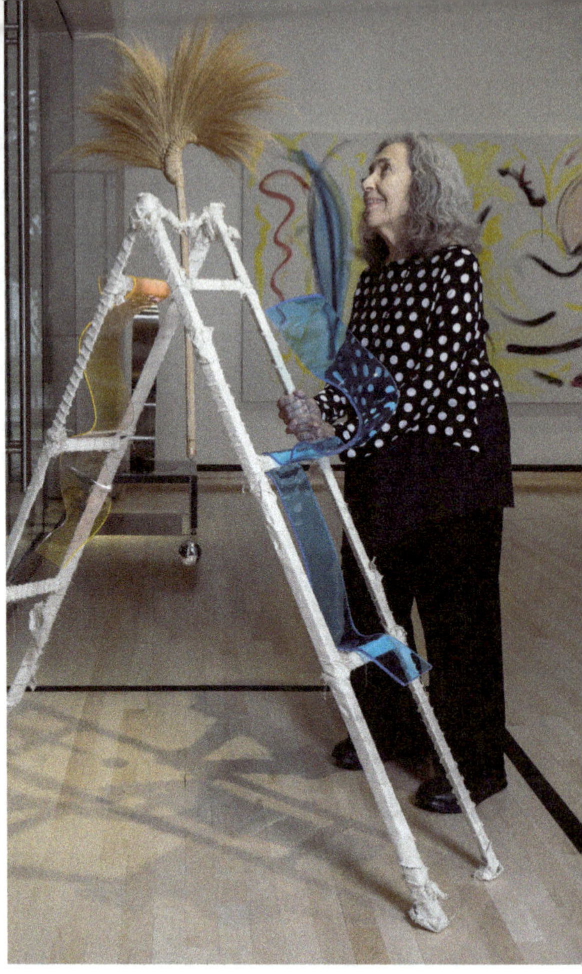

Rita with her found object sculpture *Dance of Destiny*, 1973, opening of The Rita Blitt Gallery and Sculpture Garden, Mulvane Art Museum, Washburn University, Topeka, Kansas

I MUST CONTINUE TO CREATE, OR I WOULD BE DENYING MYSELF THE PLEASURE OF BEING ALIVE supportive husband. I know that my ability to express love as I've been able to do has been key to my creativity. My husband, Irwin, passed away three years ago. We were married for sixty-six years.

Because of my conviction that my family was my first priority, I've been able to enjoy being a wife and mother as well as an artist. I have felt free to create. ❖

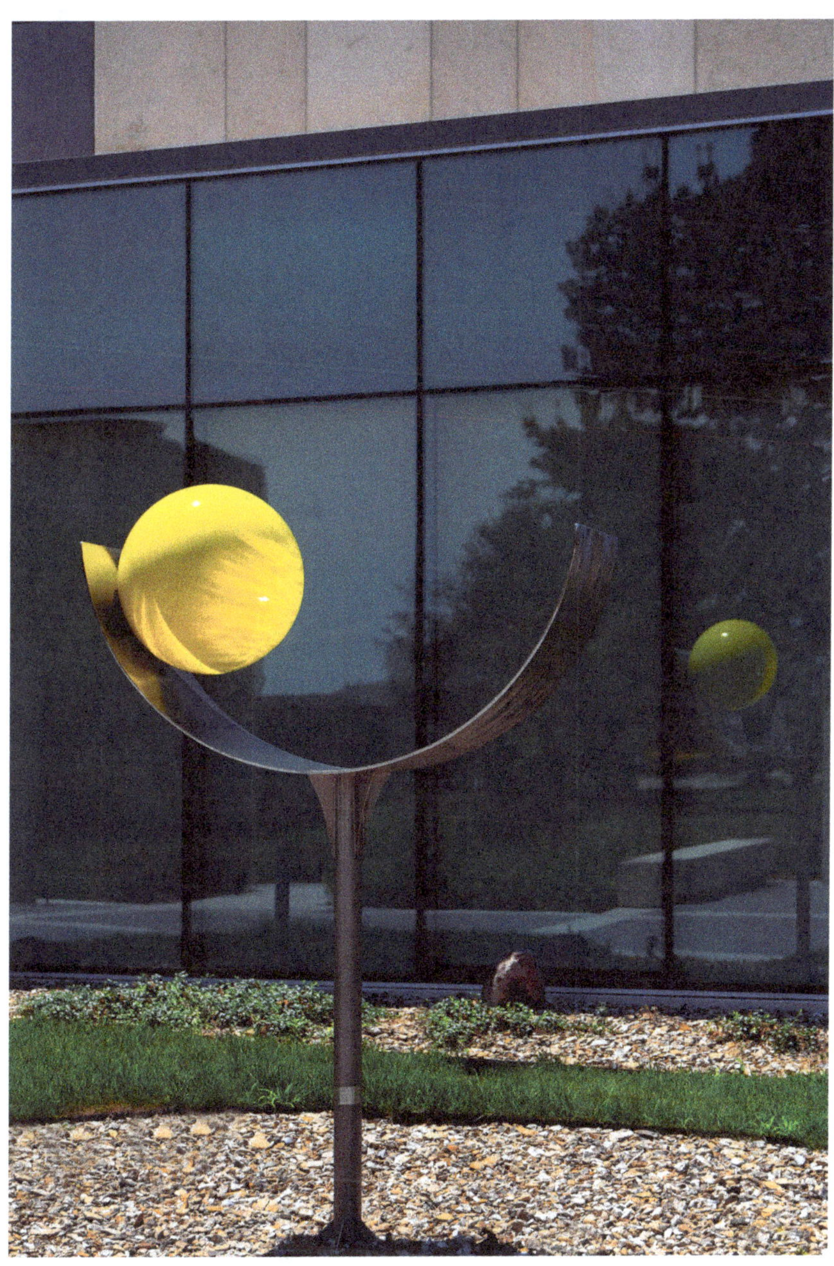

Rita Blitt, *Lunarblitt XVI*, fondly referred to as Rita's "Yellow Ball" sculpture, created in 1975, located in The Rita Blitt Sculpture Garden, Mulvane Art Museum

See *Flowers from Kitchen,* page 24

YOUNG YUN SUMMERS

Visual Artist I Collage and 3D Mixed Media Artist
Place of Birth: Seoul, South Korea
Current Location: Los Angeles, California
Age: 71

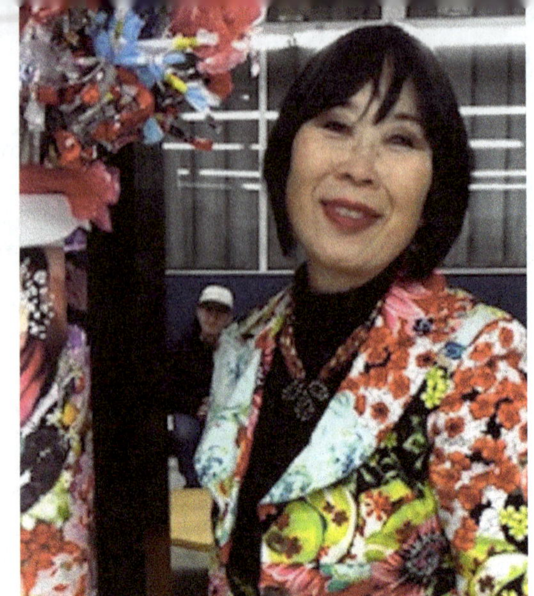

I CAME TO America from South Korea in my last year of high school. I grew up in the post-Korean War era, when the country was one of the poorest in the world. My parents fled from the North to the South before Korea was divided into two. My mom told me about their harrowing escape for the first time when she was around eighty years old. I was born in South Korea and have never met my relatives in the North. I believe my parents must have felt like refugees in their own country.

After my older brother was sent to college, my parents decided to send me, their second child, to America. We had several relatives here who wanted to help me go to school. Even though we were poor, college was something we were expected to do in my family. Everyone went to college, except my grandmother. My father died when I was about to start college, but my mother still managed to send my two younger siblings to college in Korea.

ART WAS ALWAYS WITH ME

Becoming an artist was not a stage in my life. Art was always with me. I started drawing when I was very little—even before I began school. I remember drawing in my older brother's textbooks, probably the only paper available at the time, and on the pristine white wall in a new house of old relatives. To their credit, my parents never scolded me, although I recall my older brother being upset. I carried a crayon or piece of chalk in my pocket if I found one. Maybe that's why I've always liked clothes with pockets. By the time I was in second grade, I was considered the artist in my class and the one chosen to participate in competitions. In the fifth grade, I won all the art competitions in my school, beating out boys and older students.

At my new school in America, Los Angeles High School, I was chosen to attend Art Center College of Design for life drawing classes for high school students on Saturdays, and also the drawing competition at the Los Angeles County Museum of Art. I spoke very little English and was unfamiliar with everything, but my art was the saving grace. Art was the subject I didn't have to try hard at. Even in college, I was surprised that a classmate practiced his figure drawings, because I never did. It was instinctive. It must be in my genes.

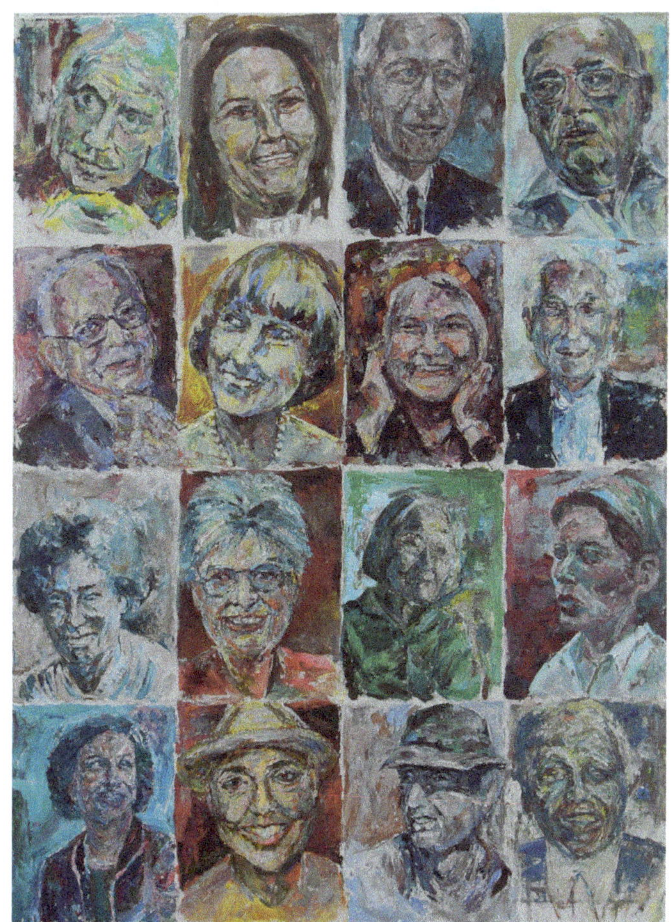

Young Yun Summers, *Ode to LA Times Obituaries*, acrylic on canvas, 36" x 48", 2014

Just about everyone in my family was into art. My father's older brother was a prominent artist in Korea, and an older cousin was a successful commercial artist in New York. My oldest aunt went to Japan to study art when very few Korean girls went to school. My father wanted to study art but, according to an aunt, wasn't permitted. I also found out art was my mother's favorite subject in school. She took up watercolor painting when she was around seventy years old. All of my three siblings liked art. One went to art school, and another went to architecture school.

I first attended LA City College, a community college, and then transferred to UCLA and earned a BA in Design in Fine Arts. Being an art major was the most natural path for me, but majoring in design was a little different. I pursued it more for a practical reason. I thought if I studied design, I would have a better chance of getting a job in the commercial art field, whatever that might be. Fashion design/illustration was one of the fields. I had a memory of my mom telling me to be a fashion designer as she watched me draw. A fashion history class at UCLA reinforced the thought that I had the aptitude and passion for it.

ALTHOUGH I WAS GOOD IN MY DESIGN CLASSES, I WASN'T HAVING FUN

When I got to college, I mostly stopped drawing as a design major, even though figure drawing had been my first favorite medium. It wasn't part of the curriculum then. My college life consisted of a lot of theories

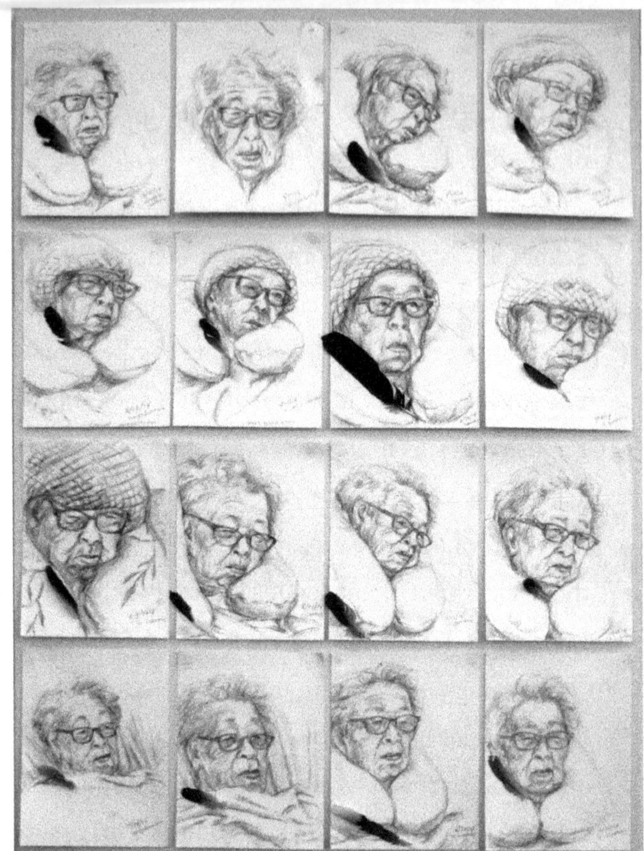

Young Yun Summers, *Toughest Bird*, charcoal pencil and feathers on paper attached to canvas with thread, 36" x 48", 2015

and art histories. My life started changing as an artist. I think I kind of died inside. Without realizing it, I even stopped doodling, like I'd lost the tools to express myself. Design was about discipline and precision, with a focus on making lettering and other things perfect. Although I was good in my design classes, I wasn't having fun. Academically, I made the Dean's Honor List twice in my first year in college. I spent a lot of energy trying to navigate everything and overcome my shyness and the language barrier.

When I graduated from college, I thought life would change for the better with my degree in hand, but I found myself totally lost after UCLA. I didn't know what to do with my degree. I wasn't prepared for a job, and I couldn't get hired with my limited English and interview skills. It was a low point in my life. I considered pursuing a job as a fashion illustrator or fashion designer. I enrolled in fashion illustration and pattern-making classes. I also had experience working at garment factories as a seamstress during school breaks. I really believed I had the aptitude and passion for it. But what did I know? I didn't get anywhere because I didn't know the field. My dream died.

I had to make a living, so I continued to work as a cook at the International Student Center at UCLA. I did some bookkeeping for a year, but I made mistakes and was fired. Being the pre-Internet era, I would search in the *LA Times* for a job. For a while, I worked touching up antique carpets. During this time, I took various art illustration classes at UCLA Extension. I just dabbled as much as I could afford as I got by on itty-bitty jobs. Then I finally got a job as an in-house graphic artist. This was my first stable job with benefits, vacation, and sick time. From there, I got another graphic artist job, and another one. I changed jobs for more creative opportunities and better pay. I ended up doing a lot of typesetting and making forms and charts. I became very good in inking! I did my best to make a boring job interesting.

I then found a job in retail advertising as a designer. I thought it would be a temporary job until I could find something else, but I got pregnant, so I stayed because of insurance and other benefits. Then my husband started having medical issues, so I remained in the job for the health insurance and the job security.

THAT'S WHEN I WOKE UP

Finally, I got back to my art. When my son was in junior high, I started thinking about saving money for his college. I read about the animation industry using artists who could draw, so I signed up for an animation character design class. I was nearing fifty. I liked the class for the novelty even though I didn't have the feel for the geometric formulated shapes.

One day, my instructor brought a life drawing teacher to the class. This is when it clicked. I thought, "Oh, this is what I like to do. I draw naturally looking at living things." That's when I woke up. I knew this was my passion before I buried it all away.

I decided to continue with life drawing classes. I was a busy working mom with a kid who had after-school music and dance lessons, but I was able to fit in my classes at nights and on weekends. Life drawing became a big part of my life. Later, I found a life drawing class at a nearby community college. One day, the teacher told me, "You should take painting since you are so good at drawing." I thought, "Painting? It's so messy and takes up space." It wasn't until my son went to college that I decided, "Why not?" My husband was in and out of the hospital too. He had been a painter (we were fellow art students in college), so I pulled out his old paint tubes and brushes. I started my painting career in my fifties. I was fired up. I knew I wanted to do it.

I felt so happy when I was painting. I didn't have a studio at home then. I started out small, on the kitchen table. As my canvases grew, I would set them up on my front porch to paint until dark after I came home from work. On weekends, I painted in the back yard. I would carry these large canvases with me to school. I remember the feelings of anticipation to work on paintings as I drove home. Something opened up in me when I was painting.

Still, it wasn't all about my happiness. I was thinking of selling my paintings to pay for my son's school loans. I was focused on getting into shows and galleries. As a mom and wife, even doing my art at this time was still for the family. I realized everything I did my whole life was for the family.

I DESCRIBE THIS WORK AS SHAMANISTIC

After I was painting for a while, I had an experience when I was at the ocean in the San Diego area that ultimately led to me being a collage artist. The tide went in, and these rocks were exposed. They looked so strange, like creatures glistening under the gray sky. I was fascinated. I decided to take photographs of the rocks and put the photographs into my painting. I made possibly fifteen paintings in this series. I describe this work as shamanistic.

I'm aware that many people believe in shamanistic spirits in nature. I witnessed that growing up in Korea. I saw shamans who would come and dance over sick people. I also saw the signs of shamanistic rituals in trees and rocks where it was believed spirits lived. Those glistening rocks on the beach startled me with their strangeness. They spoke to me, and I have vivid memories of it. There is a mystery about it. I've started painting this mystery. I painted the rocks as if they were alive.

I kept developing those paintings and looking for more ways to incorporate life into the rocks. I added more textures, but I wasn't happy. Out of desperation, I picked up one of my husband's fishing magazines and took some pictures to add to the painting. I had never done collage before. I didn't know how. I was just looking for a way to bring the rocks alive. I was really uptight at the time, and I had no idea if adding the magazine images was helping or not. I took the canvas to show to my new teacher, Doug Harvey. He looked at it and said, "I haven't seen one done like that before." Then he said, "Do all collage. One hundred percent collage."

I went home and started collaging on a new canvas. I worked on this first collage for a whole month. I spent hours at nights and on weekends. I took this collage to the teacher, and he responded in a way in which I knew it was good. From then on, I went to the next one and the next one to more than a dozen.

Currently, I only use found materials to make my collages. I'm concerned about the trash in the environment. My collaging is strictly for using up those materials that are to be discarded and to keep them out of landfills. I don't even have to go out and really look for anything. I can easily find things in my mailbox, yard, and kitchen.

As I've gotten older, I'm able to loosen up more. I used to be so careful and fearful of the imperfection and loose ends. It's mind-boggling, the number of hours I spent fussing over a piece of work. I was concerned about what teachers, gallery people, and jurors would think of my work. Now, I've gained enough confidence to use my own judgment. Since I'm creating for myself, I feel very free. I will work on a piece until I'm happy.

SINCE I'M CREATING FOR MYSELF, I FEEL VERY FREE

I also used to envy people who could talk in a fancy way about art. But now, I read and listen to the criticism to see whether or not they understand the artists. And this ties into how I used to be so concerned about money and being able to sell my work. Since I am free from any obligations, I am able to make art and think my own way. My place is a mess as I'm always collecting for my art. This is another expression of my freedom. I would love to have a big studio where I could indulge in every conceivable art size and form, a big storage space for my growing collection of recyclable materials for future projects, and a gallery space to show and share with other artists.

I found out if I did things to make me happy, then other people would respond to it. If I really put my heart into it, something about it would generate that feeling in others. It's a universal sensory thing. The way I look at art by other artists has also changed. I used to be overly concerned about the technique and skill and judged accordingly. Not anymore. Something can be technically so wonderful, but if there is no human emotion or feeling conveyed, that piece will be like a beautiful decoration. I want to create art that shows the emotional journey and doesn't hide it. ❖

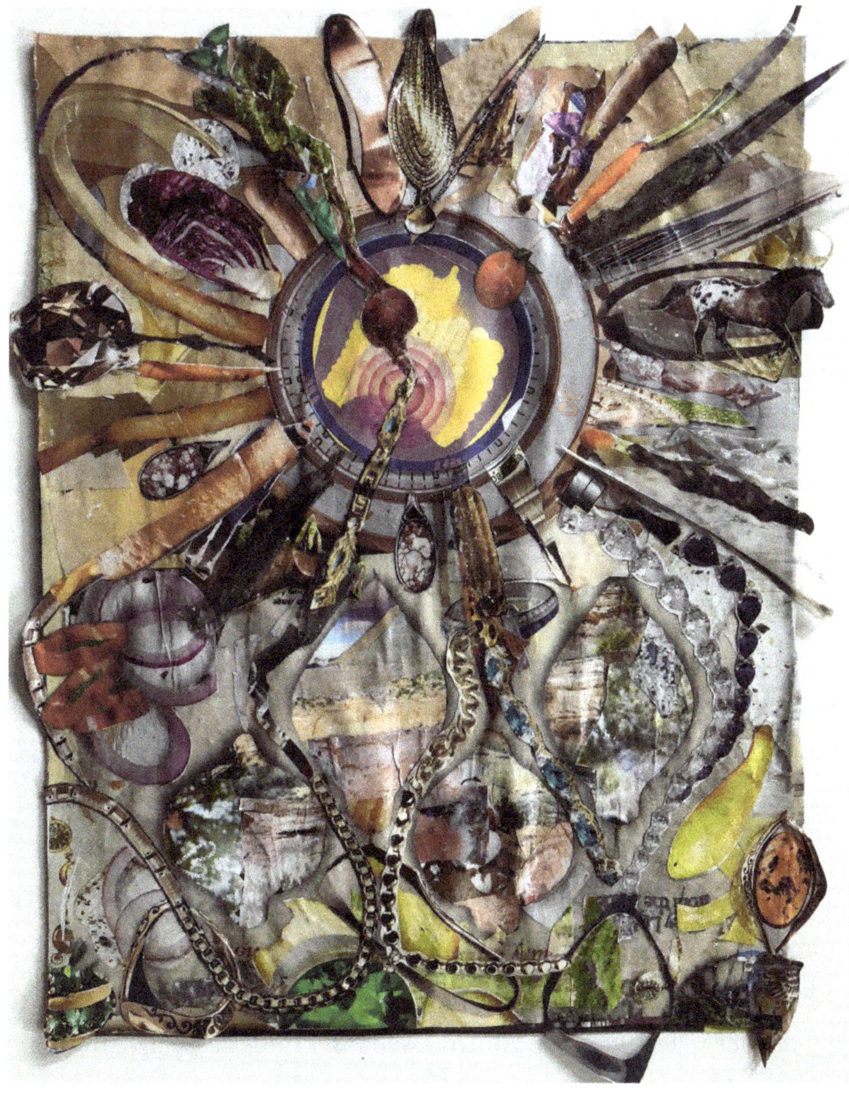

Young Yun Summers, *Time in the Pandemic,* collage on cardboard ads, 10" x 14", 2020

See *Beyond 70 - 2 Waves of Life,* page 25

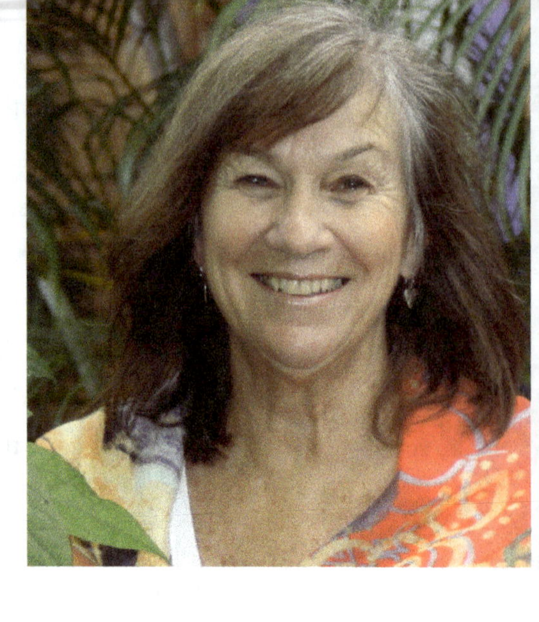

KATHLEEN HORNE

Visual Artist I Registered Expressive Arts Therapist (REAT) & Consultant Educator (REACE)
Place of Birth: New Westminster, British Columbia, Canada
Current Location: Sarasota, Florida & Cortes Island, British Columbia
Age: 75
www.expressiveartsflorida.com

THE WHOLE CONCEPT about feeling old or being old is that I'm now pretty comfortable owning my age and being an older woman. It has not been entirely smooth getting to this place. It's still evolving. I don't want to fool people about my age or deny it. I wish to embrace being a crone and an elder. In some ways, I'm more vital and engaged now than maybe at any other time in my life.

My journey with art is inextricably linked with my journey of healing. As a child, I drew, painted, danced, put on plays, and sang. I have an older brother who was and is still an extremely gifted artist in many ways. He was an incredible realistic artist from a young age. He drew pictures of wildlife. He could draw anything without any apparent laboring. It was as if his drawings appeared magically on the page. My brother would not begin with a sketch. He could start with a foot of a lion down in the corner of the page and work up the leg until he would have a perfectly proportioned and beautifully detailed lion.

HE GAVE ME [A] GIFT THAT WOULD SHOW UP LATER IN LIFE AS A HEALING SYMBOL

I am four years younger than my brother. I thought that the realistic art he was creating was what "art" is. I didn't know that there were other ways to express yourself as a visual artist. I watched what he did and tried to draw that way. My family was kind and supportive, but I knew I didn't have that thing he had. They would say things like, "Oh, that's nice too, honey." I was maybe eight or nine when I put all my visual art supplies away. I don't remember making a conscious decision, but I remember painting a robin that was quite realistic and being happy with it. That is the last thing I remember drawing or painting. From about age nine to age forty, I believed I was not artistic in the visual sense.

Another significant thing that happened when I was young is that my grandfather taught me how to use a compass. He showed me how to create the design in the middle of the circle that I now recognize as the center section of the flower of life. He didn't use the word "mandala." He didn't use the words "flower of life." I doubt that he'd ever heard those words. I was really captivated by drawing with the compass and coloring my designs in intricate ways. I also stopped doing this, but I always feel like he gave me this gift that would show up much later in life as a healing symbol.

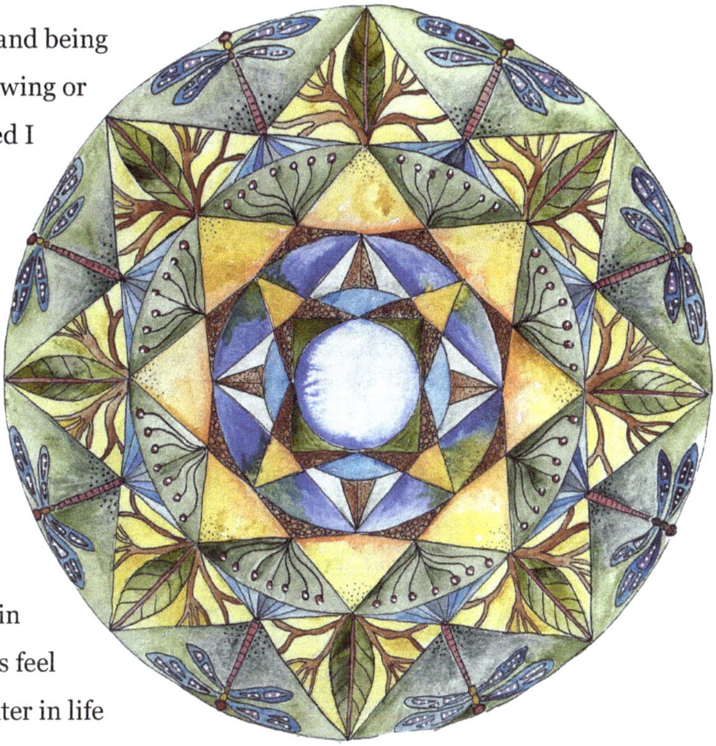

Kathleen Horne, *Clarity at the Center*, watercolor on paper, 2020

During the long years when I was not creating visually, I did some writing. I was more comfortable expressing myself in other art modalities. I studied psychology. I dropped out of the university and had a family. Then I went back and finished my degree. Eventually, I got my master's degree, and I became a therapist. I was happy being a therapist and believed I was decent at it, but I also felt like something was missing. I wasn't exactly sure what that was. Some things then happened all around the same time in the early 1990s, when I was in my forties.

I was working part-time as a counselor in an art college, which meant I was surrounded by all this creativity. Being a staff member gave me opportunities to take classes for almost no cost. I took a big risk and enrolled in a couple of classes. I had a major eye-opening experience. It was an awakening. I discovered there are ways I can express myself in visual art. It was an exciting time. I remember moments of putting an image through a press in a printmaking class and taking it out when it came through. I was literally jumping with excitement.

I WAS LITERALLY JUMPING WITH EXCITEMENT

Around the same time I was working at the art college, I was also a therapist and supervisor of a program with children who've been sexually abused. I received a grant to bring art students from the college to work with the children. It was amazing what happened when art was introduced into the children's therapy. Their healing escalated in a beautiful way.

With the therapy program blossoming into this amazing and powerful vision, I knew this was the right pathway for me to take. I didn't know what it was going to look like. At the same time, I was going through some difficult personal transitions. I would wake up in the middle of the night and feel that I needed to make art. I had to express myself visually. I started with collage and then used some of the techniques I was discovering in my art classes. This became an essential part of my own healing journey.

Another part to this time of my life is that I saw a little ad in a magazine. It read something like, "Certificate in Expressive Arts Therapy for practicing psychotherapists at California Institute of Integral Studies." I felt tears on my cheeks. Although I knew what art therapy was, I had not heard of expressive arts therapy. Mountains moved, and I found myself in that program in three weeks.

I FELT TRANSFORMED INSIDE

This was a huge investment. I was living in Florida. I didn't have the money or time, but little miracles happened. A client who hadn't paid me for about five years all of a sudden paid me. More tiny miracles happened. And then there I was in California. After the first three-week session, when I came back to Florida, people would ask me, "How was it?" I would stand there with my mouth open. I wondered if I even looked like the same person when I felt so transformed inside.

The expressive arts program felt like a year of therapy, a year of graduate school, and a beautiful retreat/vacation. I was beginning to entertain the idea of calling myself an artist. I brought the expressive arts into my therapy practice as much as I could. Eventually, I met people who became my partners in Expressive Arts Florida Institute, a business and training program we founded. I would have been close to age sixty at this time. I realized the expressive arts were such a gift to the world that I didn't want to practice it only within the therapy paradigm. I've also been fully engaged in my own art practice as a visual artist since then. I don't really separate my work and my art since everything comes from the same place.

Within the context of my own journey, the expressive arts is a reunification of the artist archetype and the healer archetype. I

WE HAVE AN ENTRY POINT INTO A DEEP WELL OF INNER WISDOM

believe that through our creativity, we all have this entry point into a deep well of knowing and inner wisdom. By engaging in the arts, we make this visible to ourselves, and we embody it. Of course, this is a very old idea going back to indigenous ways of knowing. Although the profession of expressive arts is relatively new, the well of wisdom on which the field is built is ancient.

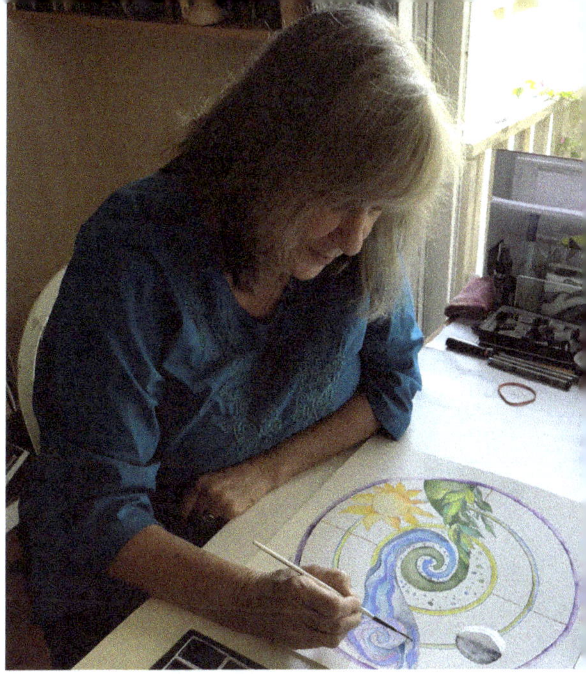

Kathleen painting a mandala, 2021

In the expressive arts, all the arts modalities—visual art, movement, writing, rhythm, sound, music, drama—are interwoven and interrelated. All forms of creative expression arise from the same source, and an integrated approach offers myriad opportunities for growth and transformation. By practicing the intermodal arts, we find our way to a deep knowing and healing. We are able to connect to our inherent inner wisdom and healing power. This can be practiced in so many different settings and with diverse people. It's important for therapists and facilitators using the expressive arts to understand the depth and scope of the power. With this understanding, we introduce it in ways that are going to serve the purpose of the person or group that we're working with.

When I think of my creative life as I've gotten older, what comes to mind is that I've never been much of a planner. I see my life journey as a meandering path. This journey is similar to starting an abstract painting and not knowing where it's going. I take cues from the next creative impulse. A message has been coming up for me lately. It's coming from my art. The message from my art is that now is the time for me to do the heart of the work.

NOW IS THE TIME FOR ME TO DO THE HEART OF THE WORK

When I think of my forties, fifties, and sixties, the image I have of myself is where I'm standing on the top of a hill with my arms wide open. This image says, "Yes, I want it all." Anything I could do and anywhere I could go to spread my work that fed me and moved through me as a life force, I wanted to do it. Start a business? No problem. Start a training program? No problem.

This was the same thing taking place with my own art practice those years. One day, it was mixed media. The next day was mandalas. Then it was watercolors, or I found myself obsessed with acrylics. It was all over the place, but in a good way. What's happening now though is I feel a rhythm of my life at seventy-three that is very different than forty-five, fifty-five, or sixty-five. I want to distill everything.

I'm spending my time, energy, and resources in the purest way that I can practice my work. I'm asking, "What is really important now?" In my expressive arts profession, my heart and my gifts are aligned with teaching and facilitating and also moving more into writing about this journey. I'm also noticing that my lifelong love of immersing myself in nature, my connection to the earth, and a commitment to sustainability are coming together in my practice. Maybe it's partly because of the pandemic. It is certainly because of the climate emergencies. I recently completed certificate training in ecotherapy and ecopsychology. I feel a sense of more integration coming.

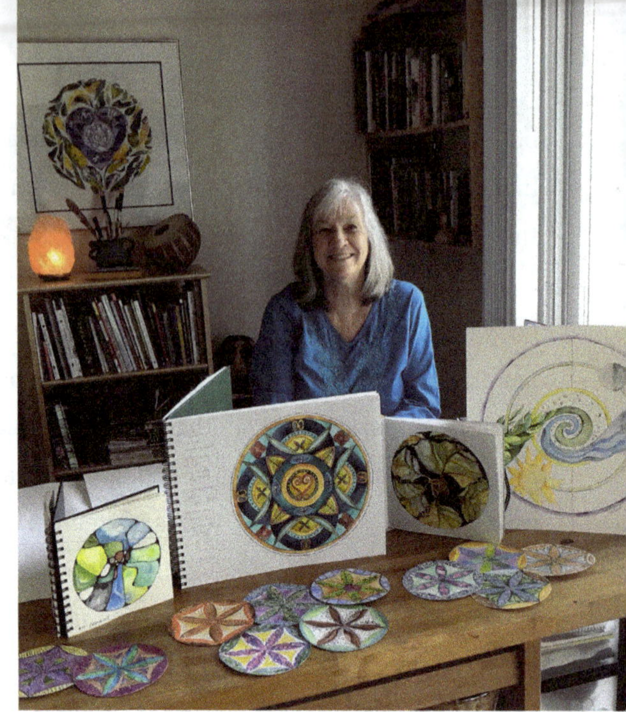

Kathleen with some of her mandalas, 2021

With my personal art practice, this idea of doing the heart of the work means increasing my artistic focus. One way of doing this is making my home art practice a priority and setting aside more time. Another is looking through this body of work of mandalas that I've created for many years. I'm documenting those and continuing to create mandalas in a more intentional way.

I also find myself increasingly drawn to the textile arts, especially anything that I can stitch by hand. This is interesting because a long time ago, when I was a young mom and I was disconnected from myself as an artist, I spontaneously started doing free-form embroidery. This interest in textiles almost feels like a full circle coming together.

If I had the means to do anything with my art at this stage of my life, I would have a simple little creative healing studio in a natural setting with a lot of outdoor space. I would spend my days there, following whatever creative impulses arise. My mandalas would be on the walls inside, and likely outside too. Sometimes, others would be welcomed to join me, and I might be a collaborator or a guide, or we might just work alongside each other. There would be no need for monetary exchange or categorization of services. Creative expression would be our meeting place. I would also have time to create in solitude, to spend a lot of time with my family, and to wander and explore the natural world.

IT'S TIME TO FIND A DIFFERENT RHYTHM

I'm not going to, and I don't even want to keep up the kind of pace that I had as a younger person. It's time to find a different rhythm. My creative life needs to be a part of this new rhythm. I perceive the time I have as precious and want to treat it that way. This includes time for my family, my partner, my creative work, and my connection with nature. This time is a distillation and integration of these different elements. My challenge with this evolution is to continue to distill the essence of my work into a purer form.

When I was a younger woman, even though I've never been much of a planner, I believe I always pictured myself as being vibrant, alive, adventuresome, and creative as an older woman. My grandmother lived to one hundred and one, and I have an aunt who is a practicing artist in her nineties. My mom and these other women in my family never seemed to consider themselves old.

I honestly do not consider myself old. I'm kind of surprised when I get my age mirrored back to me from other people, or sometimes when I look at myself in the mirror or see a photo and I am taken aback. I certainly don't feel old inside. I remember being young and sometimes making assumptions about older women based on their appearance. When I think about those women now, I realize how limited and stereotypical my thinking was. I wonder now what was going on inside of them. We are all simply fuller, wiser versions of our same younger self, each with our unique and special gifts and wisdom. ❖

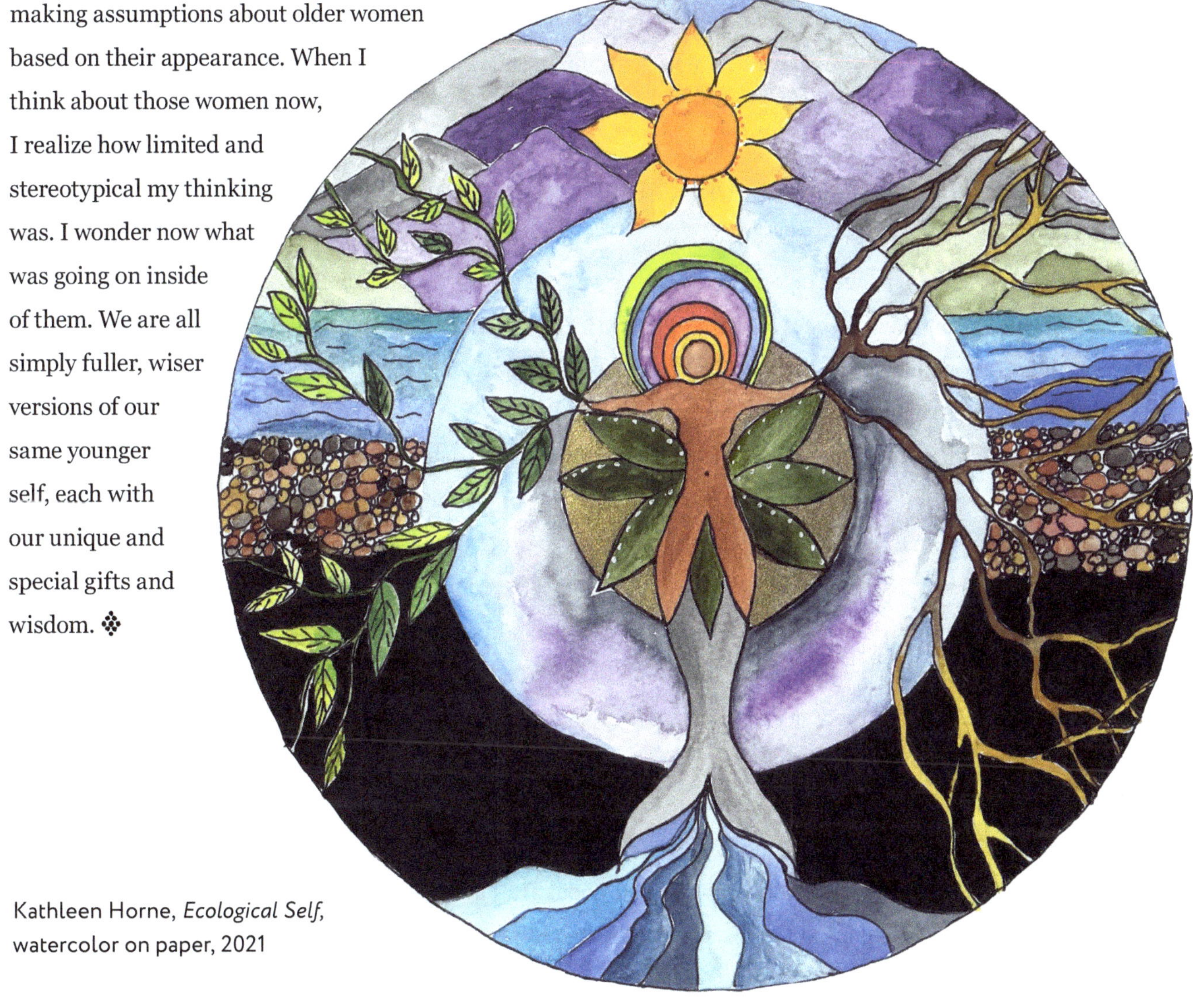

Kathleen Horne, *Ecological Self,* watercolor on paper, 2021

See *Miss Lucy,* page 26

PHYLLIS I. THOMPSON, PhD

Monotype Printmaker | Mixed Media Artist
Place of Birth: Washington, DC
Current Location: Buffalo, New York
Age: 76
www.phyllisithompson.com

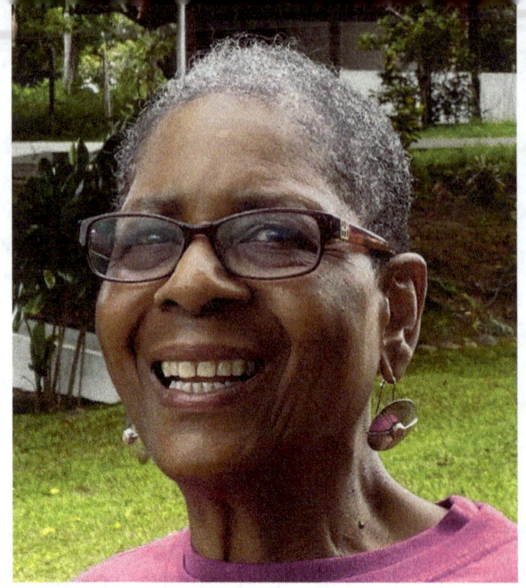

IF I COULD change something about my art practice at this point in my life, I would live near the ocean and walk most mornings before working in my studio. I would watch the sun come up, listen to the sound of birds and the water, and absorb the smells of the air and plants. In this way, I would reinforce my connection to the universe.

> BEYOND FUN, I DISCOVERED THERE WAS SOMETHING SERIOUS ABOUT ART.

I didn't realize I was an artist until high school. However, from a young age, I liked to draw, color, and make things, just like so many other children. My parents and teachers noted my artistic activities. I remember my third-grade teacher in particular. She would praise me and my artwork. With this teacher, I ended up creating bulletin boards with cursive lettering that I cut out for the headings. I just loved it. As I went into fourth and fifth grade, I was the star artist in the class.

Throughout my elementary and secondary years, I attended Philadelphia public schools. My sixth grade teacher recommended me for a Saturday program at the Samuel S. Fleisher Art Memorial. The program, run by professional artists and teachers from the Philadelphia area, offered painting, drawing, and sculpture classes. My parents supported me taking the trolley car from North Philadelphia, where I lived, to South Philadelphia, a distant part of the city. My mother went with me the first few times. This was a rite of passage for me. I was twelve years old and had never traveled so far alone on public transportation before.

I started to see the visual arts as something that was a real occupation. Beyond fun, I discovered there was something serious about art. I attended this Saturday program from sixth grade to eleventh grade. The teachers were artists, and the artists were teachers, and there were specialty areas in which they exceled. There were exhibitions all the time showcasing various artists' work. This was reinforcement for me. When I brought anything I created home, my mother would frame it and put it up on the wall. This was another form of positive reinforcement I received.

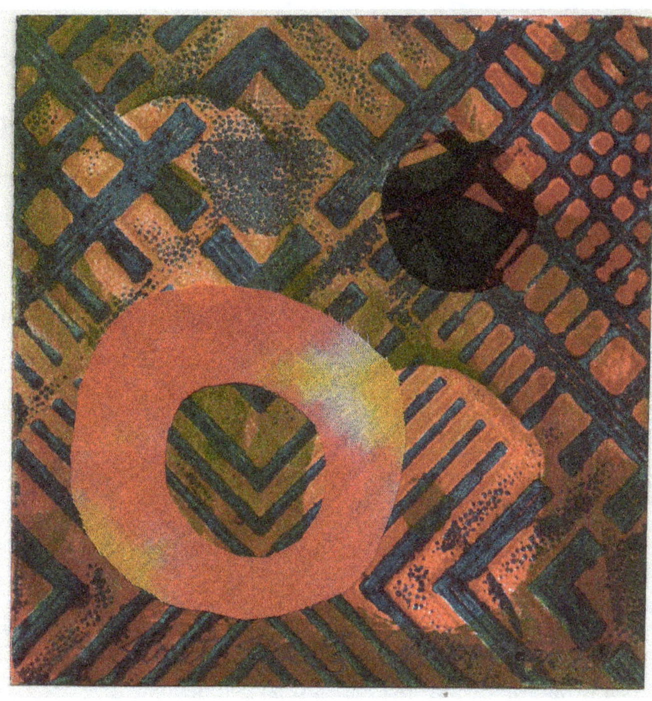

Phyllis I. Thompson PhD, *Secret Space #3*, mixed media monotype, 6" x 6", 2019

In school, we were referred to as "disadvantaged children." We learned this meant that we were poor and most of us were Black, except for maybe a few Latino students. There was an effort on the part of the teachers to really work with us and not pigeonhole us because of poverty or a lack of exposure. They got us out into the city to attend cultural events. Philadelphia had a lot to offer. It was a very nurturing place.

In high school, my art teacher selected a small group of us, maybe four or five, who were serious about the visual arts. We were prepped to go on to higher education. We visited art schools and prepared portfolios. I ended up attending the Philadelphia College of Art that is now called the University of the Arts.

[THE] WORK REQUIRES CONCENTRATION AND FLOW

At the Philadelphia College of Art, I wanted to major in fiber textiles, but they didn't really have a formal program. From early on, I admired family quilts and coverlets created by my grandmother. I appreciated the sculptural doilies my mother crocheted and the scarves and hats she knitted that could also be admired on the wall. My grandmother had a particular process she used to create a yo-yo. It's a 5" fabric circle that's gathered in the center, and you connect the circles until you have a large coverlet for the bed. When I was a little girl, I remember her sitting on the porch and making these little circles. She would have hundreds in a paper bag. I believe it is because of these memories that I was interested in majoring in fiber textiles, but since it was not available, I ended up in printmaking, which was my second choice.

When I applied to Tyler School of Art at Temple University for graduate work, I wanted to major again in fiber textiles, but I was not able to because my undergraduate experience was not related. Fibers was my minor, and I majored in printmaking again. Some of my creations were reminiscent of woven fiber pieces. I like repetition. I like the repetition that is found in weaving even though I do not weave. I connect this repetition with what my grandmother was doing over and over with her little yo-yos. This work requires concentration and flow. You can be completely removed from your thoughts, so it becomes mindless in a way as your hands work, and that is a good thing. I find that sometimes when I am drawing, I make marks without thinking about every mark I am putting down. Sewing and drawing are similar activities to me.

For a while after graduate school, I was teaching at Cornell University. This was an influential period for me. I would go down to New York City regularly, and I met a number of artists there who were part of a movement to make the art establishment more inclusive of women. There was an emphasis on women's work (craft) being viewed as high art, as opposed to it being viewed as low art and insignificant in the art world. I took a leave from the university and lived in New York City all of 1977. I rented a loft space in Chelsea. During this time, I visited the artist Miriam Schapiro in her studio. She created colorful, patterned collage paintings with craft materials such as quilts, flowers, fabric, dolls, and crocheted pieces. I also admired the work of Faith Ringgold, Judy Chicago, Betty Saar, and Alma Thomas. All of these artists embraced color, pattern, cultural icons, and so-called "women's work" in their images. Living in New York City was so reinforcing of my interests.

WORKING WITH MEMORIES BECAME CENTRAL TO MY ART

I remember my mother saying that she would rather crochet than eat. She said that when she was growing up, all female children learned to crochet. She loved it. She was also an excellent seamstress and made our clothing when we were children. Even though I was left-handed, she taught me to knit and crochet. My memories from childhood surfaced during my time in New York City.

Working with memories became central to my art. When my mother started to lose her memory and moved in with my sister, I went to her house to clear things out. I found many

Phyllis I. Thompson, PhD, *She Liked Patterned Cloth #1*, monotype, drawing, collage, 11" x 15", 2015

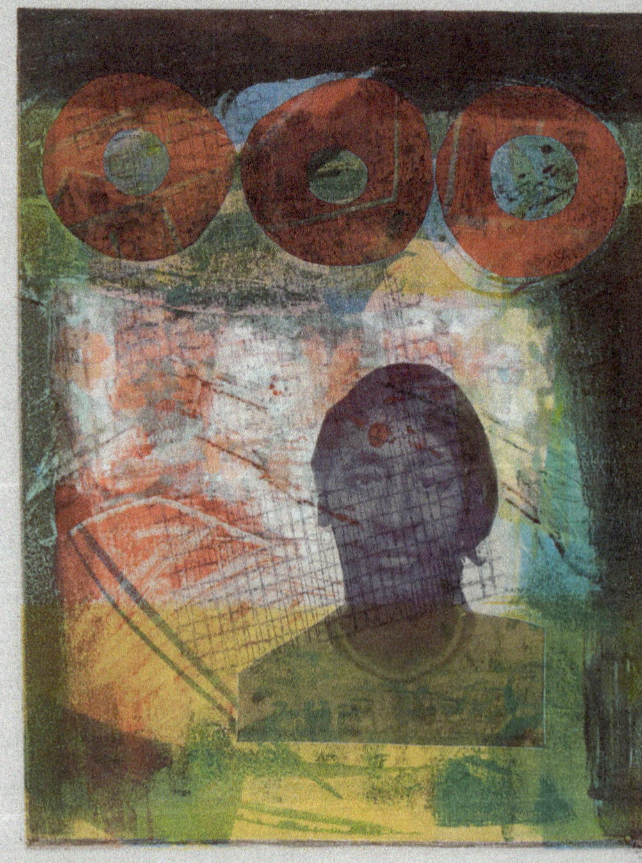

boxes of photographs under her bed. Some were very old and peeling. These were ancestral images of people I did not know. The photographs had been brought by my mother from her mother's house in Maryland. This was such a find for me. I took all the photographs plus quilts, doilies, and other things she or my grandmother created back to my home.

There was a sadness with all of this, but recently, I started to look at the photographs and use them in my work. I wanted to connect with my ancestors and give them a new life. I also use circles a lot in my art, and the circle symbol is reminiscent of my grandmother's yo-yo circles.

Another part of my story is that I had children later in life—or what was considered later back then. I believe I was thirty-five or thirty-six and thirty-eight when I had my children. I had been independent for so long and working on what I wanted to do when I wanted to do it, so it was a big transition. During that time, I was really conscious of certain women who were active with their art even with children. I went through a lot of doubt. You receive messages that if you are a real artist, you take a corner of your kitchen table as a workspace and don't ever stop working. I was aware of other women artists who did not have children or had them when they were much younger. It was difficult at times because I didn't have the energy between trying to make money and take care of the children to consistently make images. I had to come to grips with it.

WHEN I GRADUATED, IT WAS THE WHOLE FAMILY'S DEGREE

I taught middle school for about five years during this time. Interacting with other art teachers and their students helped me recognize the need to prepare art students who wanted to teach youth, especially in urban settings. I started looking into career options and was attracted to academia again. I found myself going back to school in my late forties at the University of Wisconsin, Milwaukee, where I completed a PhD in Urban Education with a focus in Art Education. I believe I was fifty-three or fifty-four when I finished my dissertation.

I worked as a teaching assistant for the art education department while earning my degree. Even though I had a fellowship, we needed the money, so I had to teach additional courses while in school to make ends meet. I attended my classes at night and taught during the day. At times, I'd take my kids along with me to class in the evening.

Phyllis I. Thompson, PhD, *Evolving Memories #4*, mixed media monotype, 12" x 24"

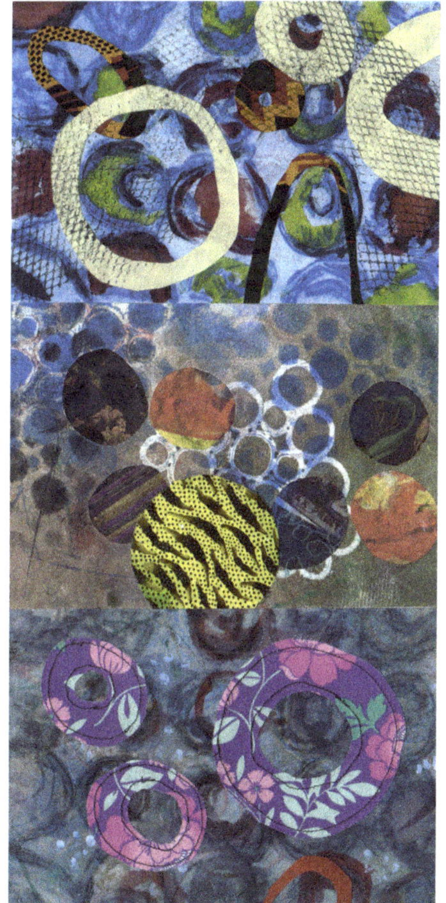

I was married, and my husband was very helpful and supportive, as were my children. It was tough, but it worked out. When I graduated, it was the whole family's degree.

While writing my dissertation, I taught full-time at the University of Wisconsin. I was not in the art studio; I was focused on writing and publishing. After graduation in 2001, I taught at Kutztown University for two years and finally retired from teaching at Buffalo State in 2018. Something happened to me when I was teaching at Buffalo State. I went through some emotional changes and depression. I realized it was because I really wasn't doing all that I wanted to do. I was neglecting that artist part of me, and it made me sick. I needed to return to my art practice.

I'M A PART OF OTHER PEOPLE

I don't believe the basic content of my work has changed a lot since getting older. My marks and symbols—that is my visual vocabulary—has expanded and grown but stayed with me, and my interest in printmaking, fiber processes, ancestors, and memories has persisted. There was a time in the 1970s and 1980s when I was working on paper almost exclusively, making oil pastel drawings and etchings. I also moved into sewing wall compositions with hand-dyed Pellon and fabric and making quilts. Most recently, I've been making monotypes. A monotype is a single print taken from a design created in printing ink on a flat glass surface. The design can be printed on a press or by hand. I'm attracted to the monotype process because of its indirect method of producing a printed image that leads to elements of surprise. No matter how much I plan, surprise is part of the process. Making a monotype is akin to collaging, painting, and drawing on paper.

One major change in my images is the use of realistic subject matter via photographs. Previously, my work was exclusively color, shape, pattern, and texture. Now, I am more literally telling visual stories with my monotypes.

I've also been moving toward celebrating my travel and special things I've collected over the years in my art. I take photographs of these special things, such as a platform shoe collection from the 1970s, and use the photographs in my work to give these objects another life. All of this is connected to memories, including photographs and artifacts from my travels. It's about resurrecting an experience or a memory that is part of me. These experiences make me who I am. When I remember and

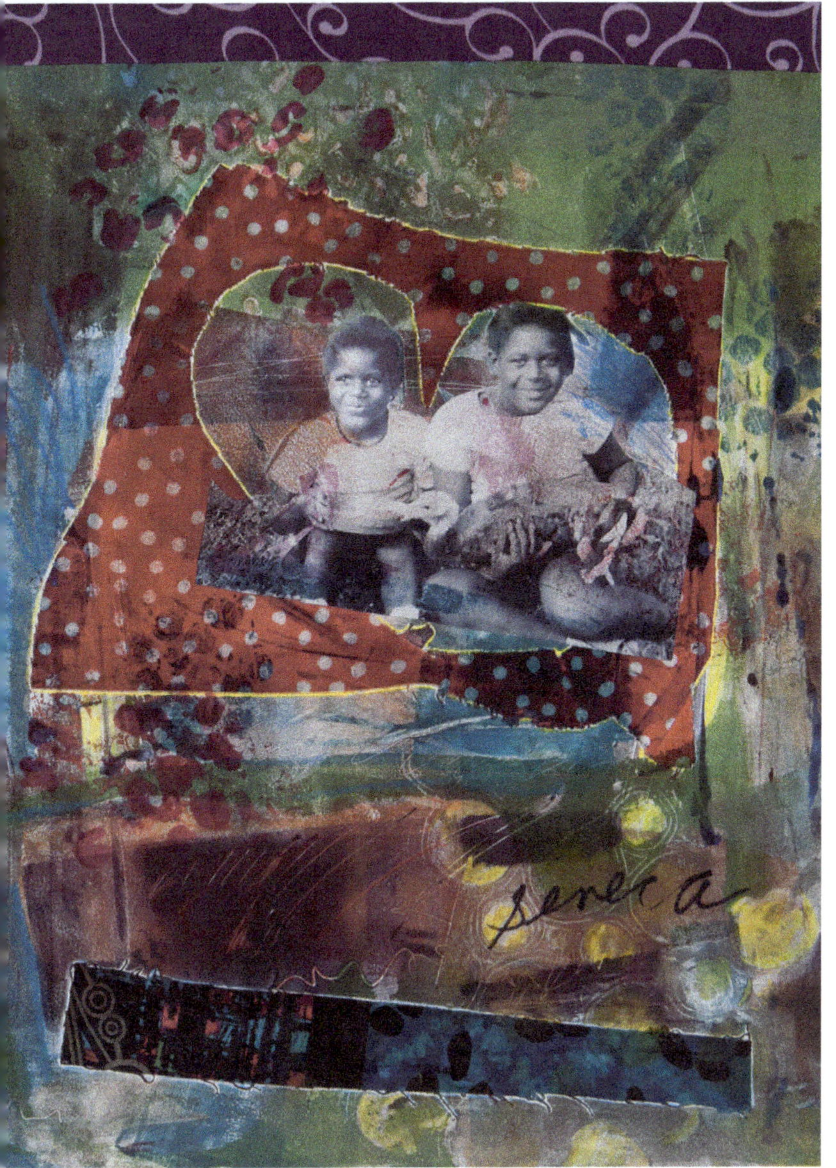

Phyllis I. Thompson, PhD, *What We Did One Day*, monotype, collage, drawing, 13.25" x 16.75", 2017

revisit them, they become more meaningful. People may be able to relate or respond to my memories and experiences in the world through my art. It's an expectation that there will be a connection, even with our similarities and differences, because I'm a human being. I'm a part of other people.

I have focused a lot on the women in my life in my art, but I've also focused on my father. The photographs I have continue to help me work through issues with him as I create. Even though my father is no longer here, I can find answers by looking at a photograph, such as the image of a car he owned. Contextual information surrounding the period starts to flow, and I reconsider it with new insight and maturity. These pieces of memory are my collage material. Working with memory in this way, through my art, I can answer some questions I've had about my early life and my parents in particular. It can be really positive to rethink an early situation in your life. I've considered writing stories about the insight I've gained into specific life experiences while making images. I remember being young and seeing older visual artists who were active and still having shows. I wondered if I would be like that. I will continue with my art throughout my seventies and when I'm eighty and ninety.

AGING ARTISTS [ARE] NATIONAL TREASURES

When I consider the larger context of art and ways to support artists, I believe artists who pursue formal education should be taught how to not only survive but prosper in their particular disciplines. It seems to me that millions of people pursue careers in the arts, but few really develop and grow. So much success is based on chance, luck, and who you know. If I could, I would also pass legislation that recognizes aging artists as "national treasures" and provides them with the necessary resources to continue their art practice without struggling for the rest of their lives. ❖

See *Danza Ocelotl,* page 27

YREINA D. CERVANTEZ

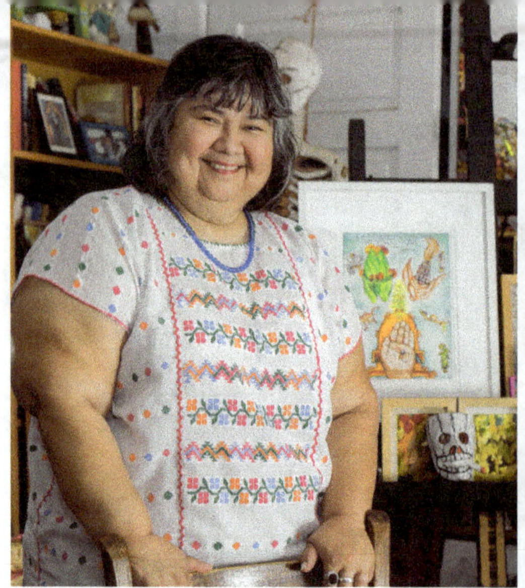

Visual Artist | Painter | Printmaker | Muralist | Educator
Place of Birth: Garden City, Kansas
Current Location: Los Angeles, California
Age: 70

I'M A THIRD-GENERATION Chicana from a working-class background. I was born in Kansas and started school not long after Brown v. Board of Education had passed. From a young age, I was aware of discrimination and racism. I saw early on that the kind of attention you got in school depended on your ethnic background. I didn't know how to name what I saw, but the prejudice was certainly something that I felt and experienced.

ART PROVIDED A PLACE OF SOLACE

When I was seven years old, we moved from Kansas to a rural agricultural area in Southern California. I lived on a turkey ranch at the foot of Palomar Mountain, close to the La Jolla, Santa Ysabel, Rincon, and Pala Indian Reservations. Here, Native peoples were the original caretakers of the land, white growers usurped the land, and mostly Mexican migrants worked on the land picking avocados and citrus. You could see the class divisions. In school, it was a polarized situation. There was also a lack of equity in terms of the way children were treated, depending on whether you were white, Mexican, or Native American. White children received more positive encouragement and guidance.

My parents were conscious of these issues, and they were aware of the civil rights movement in the 1960s when I was in elementary school. Because they had grown up in Kansas facing similar conditions of segregation and discrimination, they identified with and were supportive of the African American civil rights movement, and later, the Chicano movement when it became more prominent. I am forever grateful to my mother and father for their compassionate insight, and for teaching their children to be understanding and accepting of all people.

Throughout elementary school and up to high school, I was drawing and painting. Art provided a place of solace, my sanctuary. When we were living on the ranch, I painted landscapes and desert scenes in watercolors that were inspired by Aboriginal paintings I had seen in the *National Geographic* magazine. My mom was also very artistic and had wanted to attend art school to pursue her talent, but it wasn't an option for her. I remember coming across her drawings and different things in her scrapbooks, including calligraphy. She had beautiful handwriting. I was lucky that my parents encouraged my interest in art. This was so very important.

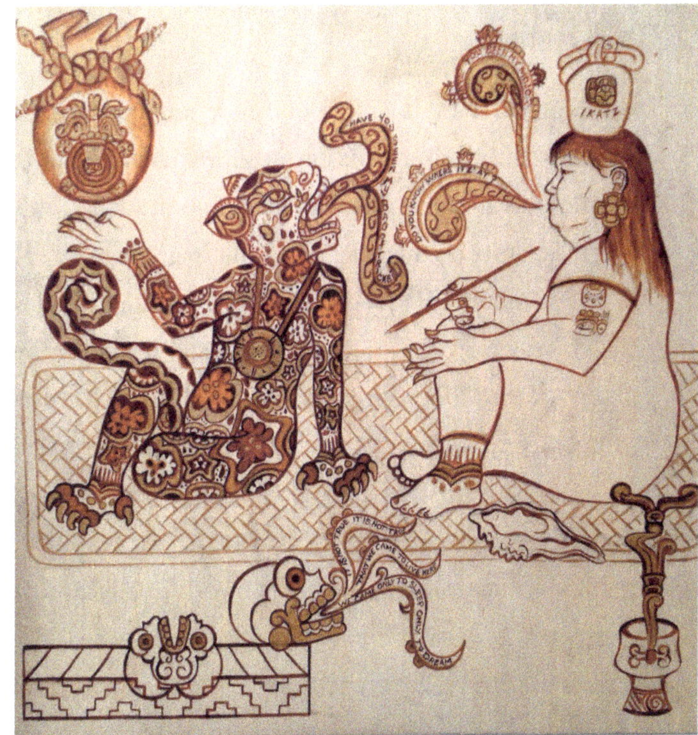

Yreina D. Cervantez, *Do You Know Where ITZ' AT Searchin' for My Mojo*, acrylic on wood, 2014

I WOULD BE THE FIRST IN MY FAMILY TO ATTEND COLLEGE

I attended Fallbrook High School for two years. Then, in the summer of 1968, my family moved to Orange County—the county next to Los Angeles that is known to be politically conservative. I attended Westminster High School for my junior and senior year. It was the beginning of a militant Chicano movement with a burgeoning art scene, great activism, and outreach into the community. I did well in school and thought about going to college for the first time. My parents encouraged this, but we didn't know how to navigate it as I would be the first in my family to attend college. I was fortunate to get support from many good people, including Ms. Jean Cavanaugh, our school librarian and MEChA sponsor, and Professor Vivian Hall, as well as my high school counselor and the outreach extended from the MEChA students at Cal State Long Beach. Through them, I became more informed of the possibilities for continuing my education. College programs such as EOP (the Educational Opportunity Program) and financial aid assistance and scholarships were vital in providing much-needed resources to students of color.

When I finally decided to go to college, I only applied to one school: UC Santa Cruz. This is because I saw an article about the university in *Life* magazine that made it look ideal. I can remember the photograph in the article to this day. It showed a professor in a classroom sitting at a table with maybe six students within a beautiful nature setting. I said, "I want to go there."

At Westminster High School, we started the United Mexican American Students (UMAS) that later became *Movimiento Estudiantil Chicano de Aztlan* (MEChA), translated as the Chicano Student Movement of Aztlan. My participation in MEChA was key to developing my political consciousness. Our sponsor, Ms. Cavanaugh, was a fabulous, intelligent, and progressive librarian with a delightful sense of humor. She was down to earth, not afraid of the Chicano students, and very respectful. Ms. Cavanaugh treated everybody equally. We unanimously agreed on having her as our sponsor. She was a mentor for all of us.

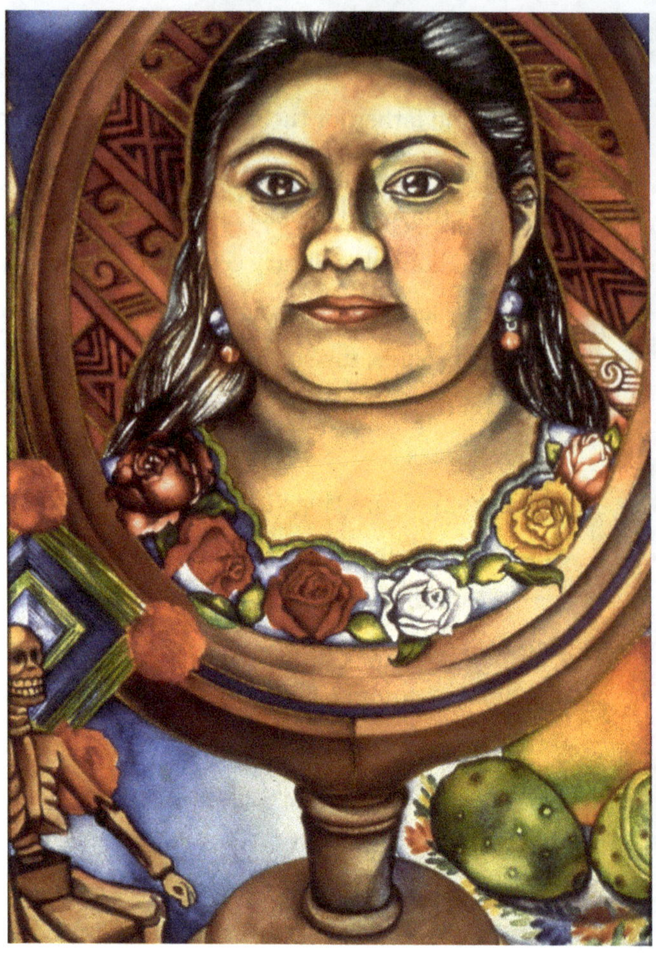

Yreina D. Cervantez, *Disfrutamos la Fruta De Nuevo*, watercolor, 1993

Another very important person at Westminster High School was English teacher and progressive advocate Vivian Hall. She later became politically active in Orange County, and in 1976 was a Democratic nominee for Congress in the 40th Congressional district. Mrs. Hall was this spunky and feminist Jewish woman, and we remained friends throughout her life. Coincidentally, her daughter Lorna was a student at UC Santa Cruz, and Mrs. Hall said to me, "Oh, you must go visit the campus and meet some of the professors." This never occurred to me, and I had never flown on a plane! Through the help of those two incredible women, I was able to visit the campus and meet with some professors. Our campus MEChA generously paid for my airfare. It's important to mention these early examples of support and encouragement that helped me get to the university and pursue my career as an artist. Networking and making connections are things that perhaps are taken for granted by people from affluent families or people with college educated parents. Hopefully, with the coming generations of students of color, we can pass on this kind of guidance and networking.

THE PERSONAL IS POLITICAL

I was accepted to UC Santa Cruz, and a California Opportunity Grant that I applied for provided a stipend that paid my tuition for four years. I learned a lot from my instructors at UCSC, including Professor Eduardo Carrillo, the only Chicano art professor I've ever had. Unfortunately, Mexican art or art by artists of color was missing in the curriculum. Most of the art classes were taught from a Eurocentric perspective. Nonetheless, I did have some very good professors, such as Professor Hardy Hanson. In my freshman year, I had an experience that blew my mind when Professor Hanson took us on a field trip to Stanford University. There were two exhibits, one on of the work of graphic artist José Guadalupe Posada, who is known as the father of Mexican printmaking. He influenced many artists who came after him, including *Los Tres Grandes* (muralists Rivera, Siquieros, and Orozco) and the *Taller de Gráfica Popular*, the Popular Graphic Arts Movement founded in Mexico in the 1930s. In another gallery, there was also an amazing exhibit of German Expressionist artist Käthe Kollwitz. The work of both of these artists really helped cultivate my interest in printmaking.

In class, I learned more about the artwork of Käthe Kollwitz, a great sculptor and printmaker. She was persecuted by the Nazis because of her progressive work and anti-war sentiments. My discovery of Kollwitz was significant because she was a woman addressing issues of the working class and social justice.

I often had to do my own research to discover artists of color as at the time, there was very little accessible information on the subject at school. I eventually found some information about Frida Kahlo, though there was not much available about her or any other women artists of color in Latin America, the United States, or elsewhere. Both Kollwitz and Kahlo did amazing self-portraiture. I also started doing self-portraits as part of an assignment in Professor Hanson's class. At times, I questioned whether my self-portraits were relevant or political enough. I began to understand, also through feminist studies, that the personal is political. The work of Kollwitz and Kahlo further encouraged and inspired this understanding. I continue to create self-portraits today. Along with the personal, I often include cultural and political elements, which go beyond the individual and resonate with the larger community in what Chicana feminist writer Gloria Anzaldua refers to as "Auto-Historia."

I remained politically active throughout college. There were Third World coalitions, anti-Vietnam War demonstrations, and this was also the time that various boycotts on grapes and lettuce were taking place in the US, protesting against unjust labor practices. Chicana/o students from the university would join the farmworkers striking in the fields. One summer, I worked with the United Farm Workers in San Francisco during the boycott on Safeway grocery stores.

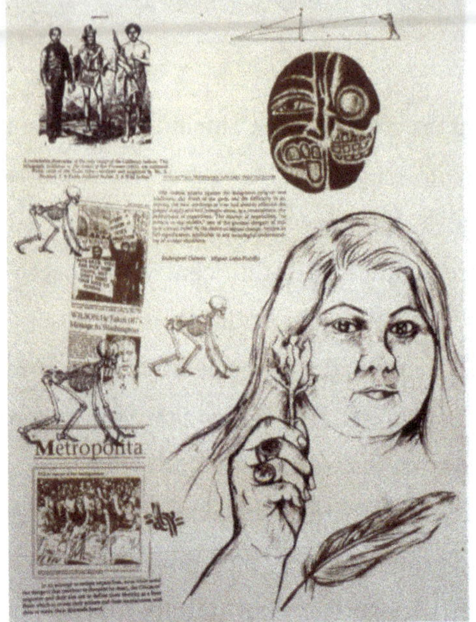

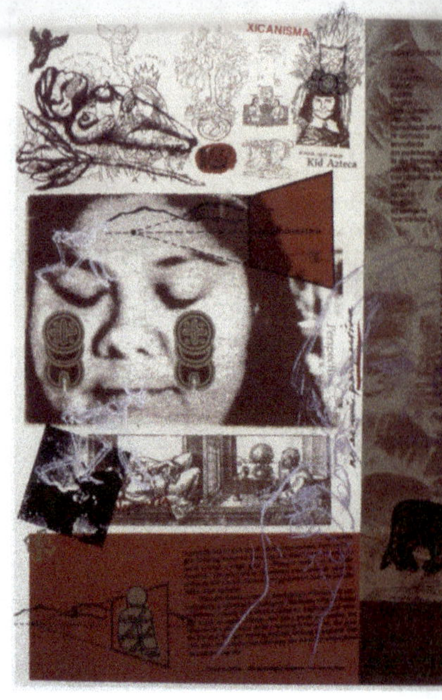

Yreina D. Cervantez, *Nepantla*, triptych lithography, 1995-96

Chicana artists and early Chicana theorists and writers were working in parallel ways. The writers put words to our lived experience, and artists were articulating it visually. Many of my Chicana artist peers were very important to me, as well as several Chicana poets, writers, and feminist theorists, including Frances Salomé España, Gloria E. Alvarez, Cherríe Moraga, Gloria Anzaldúa, and Ana Castillo. These visual artists and writers were inspirations, and the written word is evident in much of my art. I often use text/symbolic language in my work, which is part of the Indigenous (Mesoamerican codices) and Latin American art traditions.

NEPANTLA MEANS "IN THE MIDDLE". [THE] MIDDLE STATE CAN APPLY TO THE EXPERIENCE OF COLONIZATION

Another theme in my art is the concept of *Nepantla*. I believe I was introduced to the term through the filmmaker Lourdes Portillo and filmmaker/poet Frances Salomé España. Later, I read about *Nepantla* through the writings of Anzaldúa in her book *Borderlands La Frontera*, and also in the work of Mexican scholar Miguel León-Portilla who wrote about *Nepantla* and the worldview of indigenous cultures in Mexico. In his book *Endangered Cultures*, he talks about the origin of this Aztec/Nahuatl concept. Translated very literally, *Nepantla* means "in the middle." This middle or in-between state can also apply to the experience of colonization. When a people are forced to endure the violent processes of colonization, their infrastructures, cultures, religions, art, libraries, and philosophies are systematically destroyed. Those who are subjugated have previously

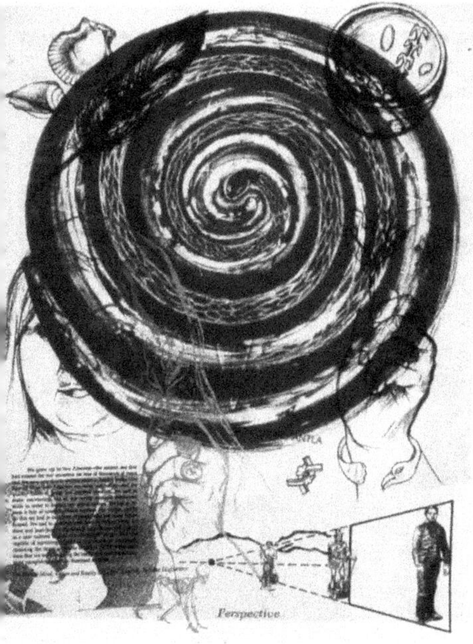

grown up with a completely different and unique worldview but are coerced against their will to accept the imposed and invading culture. As a matter of survival, those colonized and impacted attempt to reconcile both opposing cultures and live "in between." I have always taken *Nepantla* to mean "torn between." But *Nepantla* has a very complex history, and Anzaldua has reclaimed and redefined the meaning of *Nepantla*.

In Anzaldúa's writing, you see her understanding of *Nepantla* evolve over time. In the book *Borderlands*, I interpret her discussion of *Nepantla* as the tension of being torn between cultures and different values. This creates self-doubt and confusion, but through the awareness of culture and history you begin to understand the roots and complexity of your identity and experience and can come to terms with it and embrace it. So then, *Nepantla* is reclaimed as a place of awareness, acceptance, and positive transformation for everyone, especially those who have been colonized. Anzaldúa was also a queer theorist, so she took this one step further in her writings to emphasize *Nepantla* also as liberating space of possibility and creativity for LGBTQ people.

In my own work, I have also created a lithograph titled *The Nepantla Triptych, 1995–96 (Nepantla, Mi Nepantla, Beyond Nepantla)*. This artwork deals with the theme of colonization and the complexity of identity, but it is also about spirituality and transformation. I have been working as an artist now for almost fifty years. My artwork is informed by Native Mesoamerican mythology and cosmology, Mexican art traditions, Chicanx self-determination, women's history, as well as themes of environmental justice, globalization, and international struggles for human rights. My art is imbued with layers of symbolism and meaning. I work to express and connect with a contemporary Xicana indigenous worldview and philosophy.

After completing my bachelor's degree in art in 1975 from UC Santa Cruz, I returned to Southern California to work in community. Specifically, I worked as a Comprehensive Employment and Training Act

IT WAS IMPORTANT TO HAVE FOUND A PLACE THERE

(CETA) artist-in-residence with young women, single mothers, and so-called gang youth in East Long Beach. I later apprenticed with muralist Judy Baca at the Social and Public Art Resource Center. Eventually, I worked at Self Help Graphics as an artist-in-residence. Sister Karen Boccalero, the founder and former director of Self Help Graphics, was another influential source of support in my life. It was important to have found a place there, especially since mainstream galleries were not really open to exhibiting Chicano art. Self Help Graphics was focused on encouraging, supporting, and providing resources for Chicana/o/x and Latinx artists.

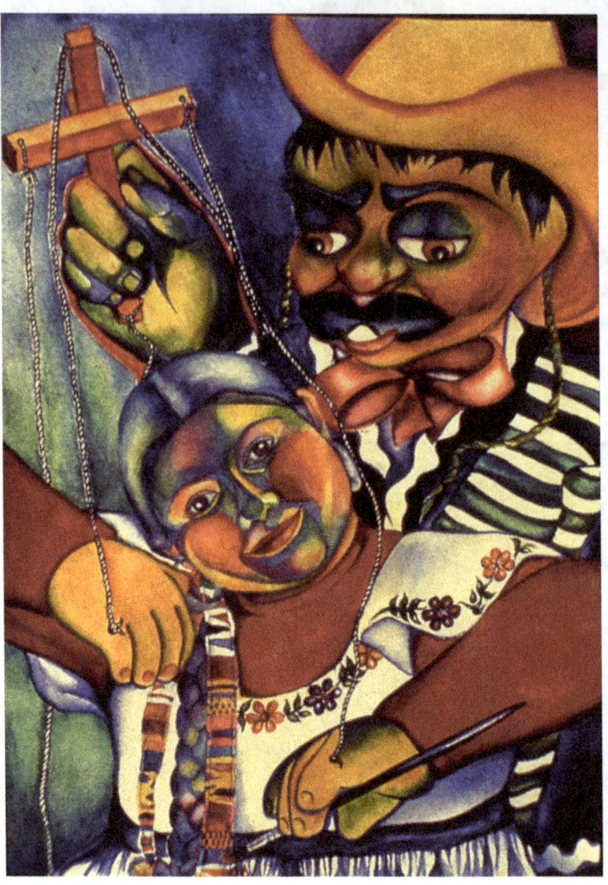

Yreina D. Cervantez, *Titere Titere*, watercolor, 1987

Mentors, such as Sister Karen, are incredibly important to acknowledge. Another person who was very supportive of my art, career, and teaching was Dr. Shifra Goldman. She was also a wonderful mentor and a very accomplished art historian, one of the first to take note of Chicano art and write about it in a scholarly manner.

After being an artist in community for nearly twelve years, I wanted to go back to school to get my MFA. Education has always been a double-edged sword for me. It was a place where I found opportunity, yet art departments especially were limited in their Eurocentric perspective and narrow mainstream attitudes. I applied to UCLA in 1986 and was accepted into the graduate program. Considering that many years had passed since receiving my BA, I thought conditions must have improved, especially in such a "multicultural" population and city as Los Angeles. Although UCLA has an international reputation, it was not what I expected. I had hoped for a more diverse representation of faculty, but the art faculty was predominately white and male. Unfortunately, I found that many times the perspective on my work was uninformed and condescending. Some professors made assumptions about "ethnic art," seeing my art as "folkloric" or decorative and not understanding the symbols or being really interested in the meaning. To say the least, it was discouraging. With the help of my own support system of friends and artists, I eventually got through the program. The UCLA MFA program was three years long. What got me through everything was remaining rooted in community and being part of a women's collective called ESA, *East Side Artistas*. Other members of this collective included Gloria E. Alvarez, Frances Salomé España, Marialice Jacob, Norma Alicia Pino, and Kay Reiko Torrez. They were very important allies for me during this time.

In 1989, for my final graduate thesis project, I painted a mural in Echo Park titled *La Ofrenda*, ("The Offering"), which was dedicated to immigrants, political refugees, laborers, and the important role that women make in creating positive change. United Farm Workers cofounder and former vice-president Dolores Huerta is a central figure in the mural. *La Ofrenda* has since been restored and designated a historically significant mural in Los Angeles.

[I WAS EMPOWERED] TO TEACH WHAT I NEEDED

The experience at UCLA led me to want to teach about Chicana/o art in a way that is thoughtful and respectful. Faculty in art departments have not often been interested in teaching Chicana/o art. If taught at all, it is usually a topic for a few days in an art history class. When a tenure track position opened up to teach Chicana/o art in the Chicano Studies Department at California State Northridge, I applied. I taught in the Chicano Studies Department for twenty years from 1999 to 2019. This department created a welcome, affirming, and safe space where I could teach, and my qualifications, aesthetics, and base of knowledge were acknowledged. More than that, Chicana/o art was appreciated and respected by my colleagues. My position as instructor gave me the confidence and opportunity that empowered me to be able to teach what I needed. I taught both studio and lecture courses in the manner that I felt they deserved. The Chicano Studies Department at Cal State Northridge is the first and largest in the nation. It is also one of the most progressive. I am honored to have been a faculty member there.

I have been very frank about the obstacles of racism and repeatedly mentioned the lack of representation in the educational system, and as a direct result of this problem, the lack of opportunity and negative effect on artists of color. There have been some changes in education, but they have been slow and hard-won. However, I am very hopeful that there will continue to be significant changes in education in general, and specifically in university art departments. Now, we are finally beginning to see some more representation in different areas of art, and there are younger generations of very impressive and powerful Chicana/o/x and Latinx visual and performance artists, writers, professors, art historians, and arts administrators that are making a great impact. I remain optimistic for the future.

YOU NEVER RETIRE AS AN ARTIST

While teaching full-time, I faced the challenge of finding a balance with my creative life. I think this is a common concern for all teaching artists. When you reach a certain age, you realize things are finite. You have limited time. I've experienced issues with my health in terms of my mobility and not being as physically active as I used to be. I decided to retire from teaching in 2019. As for the creative life, as far as I'm concerned, you never retire as an artist. I want to use the remaining time I have in the best way possible.

I would like to have a more functional studio. There are things that I can focus on now that I wasn't necessarily able to attend to when teaching and dealing with other responsibilities. I want to make a situation for myself where I can be the most creative in terms of my environment, health, and connections to my community.

I'm currently in a transition as I deal with health issues and coming back into a rhythm with my work. I'm allowing myself time to reflect and replenish. I have no intention of stopping. I may slow down as an artist, but I will stay connected creatively and work as long as I am able. There is always more to learn.

When I think of life beyond seventy, I want to create other bodies and portfolios of work. I have been very fortunate with my professional life as an artist. My work has been exhibited internationally, nationally, and locally. In 2017, a survey of my over forty years as an artist was exhibited at the Vincent Price Museum at East Los Angeles College. My work is in various collections, including the Smithsonian American Art Museum in Washington, D.C., the Los Angeles County Museum of Art; the National Museum of Mexican Art in Chicago; and the University of Texas at Austin's Blanton Museum of Art. As I said before, I want to continue with my artmaking—drawing, painting, printmaking, and hopefully murals. I always wanted to paint a fresco mural. I still do! ❖

Yreina D. Cervantez, *La Ofrenda* mural restored, Los Angeles

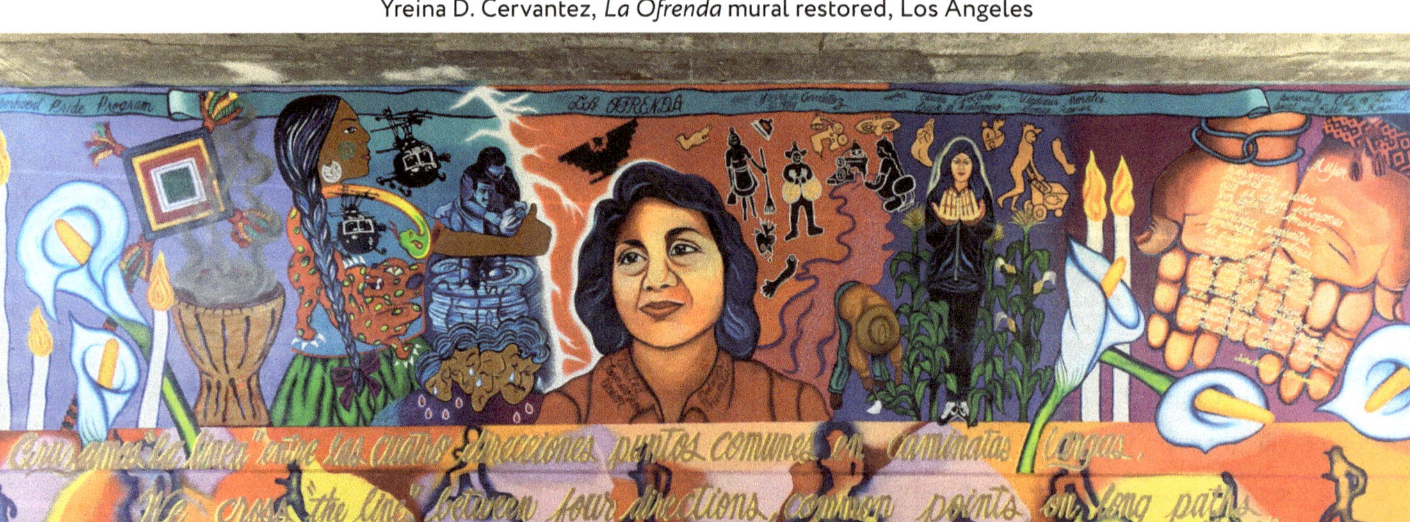

See outtakes from *Monkey Moon,* page 28

NANCY WANG

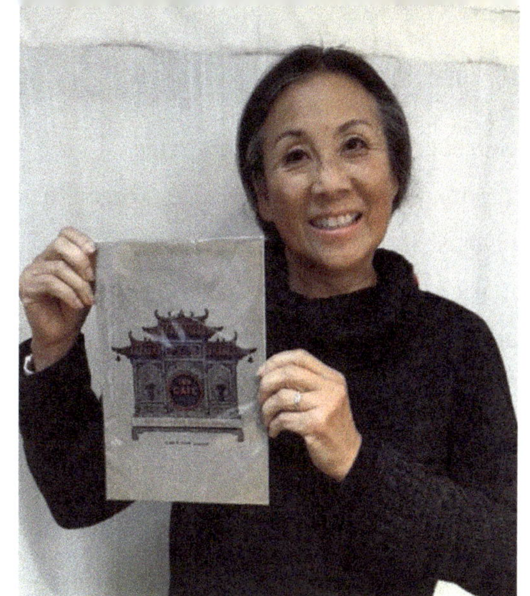

Performing Artist | Storyteller | Writer
Dancer/Movement Performer
Place of Birth: New Orleans, Louisiana
Current Location: San Francisco, California & Eastsound, Washington
Age: 79
www.ethnohtec.org

I HAVE A memory from elementary school of being on the stage and popping out of a pretty wrapped box while twirling and singing. I was maybe ten years old, and though I was nervous, I think I liked it! I believe I found my passion at that point forever! I had always wanted to be a dancer, but now I also wanted to be a singer. I wanted to perform!

Both privately, in my heart and mind, and somewhat out in the world, I made it clear that this was one of my passions. (I also became a psychiatric social worker.) My parents didn't squash this performance passion, but they didn't exactly super-support it either.

So, I dabbled, and then once out of school and on my own, it was my life to lead! I became a professional performer after I graduated. I took classes at the San Francisco Performing Arts Workshop, and its founder and dancer Gloria Unti became my teacher and my mentor. I learned pretty much everything I know from her in terms of teaching, creating, choreographing, and the art of performance in theater and dance—all of which I apply to my present-day art form: storytelling.

I FOUND MY TEACHER

I took my first class with Gloria in 1972. I had been searching for a teacher, but all I could find was jazz. I wanted modern dance. Then I saw some of her students perform a satirical theater movement piece at an outdoor festival, and that did it! I found my teacher. At class, she saw my talent and took me under her wings. She became my mentor and my West Coast mama. I taught there, performed, and choreographed for our company.

Nine years later, I married and began to create performances with my husband. We started in traditional southern Filipino bronze gong music and dances with a school and a performance company. Then, about five years later, we started our nonprofit company Eth-Noh-Tec, a kinesthetic storytelling performing arts company. Our mission is to build cultural bridges that celebrate diversity and create compassionate communities through the art of storytelling. The name *Eth-Noh-Tec* means the weaving (tec) together of distinctive cultural elements of the East and West (eth) to create new possibilities (noh). We are well-known in the San Francisco Bay Area performing arts and storytelling community and within storytelling communities across the country and around the world.

As a story arts company, our performance work can be seen on YouTube. We also deliver workshops and have cultural products such as books, DVDs, and CDs. We tell stories at storytelling festivals, museums, theaters, conferences, and colleges and universities throughout the country and in Europe and Asia. We even performed for both the Clinton and Obama inaugural celebrations. Although storytelling is not as well-known as dance and theater or opera and ballet, there is a huge following for storytelling.

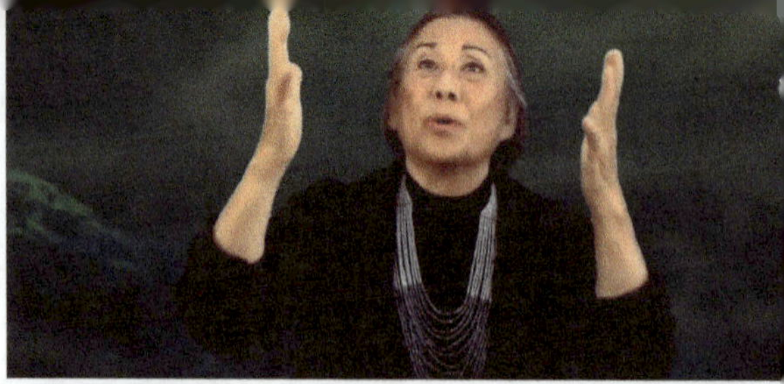

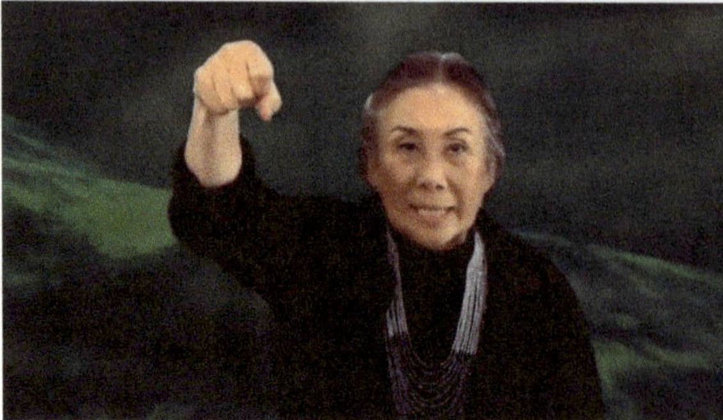

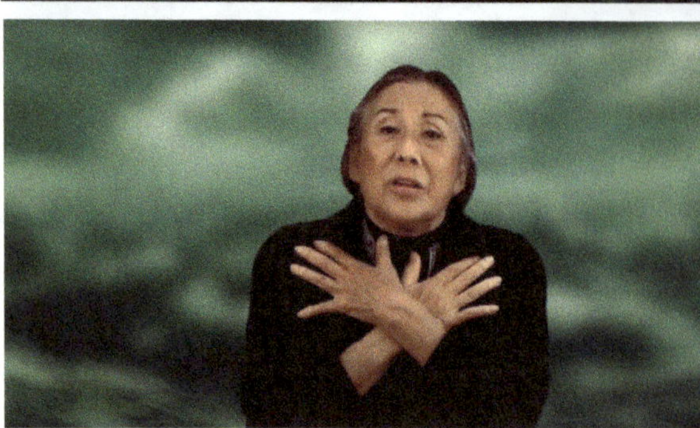

Nancy Wang, video outtakes from *Red Altar Novel, Chapter One*, 2017

WE ALWAYS FOUND A WAY TO SURVIVE

Because of my dance-movement background, Eth-Noh-Tec has a unique style weaving movement, music, and the spoken word. In the storytelling world, we are also unique because we are two tellers telling (my husband and co-director), also known as tandem tellers, and, because we are Asian, not a common commodity in the storytelling world, which is ninety-five percent white. Now, many years later, there are several other wonderful Asian American tellers. And since a storytelling festival will usually only have one Asian, one Black, and maybe one Latina or Native American, it has become more rare for us to be the one Asian on the stage among ten to twenty other tellers. Still, in the beginning—for us in 1987—we were in the right place at the right time. The demand for diversity hit the American storytelling world.

Eth-Noh-Tec tells ancient Asian folktales, legends, and mythology from throughout all the Asian cultures and ethnic groups. These include Siberia and Afghanistan. Asia is huge with East Asia, West Asia, North Asia, and Southeast Asia. There, cultures are all rich with folktales, mythology, and legends. Of course, every culture around the world has stories. In fact, storytelling is probably one of the very first art forms of our human existence—including the famous pictographs on cliffs and in caves around the world.

We choose our stories by the messages and values they convey. For someone new to storytelling of the traditional verbal form—not movies, not books, not opera, not a TV series—it is wise to start by studying folktales to tell. This ancient story "telling" art form is what I'm referring to. Even if the folktale book tells the story in three paragraphs, there is already a beginning, middle, and end—the primary structure of a tale. It trains you how to create a good story. Everything is already there. All you need to do is fill it in by extending, expanding, and deepening it, shaping it to your personality.

We look for how a story may connect to a contemporary issue. We just did performances of *Monkey King and the Pure Hearts*. It's a story about a king and a beauty who was not quite a queen yet. In order to keep her beauty and the king under her spell, and with the promise of curing his ailments, they kidnapped the children of the village, caged them, and readied them for the elixir, which would contain 1,111 hearts of 1,111 children. You can see how the story ties into what has been happening at the U.S.–Mexico border with children being put in cages.

Nancy Wang, video outtakes from *Asian Tales of Terror*, 2020

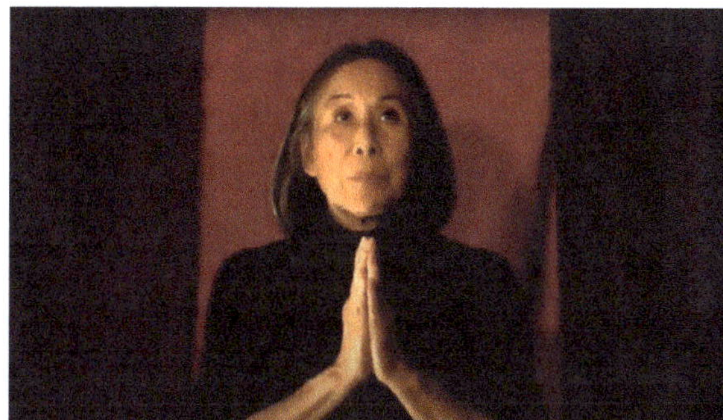

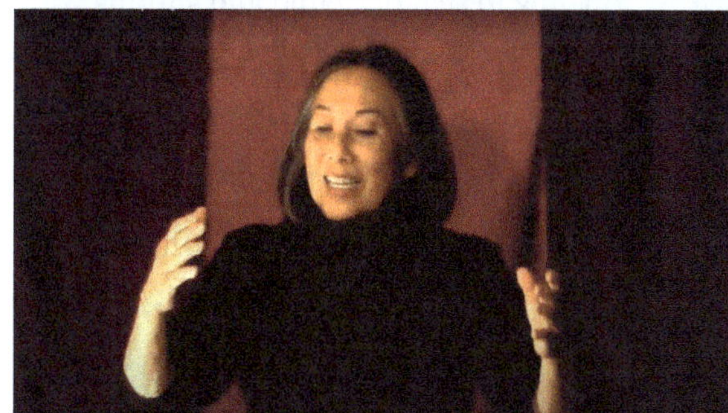

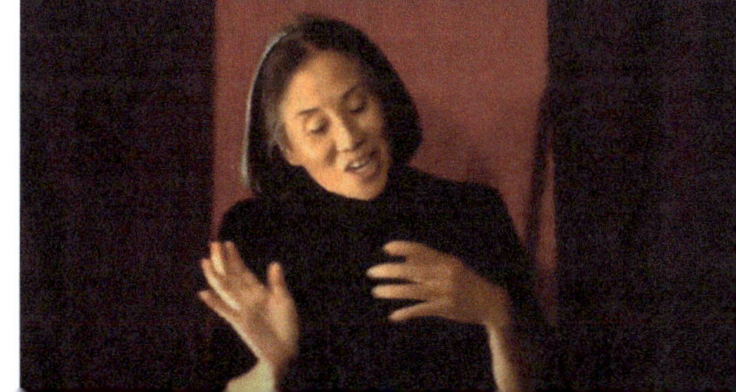

Besides ancient tales, we also tell contemporary Asian American inspirational stories. One of these stories I created is about three generations of my ancestors. The first generation of six teens started a fishing industry in Monterey County in the Bay Area in 1850. They had to constantly reinvent themselves for survival because of prejudice and racist laws that were passed against them. For example, Monterey passed a law that only the Chinese were forbidden to fish during the day. Since we were only allowed to fish at night, we reinvented ourselves by starting the squid fishing industry. They soon encountered new laws preventing the drying of the squid. So then, my ancestors resorted to gathering all the rotten fish and innards that the Italians would throw out onto the public beach. They made fish emulsion and fish fertilizer and sold it to the farmers. We always found a way to survive. This story is universal in that it connects to injustice rooted in white supremacy. Good stories are a form of activism, survival, and building connections.

STORIES ARE POWERFUL

I believe stories have a way of giving hope to people even when things are looking pretty bad. Folktales have a way of providing a different perspective of how others solved a problem. Folktales take us through three phases—the beginning: who, what, where, when; the middle: the problem, the crises; and the end: the problem solving, the resolution. Human beings have always been inventive, resilient. Stories are powerful reveals of who we are as human beings. Our stories may originate from Asia, but they are universal in our humanness.

Something that comes to mind is when I've performed at schools in an area such as the Midwest of the United States and there is maybe one Asian child in the auditorium. I know how confusing and isolating that can feel. Growing up in New Orleans and Chicago, my family always lived in white neighborhoods. Even later in college, I found myself as maybe one of three Asian students, and only one of two Asian students in graduate school. So, when performing at a school and after capturing their attention, their minds, and their hearts with our stories, the fun, the humor, and the movement, when we announced, "The next story is from the Philippines," (or from China or Cambodia), we would see everyone turning to that one child and smiling with excitement. Afterward, the child would come up and say, "Excuse me, I'm also from China," or, "I'm also Chinese," or, "I'm also Filipino." They didn't feel alone anymore. And now, all their schoolmates had witnessed Asians on stage and getting them to use their imagination and their laughter. We build bridges through our stories and through our persona on stage. I would see this validating experience for children all over the United States and abroad, wherever there was that one lone Asian child among a different majority population.

Through our performances, I've gotten to meet such wonderful people throughout the world. Storytellers and those who love storytelling are humanitarians—more so than any other art form.

Eth-No-Tec, video outtakes from *Asian Tales of Terror*, 2020

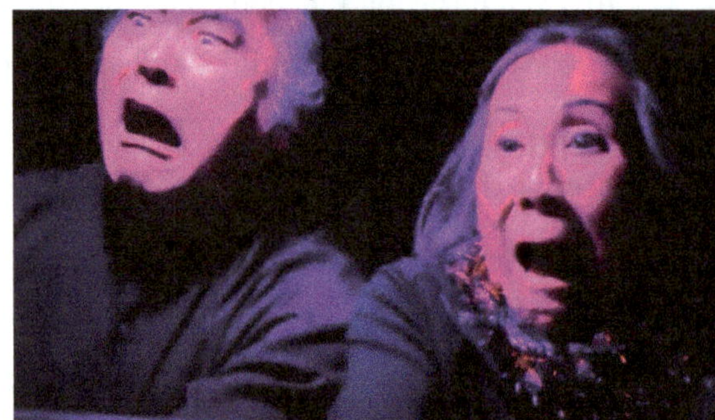

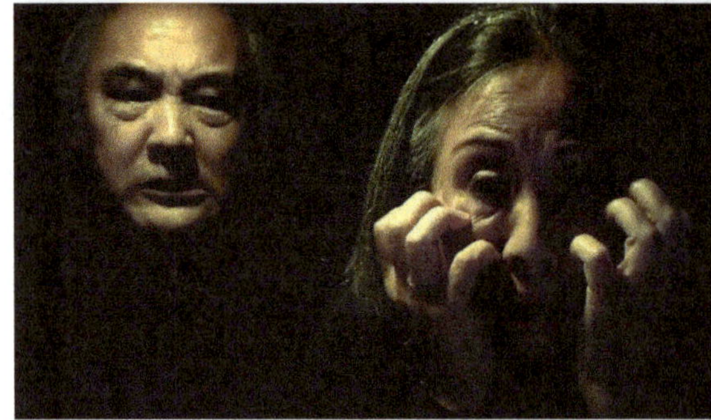

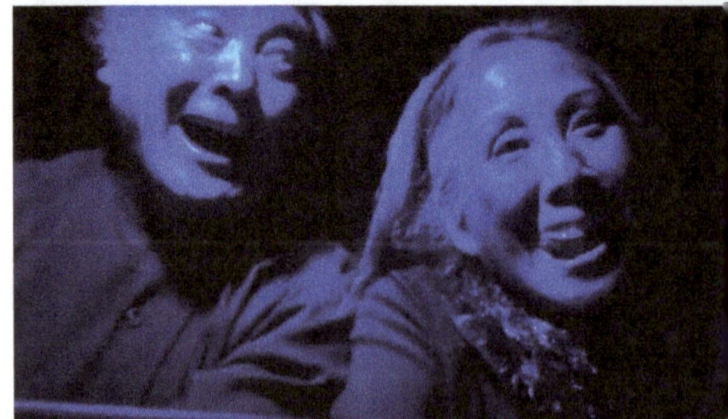

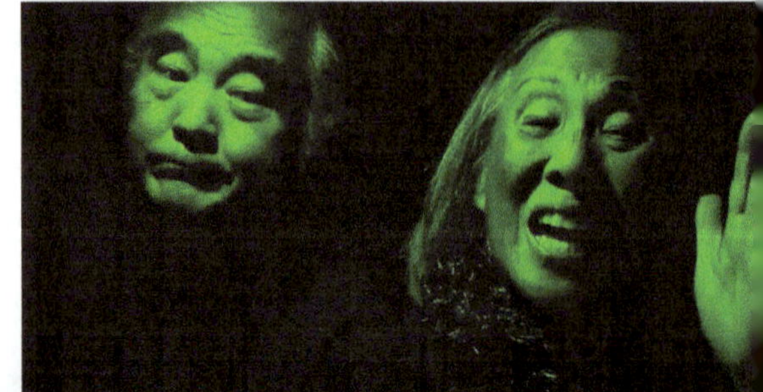

As I've aged, I've faced physical challenges. I was a dancer, and our performances are highly choreographed, but in time, I had a bad hip that finally got replaced. Then I had a bad knee, and I was on crutches. I was in pain off and on for decades. I was able to figure out how to go onstage and perform without using my right leg and not appearing to have pain. The way I perform my stories has been changed by my body. We still move, but not as vigorously!

Although things have become more physically challenging, psychologically it has gotten easier. Aging has helped in terms of my personal philosophy and psychology. I've gotten braver. I no longer care as much about what people think. I've already gone through so many transitions in my life. At this point, I dare to do things that before I would have been concerned the audience wouldn't like. I've gotten braver with my views and expressing them through story, such as my *Red Altar* piece that includes what white Americans historically have done to the Chinese. It makes connections in support of the Black Lives Matter movement. Not everyone will like to hear it, but a really good story makes one uncomfortable. So, I have become braver in how my work succeeds in breaking stereotypes.

I HAVE BECOME BRAVER IN HOW MY WORK [BREAKS] STEREOTYPES

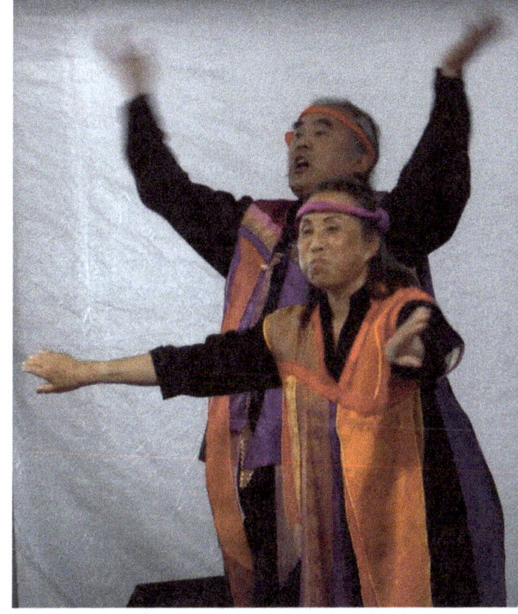

With the pandemic, I've had to learn a lot of new things to keep telling our stories, which now is telling our stories online. It's hard. Being in front of a live audience onstage, you can make a mistake, and everyone laughs and forgives. With online recordings, everything needs to be perfect because people are used to sophisticated and perfect delivery of lines in movies and TV skits. It's exhausting to keep on keeping on, performing to a camera, and not make any mistakes. Retakes, retakes, retakes!

I'M NOT DONE WITH MY WORK

This page: video outtakes: Eth-No-Tec *Live at the 2019 Storytelling Festival*

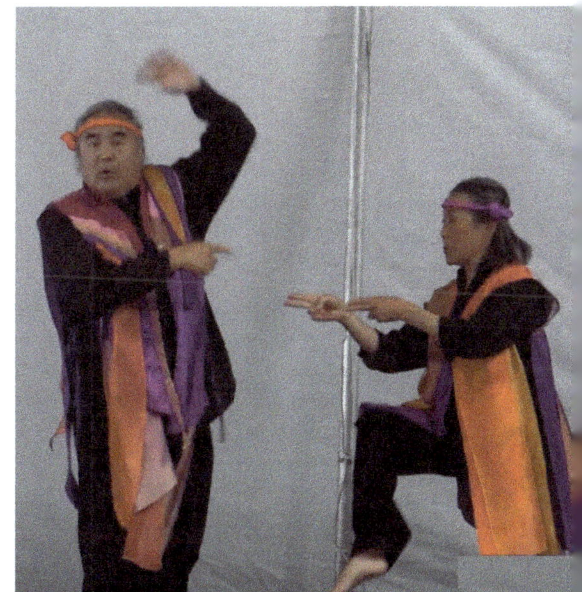

Thank goodness storytellers can be ninety years old and still be telling stories. So there's still time to get even braver, bolder. I'm not done with my work. For example, I am in the final editing of my book *Red Altar*—the story of the Chinese who started the fishing industry. I'm really excited about getting it out to fourth and fifth graders through college. Another story theater piece is on my grandfather's life. He was a famous restaurateur who may have been murdered, although the "accepted" family story is that he fell down his own restaurant's elevator shaft as an "accident." But I wonder if it was "murder." I was able to find a lot of old newspaper articles about him, the Chicago Chinatown community, and the Tongs (the Chinese mafia), as well as archived national immigration records and more. Sadly, the performance was cancelled due to the pandemic. It is waiting to become a radio play!

Now, I'm working on our Fortieth Anniversary Concert for Eth-Noh-Tec, which is going to be a retrospective of mostly who we were, how we met, how we became Eth-Noh-Tec and continued for forty years! How was it possible? There were so many indicators that shouted "implausible!" There will be dirt flying!

Am I busy? Yes! More than before the pandemic! In addition to the creative work and the usual administrative hassles, I continue to write grants and make reports on grants we've received, and, of course, we are busy learning this online technology.

When I imagine my life into my eighties and nineties, I think I'll still be doing my work. With the pandemic, everything is changing. Either you accept the challenge, or you give up and retire. I'm too full of energy and ideas to retire. And besides, most American/European storytelling is standing or sitting with a microphone. So, when I can't move much anymore, I just do it their way. It's still "telling" stories! ❖

Eth-No-Tec, video outtake: *Festival of the Moon* storytelling, 2020

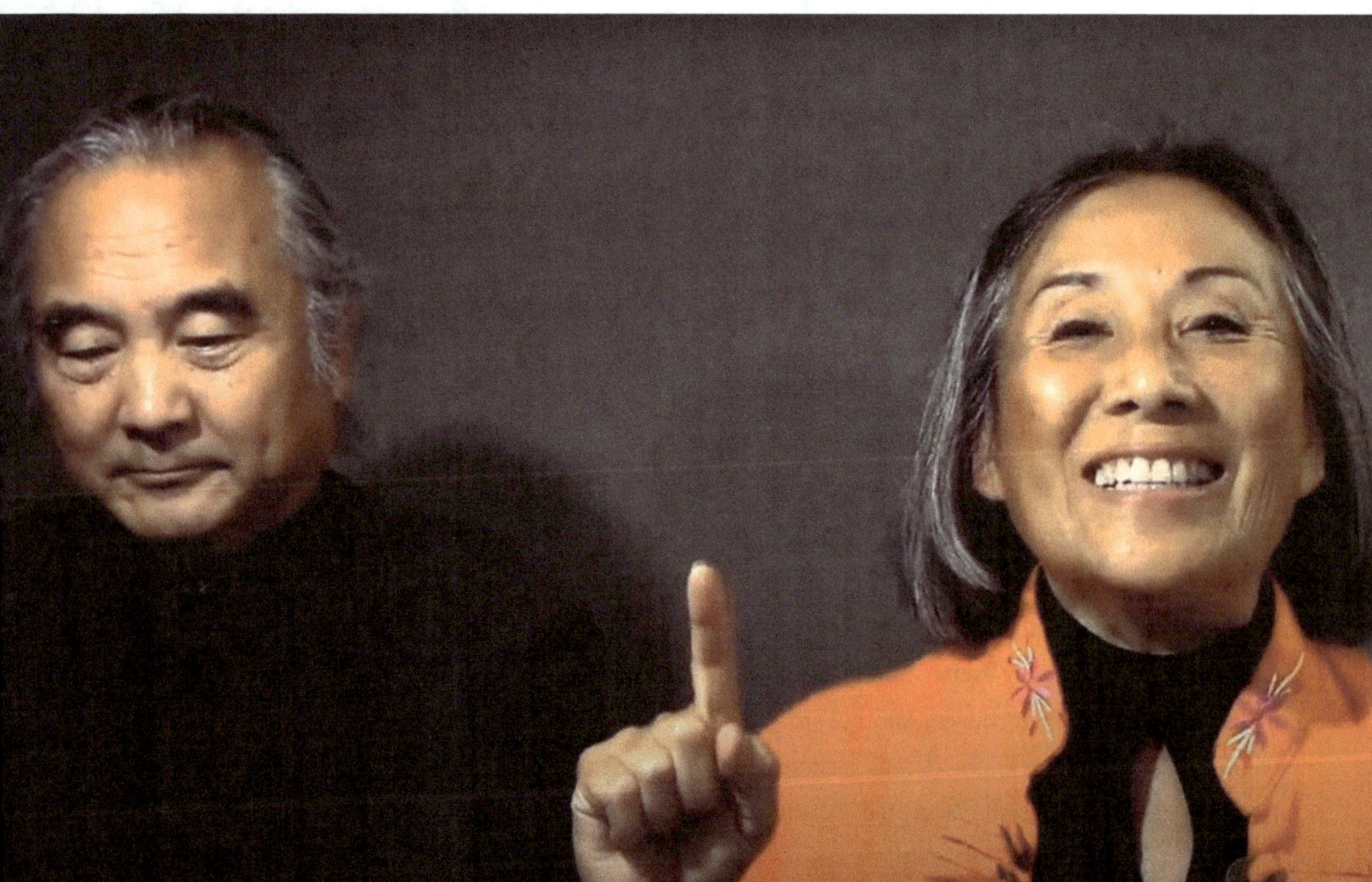

See *Rockin' It,* page 29

WENDY TIGERMAN

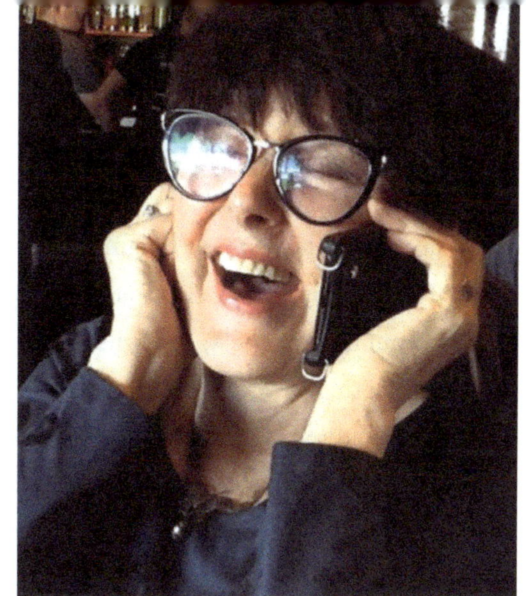

Mixed Media and Digital Collage Artist
Photographer I Writer
Place of Birth: Los Angeles, California
Current Location: Los Angeles, California
Age: 72
www.wendytigerman.com

IF I COULD transcend restraint and reality, I would travel back in time to have tea or tequila with Matisse, O'Keefe, Picasso, Rauschenberg, Hockney, Basquiat, Pollock, and Van Gogh. I would ask each of them to give me one piece of advice. Then I would either crash and burn as an artist or rocket skyward with new inspiration.

I'm very open to my art not needing a through line stylistically. I'd like to see my art grow and be more harmonious with my sense of composition. I want to allow whimsy to take root—even more than it does already. I'd like to teach more. But it's a loose plan, and I really don't have allegiance to following it. Being pigeonholed makes me chew on my hair. If I'm painting and I wake up one day and think, "I don't want to paint like this anymore, or at all," then I'll just do something else. I can always change my mind, and I can always go back to something if I realize it made me happier. I read once that Buckminster Fuller was called a "Renaissance man in a time of specialization." That comforted me. Also, some of the best personal advice I ever received was, "Choose. Then choose again."

CHOOSE, THEN CHOOSE AGAIN

Do I begin with a concept? Nah, I just start with an image that resonates with me. Color, shape, humor, intensity—all call my name. Mostly my own photos, including an album of family shots that go back to the late 1800s. Wow, right? Often, a concept shows up. But not always. In fact, the ones that start with a concept are usually sociopolitical commentary. How do I know when the work is done? Basically, I stop when I let out a tiny sigh. How do I price

Wendy Tigerman, *Clean Sweep*, digital and mixed media collaboration by TigerNoodle (Kate Knudsen and Wendy Tigerman), 2021

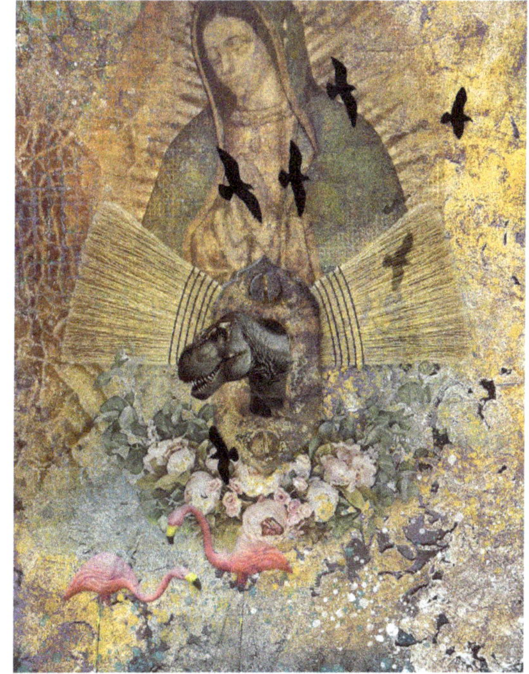

my work? I charge based on how much it's worth to let it go.

I think it was always in me to be an artist. When I was a little girl, I would lie on this long, rectangular ottoman to watch television in my shorty PJs with my chubby cheeks resting in my hands and long legs stretched out behind me. As I watched *Mr. Wizard* and *Sky King*, I drew what I saw with my feet. I would mostly concentrate on lips. I was drawing the outline of lips nonstop in the air. In retrospect, this was probably the precursor to my obsession with lipstick.

I DREW WHAT I SAW WITH MY FEET

When I got older, I graduated from feet to fingers. Most people doodle on paper, but I'd be walking around or sitting and drawing in the air. Still mostly lips. Eventually, I figured, "Well, I can't do this. People will think I'm insane." So I moved on to drawing secretly on my thigh with my finger.

Even though I've gone through extended periods of not producing visual art—except for taking photographs, which I've done since I was a child—I believe my compulsive drawing has kept me connected to seeing and creating. I still do it, but now, the substrate is my thumbnail, and I've tossed self-consciousness to the wind. Well, mostly.

When I was in elementary school, I'd sit at our kitchen table looking at the line of trees across Olympic Boulevard. I'd paint the trees using cut-up sponges and watercolor.

Once, I made something I thought was particularly ugly. So I crumpled it up and then got the idea of putting the crumpled piece of paper in the bathtub and running water over it. When I uncrumpled it, of course, I had something entirely different. I ended up ironing the paper and drawing on top of it. That was a huge and helpful discovery about turning mistakes into something that you never would have imagined.

When I went to UC Berkeley, I wanted to major in art and writing. As usual, there were two voices in me talking at the same time. One would say, "I can do absolutely anything. Just give it to me. I can do it." And the other, "Oh, God, I suck. I'm a total imposter." The next year, a gypsy fortune teller read my handwriting on the steps of the Pompidou and said, "It must be so hard to be you." Much later, a therapist remarked, "It's like you're bipolar, but you're not." Welcome to my world.

WELCOME TO MY WORLD

Wendy Tigerman, *Psychic Llama*, digital collage, 2020

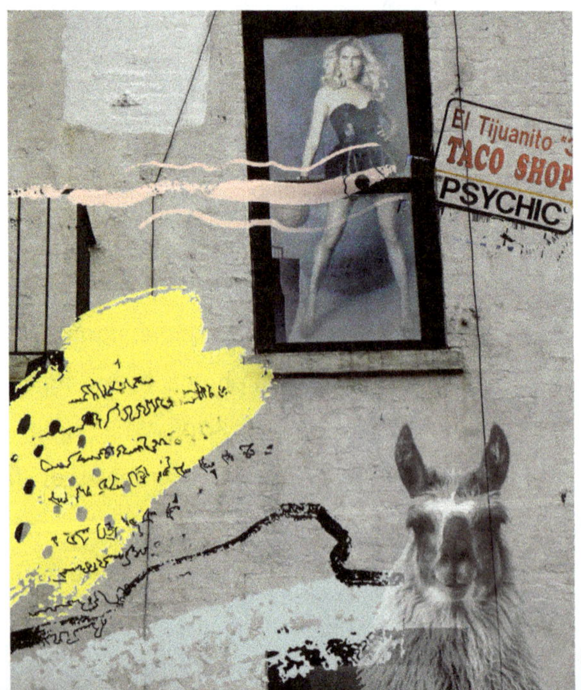

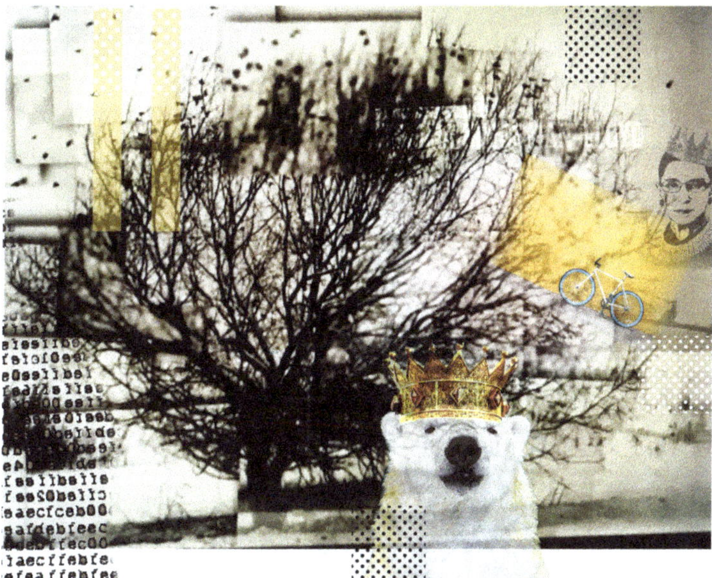

Wendy Tigerman, *Bearscape*, digital collage, 2019

In my college art class, someone told me I had to start thinking about my portfolio, because I wouldn't be able to work in the arts if I didn't have a portfolio in order to get an agent who would promote my work and get me into shows and galleries and and and...

I thought, "I'm done. This sounds terrible." Hence, I didn't do anything with art or writing for many years. Although I'd planned to be a graphic designer, the streets of 1970s Berkeley were far more seductive. I dropped out and was your typical hippie/radical/spiritual-seeker/natural-foods junkie. I even raised alfalfa sprouts and helped run a natural food store. The reality of going to school became very abstract and unappealing.

I eventually ended up working as a graphic designer though. I interned and then was hired by Communication Arts in Boulder, Colorado. When I came back to LA, no one would hire me as a graphic designer without an art school degree and the ability to design on a computer. Because of this and my still prominent aversion to school, I worked for many years as a copywriter. This work allowed me to stay connected to the worlds of art and writing. Whether it was for billboard, radio, TV, magazine, or electronic media, in advertising the artist and writer have a symbiotic relationship. As a copywriter, I often came up with visual elements, and the graphic designer came up with headlines.

CREATIVE WORK IS CREATIVE WORK

When I finally returned to "non-commercial" fine art, I realized I'd learned a lot from all my years as an adwoman. Creative work is creative work. It is just another kind of artistic practice. When I discovered how much I'd learned, my first thought was, "Oh, good. I didn't waste all that time."

THE STREETS OF 1970S BERKELEY WERE FAR MORE SEDUCTIVE

In my early thirties, I started taking acrylic painting classes with the artist Martin Facey at UCLA Extension. He was an amazing teacher who'd been mentored by Richard Diebenkorn. Martin would walk around the room and just give people great tips the whole time. I remember he walked all around and came back to me, but my canvas was still blank. Thirty minutes went by, and he returned to check on me. Still nothing. He said, "Okay, here's the deal. I'm really generous, so if you want, you can have your money back for this class. If I come back and see you've still done nothing, I'm going to throw you out because you're just taking up space." Then he said, "Just do anything. Don't think." So, I made an abstract brushstroke on the canvas. He returned and said, "Okay, now respond to that. And respond to that. Then respond to that." And these words became my creative mantra. Martin's advice has guided my artistic work for the past forty years!

ART COMMUNITY ROCKS

About fifteen years ago, I enrolled in a collage class at UCLA Extension. The teacher was also a godsend. Soon after, an artist friend turned me onto the nonprofit organization Collage Artists of America. Joining CAA taught me that an art community can be invaluable. Both in person and online, this group teaches me new techniques, cheers me on, and even tolerated me as their graphic designer and president for several years. Community rocks.

Collage remains my primary form of art. I'm always dealing with self-criticism and fear. With collage, I can create something and, if I don't like it, start over and over and over again. Mixed media collage is forgiving and allows you to be adventurous because you know you can always retrace your steps. This is especially true with digital collage, which I've been doing almost exclusively for about three years now.

Collage is also something that can be done anywhere, even without any art supplies. Once, I was in Kauai and gave myself a project: to only use found objects from the beach as the material for collage. I arranged different objects on huge leaves and photographed them. Then they were gone. It was the perfect homage to impermanence.

I NURTURE ... WHAT'S SPIRITUAL IN THE MUNDANE

I was fortunate to have studied Tibetan Buddhism with Chögyam Trungpa Rinpoche for over a decade. Inspired by my Buddhist practice, I go outside every morning, look around, and feel how breathtaking everything around me is. I nurture the part of myself that sees what's spiritual in the mundane. For me, it's about being startled by the phenomenal world and paying attention to surprises.

I also took a course called Dharma Art taught by Rinpoche at Naropa Institute in Boulder, Colorado. One of the first things I remember doing was playing with objects. Rinpoche put one thing down, and then it was my turn to place something near it. We kept at it until it felt "done." This was the same process in many ways that I learned years later in the painting class with Martin Facey. Doing something, reacting to it, and reacting again. It takes the preciousness out of it. I believe preciousness is the death of art.

This process is also about developing gratitude toward space and not seeing it as your enemy. You don't have to fill it up. You can be a witness to the details of life without bias. You can actually be playful and relax. Imagine such a thing.

Most of the plans I have at this age involve art. I'm not going to be here forever, so I ask myself what I want to get done. Sometimes, I imagine myself with long gray hair pulled back in a ponytail and being part of an artist community in Santa Fe. I'm both a loner and a people person, so I love imagining that. Part of me also wants to move to France.

I'VE NEVER BEEN MUCH FOR PLANNING

I've never been much for planning though, so I never really imagined how my life would be when I got older. Now that I'm in my seventies, I do think more about the future. (And cosmetic surgery.) Sometimes, I think, "Shit! How many more years do I have left?"

When you're younger, you can't really know what getting old is going to be like. It's totally bizarre. I'm almost seventy, but I'm so childlike. Or immature. Take your pick. ❖

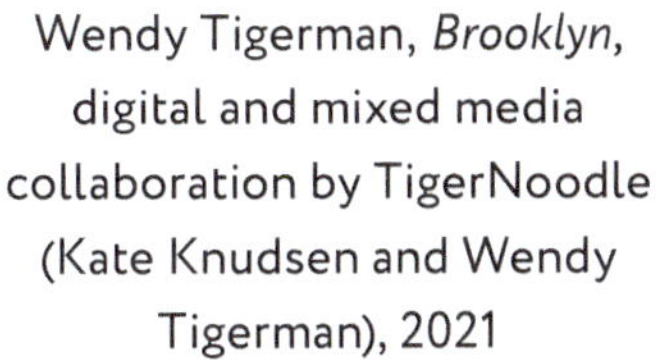

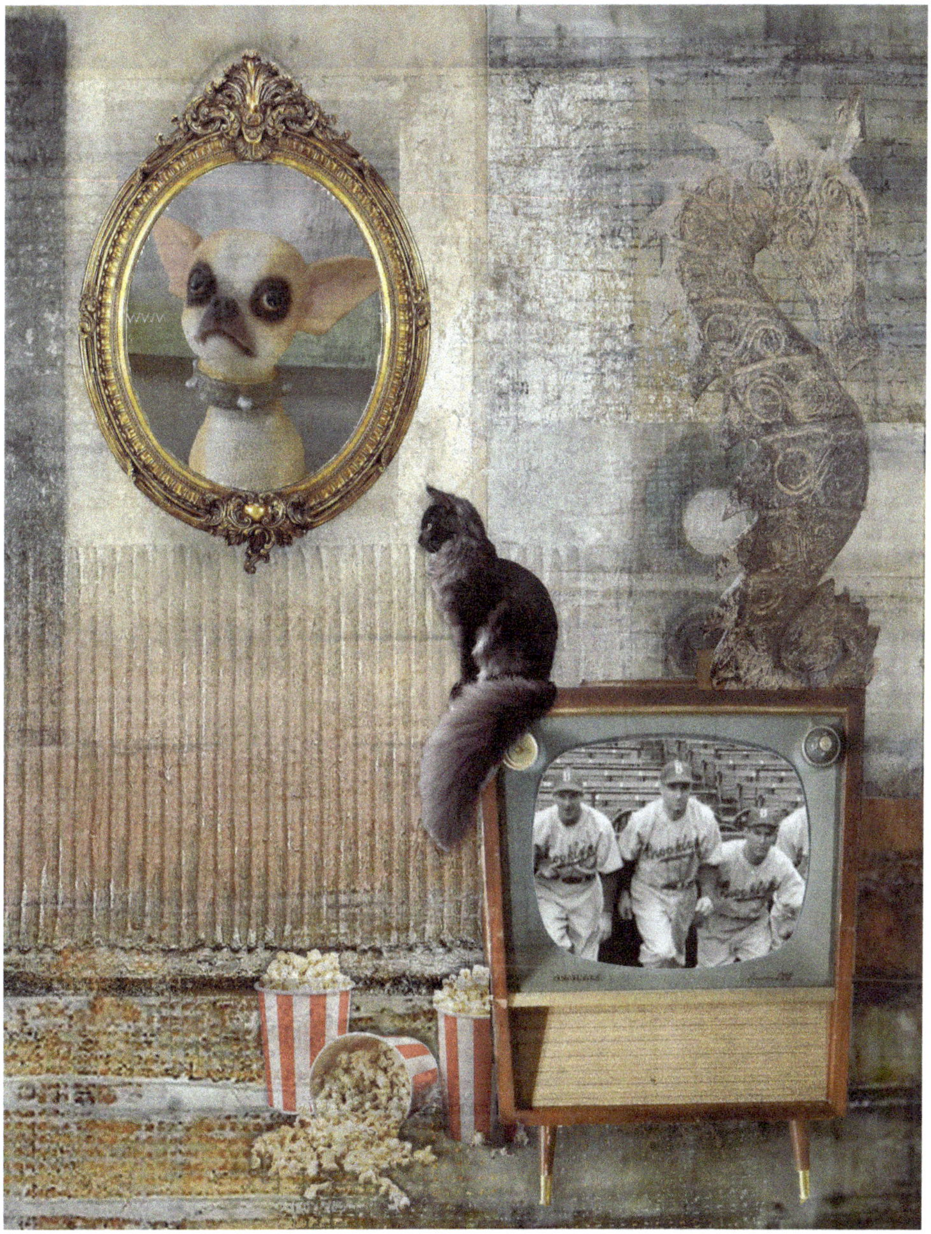

Wendy Tigerman, *Brooklyn*, digital and mixed media collaboration by TigerNoodle (Kate Knudsen and Wendy Tigerman), 2021

See *High Plains Farm, Adrian, Texas,* page 30

PAULA CHAMLEE

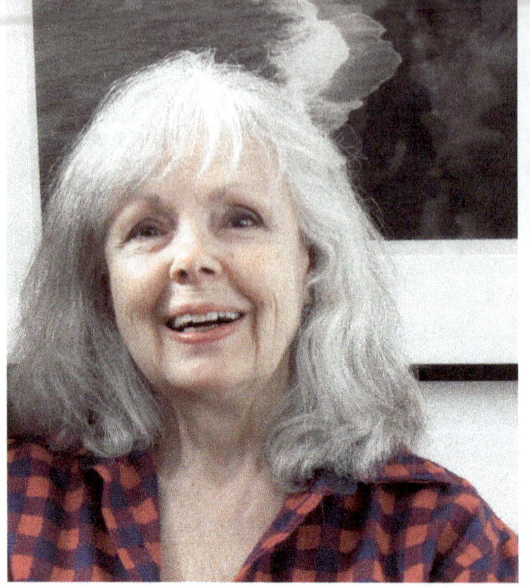

Photographer | Painter | Writer | Publisher
Place of Birth: Amarillo, Texas
Current Location: Bucks County, Pennsylvania
Age: 78
www.michaelandpaula.com | www.lodima.org

IF I COULD break the reality barrier, I would make photographs and paintings by blinking my eyes.

One never knows exactly when the creative life begins since it is formed by so many different things. I didn't experience a specific "aha moment" in my early years of "I'm going to be an artist." I always knew as a child that I was a little bit different, because I didn't think like my parents or most of the kids around me. I wanted to be a dancer, an actress, an opera singer, or anything to get me out of West Texas.

I grew up on the High Plains of the Texas Panhandle, far from big cities and fifty miles from the nearest small city. In our community school, there were no art or dance classes, but curiously, we did many stage plays, and I did lots of acting in high school and college. Even though I loved the way I grew up and it's a wonderful place, I was eager to go beyond and see the world. I had wanderlust. I knew I wouldn't be content staying in one part of the world.

I HAD WANDERLUST

When I got to college, I was able to take classes with creative people for the first time. I was there on a speech and drama scholarship, and in the theater department, I was around some wonderfully creative people. Over time, I decided the theater wasn't going to be the life for me— I wasn't cut out for it.

[I FOLLOWED] MY DREAM OF TRAVELING

After two years at Texas Tech University in Lubbock, a friend in my dormitory told me that she wanted to be a stewardess. This was back in the mid-1960s before the term "flight attendant." When I heard about her plans, it sounded fun and an opportunity for adventure and travel. I left college and started flying for Delta Airlines. My parents didn't have the money to send me overseas for a sabbatical or education, and being a stewardess allowed me to follow my dream of traveling. I loved it.

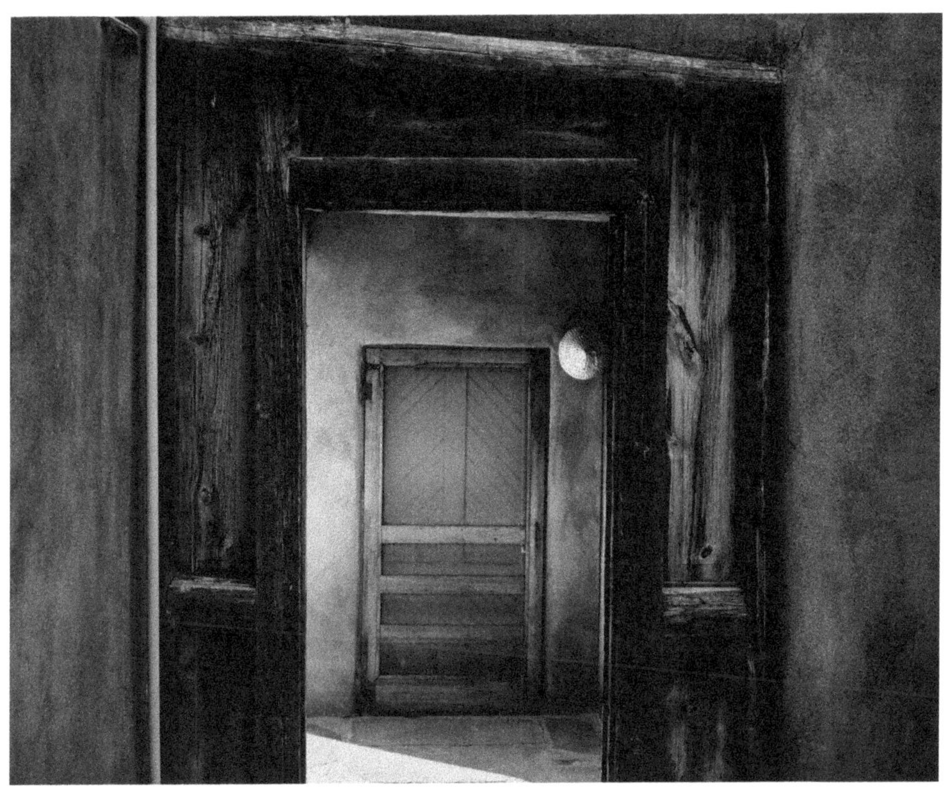

Paula Chamlee, *Near Pojoaque, New Mexico,* silver chloride contact print, 8" x 10", 1991

Back then, of course, flying was easier than it is now. As an airline employee, you could get a standby pass for any other airline, even foreign ones, for around twenty dollars. This afforded me the opportunity to go overseas for the first time. During my three years as a stewardess, I lived and flew out of two home-base cities: Atlanta and New Orleans.

I met my first husband while living in New Orleans and later settled down in Mobile, Alabama, where he was working. New civil rights laws were being passed and enforced at this time, yet the federal government was more focused on equal rights enforcement in schools than in companies like the airlines. And thus, women were being forced to retire from their stewardess jobs if they got married—the airlines were not yet complying to the new laws. I was okay with moving on to the next phase of my life.

When I first got married, I worked at a local television station as a temporary feature news reporter and also started working as a real estate sales agent. After the first four years of our marriage, I became pregnant with our first child and worked as a full-time mom as well as a corporate wife, so I stopped working professionally.

I CAN BE READY TOMORROW

In 1979, my husband was offered a rare opportunity to become a liaison in his field for two of his company's overseas locations. When he first came home and told me about the possibility of living abroad, my response was, "I can be ready tomorrow!" By then, I was in my early thirties, and we had two small children. We moved to England and Switzerland for the one-year assignment. I loved living overseas. I would visit museums when possible and was thrilled to see so much great art "in the flesh."

After we moved back to Mobile, Alabama, I contacted a good friend who was a painter and asked him if he would give me lessons. We got a few people together for a small class, and that is when I learned that I really liked painting and that I might, with training, be pretty good at it.

My youngest child was in grade school full-time by then, so I had several free hours during the day that I could devote to myself. I went back to school at the nearby University of South Alabama in Mobile and set out to finish the degree I had started at Texas Tech. I studied French and took all the art studio classes—painting and drawing, printmaking, design, ceramics, and sculpture. I also took all of the art history classes. I was meeting other artists who were either the traditional age or my age. This was my beginning of being immersed in an art environment.

Among the art history courses offered, I took a history of photography class taught by an excellent professor. On the first day that I opened the textbook, Beaumont Newhall's *History of Photography*, I was captivated by the reproductions of Edward Weston's photographs. I was completely smitten. I realized that you could use the camera to photograph something universal, mysterious, beautiful, deep, and soulful. This was photography that went beyond mere illustration. Through the university library, I began to read all of the books on photography I could find.

YOU COULD USE THE CAMERA TO PHOTOGRAPH SOMETHING UNIVERSAL, MYSTERIOUS, BEAUTIFUL, DEEP, AND SOULFUL

The university did not have a photography department, but there was a beginning studio class for learning how to develop 35-millimeter film, make proof sheets, and preliminary prints. This class was taught by the History of Photography professor in a small, decrepit building off-campus. I was constantly asking him to, "Teach me how to do this. Teach me how to do that." Finally, he said, "I've taught you every technical thing I know. Go make photographs!"

At the end of the semester, he invited some local accomplished photographers to critique our work. Through them, I was introduced to larger camera formats. I began to see photographs made with larger negatives, six-by-six centimeters or six-by-seven centimeters. I thought to myself, “That’s better.” Then they introduced me to four-by-five-inch view camera negatives, and when I saw those larger negatives, I thought, “That’s even better.” I was able to borrow a four-by-five view camera from a friend, learned how to use it, and discovered that this was a real turning point for me.

The first time I looked on the ground glass of the view camera and saw the world upside down, I felt, “This is perfect. Now I can see the world for how it looks and not what it *is*.” I realized that I could finally process visual information with less preconception or judgment about what is before the lens and concentrate instead on rhythmic structure. It opened up a new world of *seeing* for me—that everything visual can be equally interesting—and a way to see the world that isn’t possible in one’s right side up view. In 1990, I began photographing full-time with an eight-by-ten-inch view camera.

SEE THE WORLD FOR HOW IT LOOKS, NOT WHAT IT *IS*

When teaching, I often emphasize that we don’t need to rush to make negatives; instead, we need to spend time absorbing new visual relationships to expand our visual vocabulary. Thus, when we do make a negative, that accumulation of knowledge can engender fresh discovery and growth.

As an artist, I believe it’s helpful and informative to try to see the world for how it looks, not what it is. Whether you’re a documentary photographer, journalist, street photographer, commercial photographer, food or fashion photographer, it doesn’t matter. Seeing the world through a camera can be revealing and enlightening in ways that our usual binocular, right side up seeing can’t process.

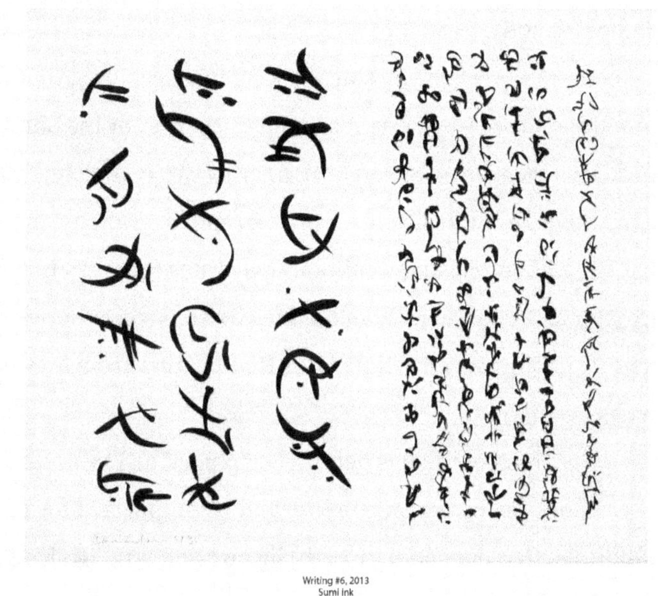

Paula Chamlee, *Writing #6,* sumi ink, 11.5" x 13.5", 2013

If we could see the world through the eyes of a young child, I suspect everything would look like luscious visual information—texture, color, line, and form. Before a child is taught to name things, there is no judgment about what the thing is. Just the act of looking can be thrilling if we don't preconceive what we think it *should* be instead of what it *could* be.

WHEN YOU START LOOKING IN A DEEP WAY, THERE'S ALWAYS SOMETHING TO SEE

With my late husband, photographer Michael A. Smith (1942–2018), whom I married in 1990, I traveled around the United States and other parts of the world making photographs. Many of my photographs have been compiled into books, including *Natural Connections* (1994); *High Plains Farm* (1996), a visual record of my family farm where I grew up on the High Plains of the Texas Panhandle; *San Francisco: Twenty Corner Markets and One in the Middle of the Block* (1997); *Tuscany: Wandering the Back Roads, Volume I* (2004); *Madonnina* (2004), a series of photographs of religious icons made during trips to Tuscany in 2000 and 2001; *Iceland: A Personal View, Volume I* (2015); and *Chicago: Lake* (2009). All were published by Lodima Press, our publishing arm originated by Michael in 1981.

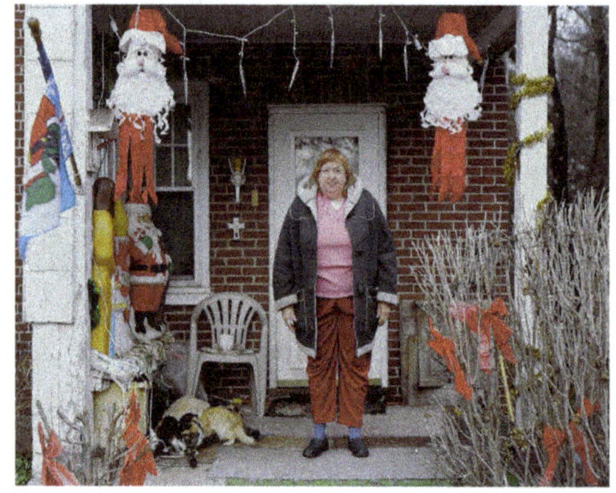

Paula Chamlee, from the series, *Celebrating Sarah*, archival pigment print from 8" x 10" negative, 2010

I believe that when you start looking in a deep way, there's always something to see—even right around the corner or in your own back yard. My *Celebrating Sarah* (2013) series was completed very close to my home in Bucks County. I photographed a woman and her yard that she elaborately and inimitably decorates for every holiday throughout every year. *From the Field* is an ongoing series I started in 2011, photographing wild plants that I gather from around my studio in Bucks County.

My creative life has definitely changed as I've gotten older. There's only so much time in life, and it's important for me to focus on the things that engender growth, inspiration, and positive energy. There are many things that have been important to me in that regard: listening to new music, seeing museum shows, reading new books, conversations about art and the art world, expanding knowledge in art history. I am interested in looking at other mediums such as the performing arts, sculpture, fine ceramics, ancient pottery, and paintings, for example. Wherever Michael and I traveled, if there was a museum anywhere nearby, we would visit the exhibitions.

IT'S IMPORTANT TO FOCUS ON THINGS THAT ENGENDER GROWTH

I find that some of these accumulated inspirations will emerge naturally to serve my working process in the studio. These mediums have certainly informed my photographing. Because my paintings, drawings, and collages are difficult pieces to resolve, I need whatever tools I can muster to lead me to what is useful for development. There is no gratification in repeating myself.

As I've gotten older, I realize that I can quickly sift through things that I perceive to be unessential and superficial. I can easily slough them off so that I can focus on what is, for me, a deeper and more meaningful place.

[I TRY] TO SEE AND FEEL HOW ENERGY MOVES IN THE UNIVERSE

I am not especially involved with idea projects, although ideas and intellect are always present. I do better when I can quiet my mind. My art is related to my interest in trying to see and feel how energy moves in the universe—something called "universal energy." In part, it has to do with the way the wind blows, how birds fly, how waves in the ocean move, how insects fly under a light, how blood courses throughout our bodies. There's something there that helps me connect with the world in a deeper way. Whether I'm photographing my parents on their farm, Sarah at her home and gardens, or an iceberg in Iceland, that interest pervades all the work. That has basically been my life's mission: trying to grasp what is beneath the surface and transmit it to my art.

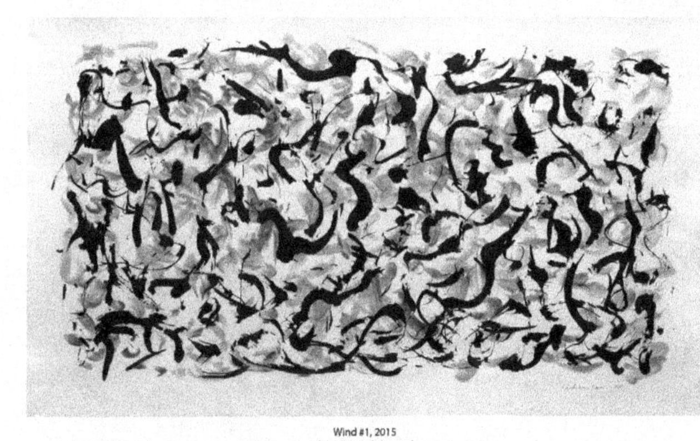

Paula Chamlee, *Wind #1*, sumi ink and charcoal, 18" x 32", 2015

One thing I've always felt is important in my photography is to not reprint old work any more than necessary. I'd rather be making new work. I continue to embrace this. I believe it's the new work that's going to lead me to discoveries that further my development as an artist.

The only thing I regret about growing older as an artist is that I don't have the stamina and energy to work as fully as I would like to. That troubles me a lot because I've always been a bit of an overachiever. I want to get things done and keep moving, although that often adds unproductive stress.

SEEING WHERE THE FLOW TAKES ME

When I was younger, I had no idea how my life would be now. I wasn't thinking about specific long-term goals. When I was raising my kids, I thought about the timeline of raising children, their lives and their education and needs, but nothing specific beyond that. When I started painting and drawing and returned to university studies, I developed a focus on making opportunities for things related to my art—further training, exhibitions, and so forth. Once I started photographing, I wanted to keep making photographs, possibly exhibit them and publish them, and to meet other photographers. There was some general planning, but I think most of my life has been about seeing where the flow takes me. I try to be open to new possibilities, and I want to give back to the world—to leave something inspiring and useful for others. Maybe that universal energy will guide me to the next step. I never know what lies ahead. I just want to keep working. ❖

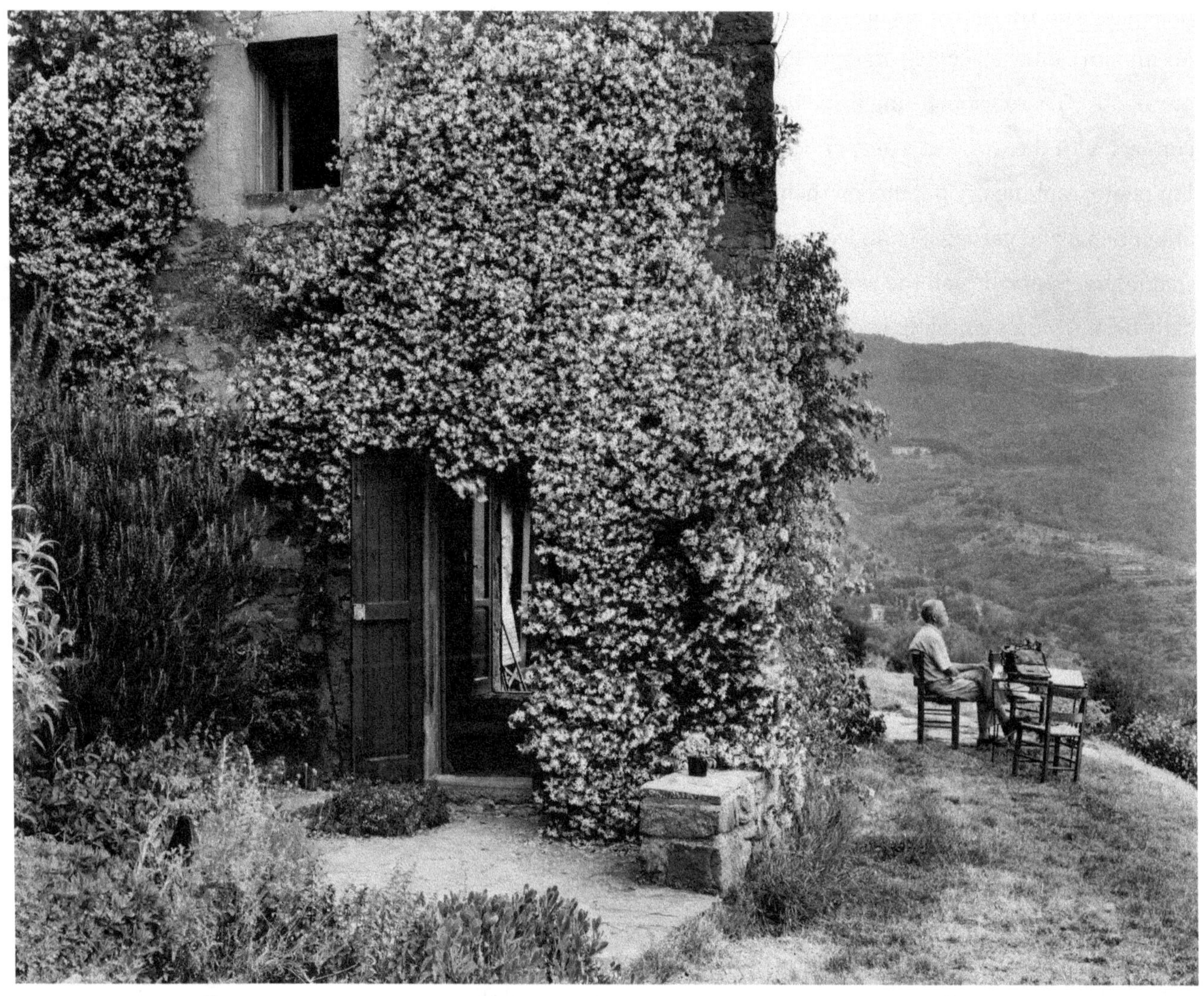

Paula Chamlee, *Cortona, Tuscany*, silver chloride contact print, 8" x 10", 1999

See *Women of Color Embracing Their Individuality Proudly and Boldly Taking Their Place in the Universe, Part A,* page 31

ROSEMARY OLLISON

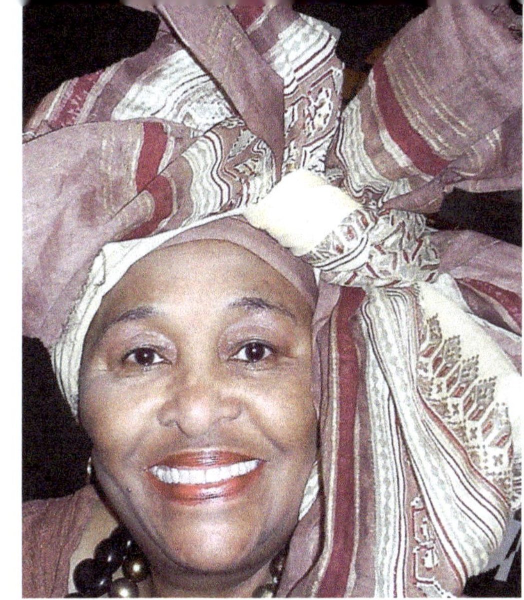

Visual Artist I Quilter I Textile, Jewelry & Wearable Arts Creator
Place of Birth: Portland, Arkansas
Current Location: Milwaukee, Wisconsin
Age: 80
www.portraitsocietygallery.com/rosemaryollison
www.gobeyondreligion.com

FOR YEARS, I didn't consider myself to be an artist. I'm a very religious person, and my frame of reference is the Bible. I read a Bible verse, Psalms 1:39, about how God created individuals. Reading that scripture and other verses made me pray to God to put me on a straight path and show me who I was. I had emotional and mental problems at the time. Some people may not believe it, but I was inspired by the Holy Spirit to go and get a sketchpad and some magic markers, which I'd never done before.

I would have been around age fifty-one when I started to draw. It was like God was showing me what was wrong within me through the images. In about a year and a half to two years, I had around two thousand images that I received. The first images were sexual, with big breasts, protruding nipples, and penises. At one point, I wondered, "How could this be coming from God?" Then I understood that God was explaining to my heart and mind that my emotional problems were from being sexually abused.

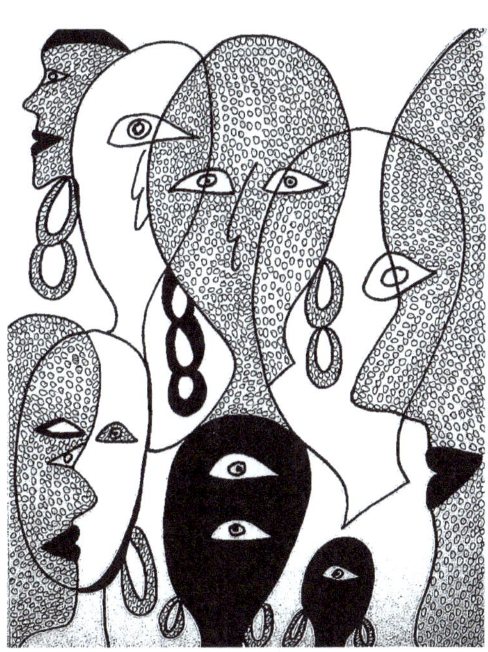

Rosemary Ollison, *Confusion in a Black and White World*, ink on paper, 12" x 18", circa 2000

I had no intention of selling my art at all, but I ended up having my first show in 1994 at age fifty-two after Tony Fikes brought artist and curator Evelyn Patricia Terry to my home to see my drawings. Many of the early images with the sexual overtones were in the show. These images brought back things that happened to me when I was younger. They were deep secrets within me that affected me mentally and caused much confusion. Once I got all of those things out, I started receiving and creating beautiful art.

My work with fabric came about shortly after the period of making the two thousand images. I used to feel insignificant and of no importance. I don't cook, and I don't drive. Compared to other women, I felt that I wasn't getting anything out of life. I was like a walking dead woman. I didn't feel that I deserved anything from God, but I believed, and I prayed. I read a scripture verse that read, "Even the little dogs eat the scraps from the master's table." I thought, "Just give me scraps or anything to help me." Literally, that's where the scraps came in. I moved away from the drawing and started working with fabric scraps. Everything I've made since is with scraps. I collect a variety of materials from thrift shops and rummage sales, including glass, leather, bracelets, beads, bones, and jewelry. There are many things that people throw away that I can take and turn into something beautiful. One of my recent shows that displayed some of my creations was titled *Prosperity in a Million Scraps*.

I WAS LIKE A PEACOCK WHOSE TAIL WAS CUT OFF AND NOT ALLOWED TO GROW

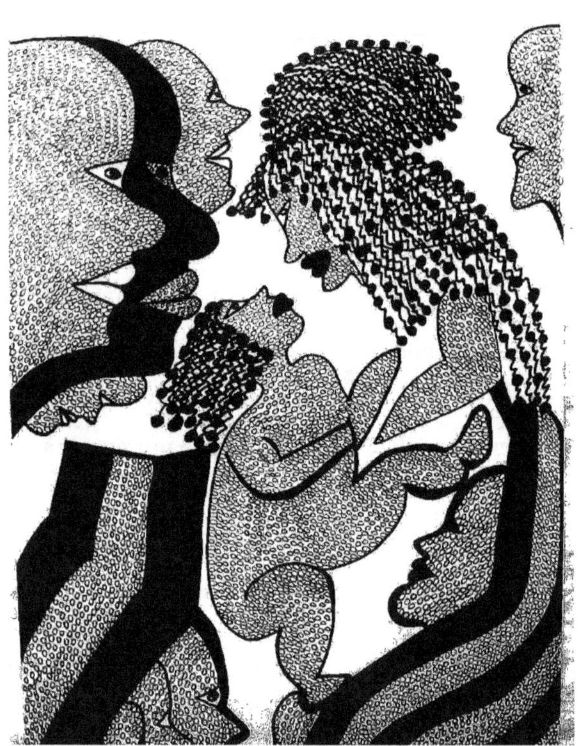

Rosemary Ollison, *Detached*, ink on paper, 12" x 18" circa 2000

Working with scraps is like creating with pieces of a puzzle. It's different from collage. God told me that I was like a peacock whose tail was cut off and not allowed to grow. I was like a puzzle of a million pieces that He would put together. Everything I make is like a work of art from puzzles. It's definitely healing.

I went from being a walking dead woman to a full human being. Over this time, God has put me together. Each time I take some pieces of scraps and put them together to create my art, it's the same as what God has done for me by making me whole.

My creative imagination never stops. Currently, I'm working with the scraps and continuing to write extensively in my journal for sometimes two or three hours a day. I've been journaling since 1984. I recently pulled out four hundred and fifty poems that I've written. I also create jewelry every day. I still draw at times, but it has to be something that my spirit leads me to do.

When I was a younger woman, I did not imagine my life would be as it is now. I had no plans. I was a battered wife. I had been convinced that I couldn't do anything. Before this, I was a sickly child who didn't start school until I was seven. I just never did anything. Still,

I AM WONDERFULLY MADE

I do not feel at all like, "Wow. Look at my life now." I can explain how I feel through a quilt I made.

I made a very large quilt that was ten feet by ten feet. The gallery picked it up, and I didn't want to be involved with how they were going to display it for a big solo show. I walked into the gallery and saw the quilt on display. Everyone was asking me questions. They asked, "How do you feel when you look at your work?" For the first time, I remembered the scripture in Psalms 1:39 where it says, "I am wonderfully made." Seeing the quilt let me know that I'm okay. I made a comment to someone, "I never thought about it, but when I look at this big quilt, I feel wonderfully made. I feel that God did not make a mistake when He made me." At that moment, I felt for the first time that I'm wonderfully made. That's now how I feel every time I make something.

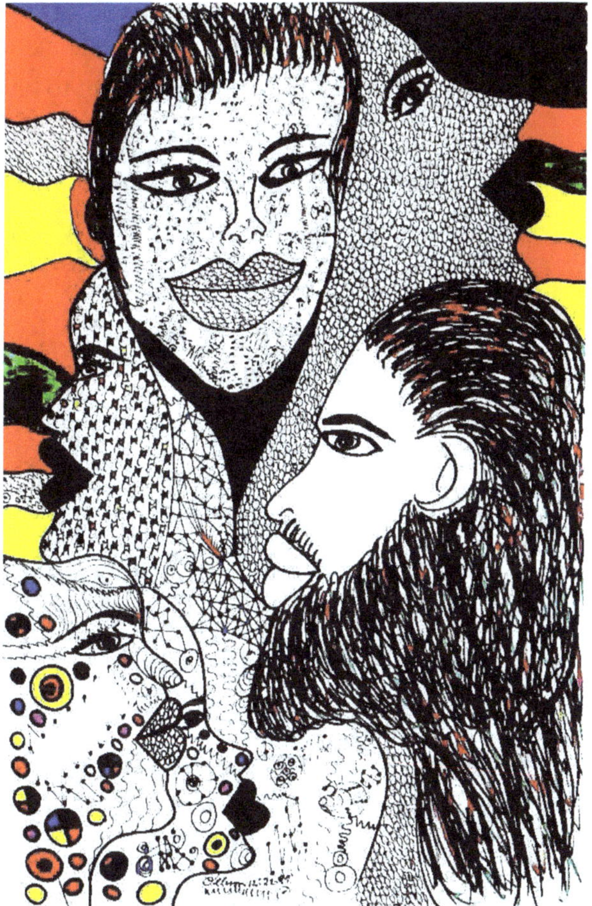

Rosemary Ollison, *One Race—The Human Race*, ink on paper, 12" x 18", circa 2000

All of my art has a meaning. I don't just do it without having something in mind; I do it in dialogue with God. Because of this, all of my art speaks to me. My art tells a story about my life. It is my story in pictures. My personal relationship with Jehovah God and my creations are my whole life. A lot of what I create is also for other people. They see what they see, and it encourages them.

I believe that God has a purpose for everything I create. I have gifts that I've been entrusted to take care of. I don't worry about where it will be used. What I create does not belong to me. The right person will come and find it. Even after I'm gone, what I create will still be here. Maybe ten or more years from now, something I create will lift someone up and make them feel a certain way.

I hear so many people say, "I don't have a gift," or, "I don't know what my gift is." I'm sure they have a gift that is needed. We all have a purpose in this life, and every individual has a gift. The creative imagination is within everyone. What hinders so many people from using their gifts is that their gifts are not considered great by the world. If you were created to be an artist and you don't do it, you're not fulfilling your full purpose. People should learn what their gifts are and just be

THE CREATIVE IMAGINATION IS WITHIN EVERYONE

free. You will never be free until you get to know yourself and become self-actualized.

My creative imagination never stops. And I know it will continue forever, because the Bible tells me that God did not create humans or the earth for nothing. He formed the earth to be inhabited with perfect individuals to live forever in paradise. Even those who have passed on in death will be raised.

I look forward to seeing my loved ones that passed on. I just lost a brother from the coronavirus. I look forward to seeing him, my grandparents, my mother and father, and people that I've known. When I'm in paradise, there will hopefully be things that I can do. Maybe I will make clothes for the resurrected ones. I believe I will still be using my gifts forever to benefit others. ❖

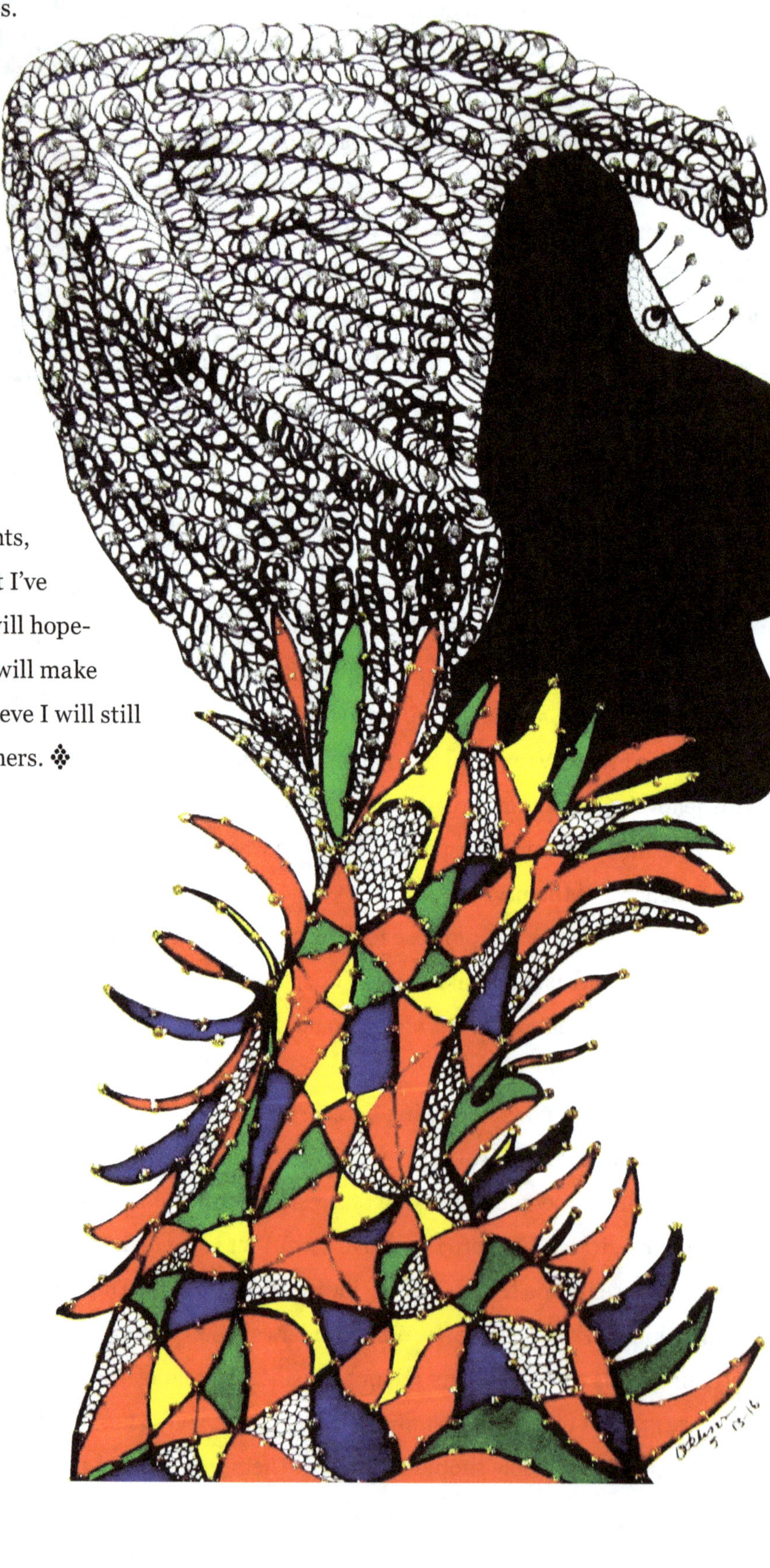

Rosemary Ollison, *Women of Color Embracing Their Individuality Proudly and Boldly, Taking Their Place in the Universe, Part B*, ink on paper, 12" x 18", 2016

See *Greeting Cards,* page 32

GWYN KIRK

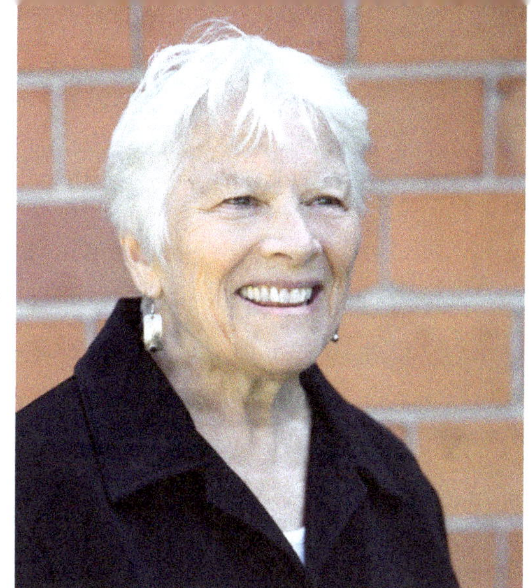

Writer | Fabric, Paper, Collage & Book Artist | Gardener
Place of Birth: Chester, England
Current Location: Oakland, California
Age: 78
www.gwynkirk.net

I THINK OF my life and work as being like a kaleidoscope. The elements of learning, teaching, activism, writing, visual art, and gardening all nurture and inspire me. When you turn a kaleidoscope, the images you see are made up of the same pieces, but in different arrangements. Maybe the purple triangles are prominent. You turn it again, and the red squares or silver dots stand out. These basic parts fit together in various ways. My interest in one area helps to feed and energize my interest in others. A kaleidoscope is also a structure that holds all the pieces together.

It's important to me to have a balance between what I do that is externally focused and what is internally focused. If things get out of balance, I begin to feel I'm short-changing myself. I didn't think like this when I was twenty-five or even fifty-five. I've taught at various U.S. colleges and universities on and off over the years. When I was younger, I often felt burdened by responsibility and the need to be "productive" in professional terms. I'm free of most of that now. It's too bad that it's often only after "retirement"—whatever that means— that we're able to keep things in better balance.

Growing up, it would have been helpful if I received more encouragement from parents and teachers about art, and more of an overall sense that making art is a valid way to spend time.

It would have also helped to know more people who were making art. This would have allowed me to be part of an ongoing conversation. I wish funding was provided for artists and writers under a broader definition, and not just for people who have gone to art school or are "recognized" as artists and writers.

Activism has been an element in my life for many years. It's wrapped up with my learning, teaching, and writing. Activism is about creating something that did not exist—a new realization, a different situation, changing the discourse or conversation, opening up fresh possibilities. Also, I think activism needs to be creative to mobilize people and to excite and inspire us, especially over the long-term.

WE TRANSFORMED THE PLACE

In the early 1980s, I was involved in a women's peace movement in Britain. It started as a protest against a plan to locate nuclear weapons at Greenham Common, a base under U.S. Air Force command. What was fascinating about that experience was that it was so creative. Women were organizing things, and there was a conscious effort to get away from just doing demonstrations or rallies. I'm not saying these aren't valuable, but what was happening there was different.

In December 1982, there was a huge gathering of about thirty thousand women from across the country. We stood together around the nine-mile fence that separated us from what went on inside the base. We were shoulder-to-shoulder in places. We decorated the fence with things that meant something to us, in opposition to nuclear weapons and war. Women brought photos of children and grandchildren, clothing, plants, colorful fabric, posters, and signs. When this material was put together, it was an amazing thing, a nine-mile exhibit, and an outpouring of creativity from women's lives.

Another part of that experience was noise: shouting, chanting, singing. You can't see very far around a nine-mile fence. You see the people near you on either side, but sound travels much farther. Our singing and chanting really brought us together and underlined a sense of unity, of community. We transformed the place. I remember this, years later, as just one example of creative activism that I've been part of.

There are also many more current examples. After George Floyd was killed, people took to the streets in Oakland during a

Gwyn Kirk, *Earth*, silk, cotton, linen, store-bought felt, leather, embroidery thread, beads, and buttons, 2002

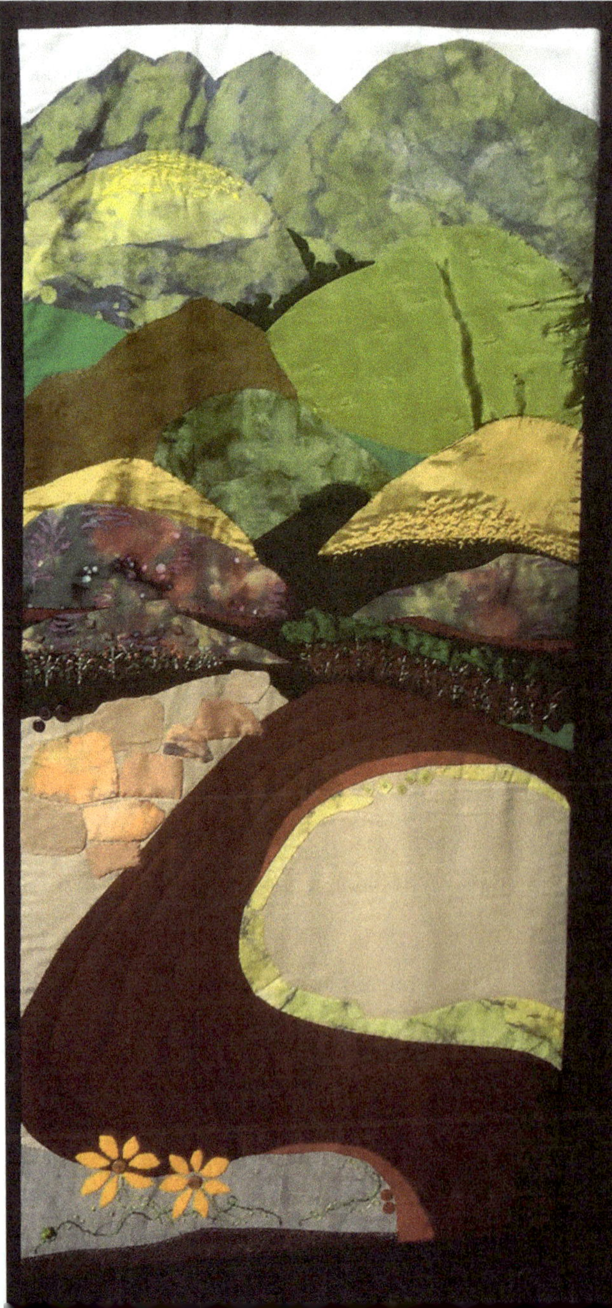

large Black Lives Matter mobilization. Storeowners were concerned about the possibility of looting and damage. They boarded up their storefronts with plywood. People painted murals on these boards. Walking around Broadway, a main street in downtown Oakland, was like walking through an outdoor gallery with positive images and messages about Black lives.

There are many overlaps between creativity and activism. Even slight interventions can change things for participants and perhaps for others. And major movements invariably grow from small beginnings.

I've always wanted beauty in my life, though this was often a rather vague yearning. These days, I'm much more conscious of how important it is for me to be creative in some way, and I see creativity quite broadly. It could be an ambitious project, or it might just mean making a quirky birthday card for a friend or placing a plant with blue flowers next to one with orange flowers to enjoy the sizzle of those two colors together. Or when you cut through a cabbage, you notice it looks like a tree inside. It's about being more aware, conscious, focused, and intentional.

IT'S ABOUT BEING MORE AWARE, CONSCIOUS, FOCUSED, AND INTENTIONAL

Another thing is time. When I was younger and busier with teaching, it was much harder to find time for creative projects. Now that I understand the importance of creative work for me, it's easier to justify the time it takes. I value it differently and allow myself to make it more of a priority.

I also realize that any kind of creativity needs the best part of our brains. There's this idea that if you are a teacher, for example, but you like to knit, sew, draw, or something, these activities are hobbies, relegated to evenings or weekends. I had to shift my thinking on this. If I want to pursue creative activities, I need to start in the morning. This is about honoring creative work with time and also with the best parts of myself—the physical, mental, and emotional energies that it requires. Creating something new is important to me. If I were to look back later, I know I won't regret not having gone to more meetings or answered more emails in a timely fashion. I will regret not having tried to explore the creative side of life as fully as I can.

Gwyn Kirk, *Handmade Book*, Arches drawing paper, decorative paper scraps, cotton tape, embroidery thread, 2017

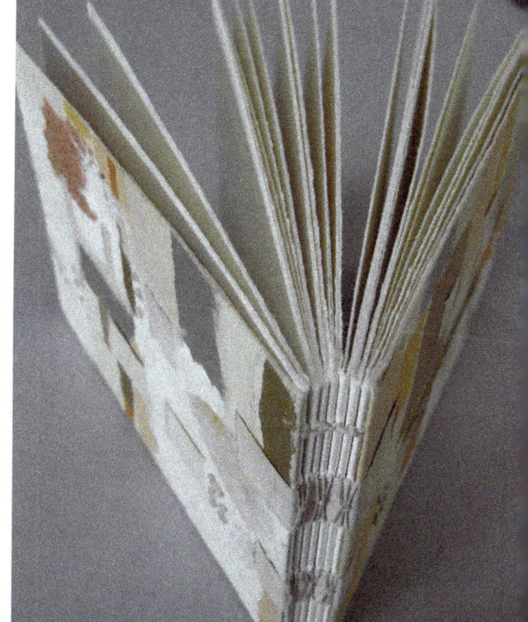

I'm currently working on several different projects. For example, I'm making small books. They're fun, with a lot of color. You can do them on the kitchen table, so you don't need a huge amount of space. I'm finding the forms, methods, and crafts that fit who I'm becoming as I grow older—my interests, skills, and capacities.

I'm excited about another book project, based on color. These are handmade artist books—zines, really. One is called *Yellow*, another one's *Red*, and a third one is *Blue*. I've started them but still have a long way to go. I'm experimenting with collage. I'm really intrigued by it. I find it challenging, like solving visual puzzles.

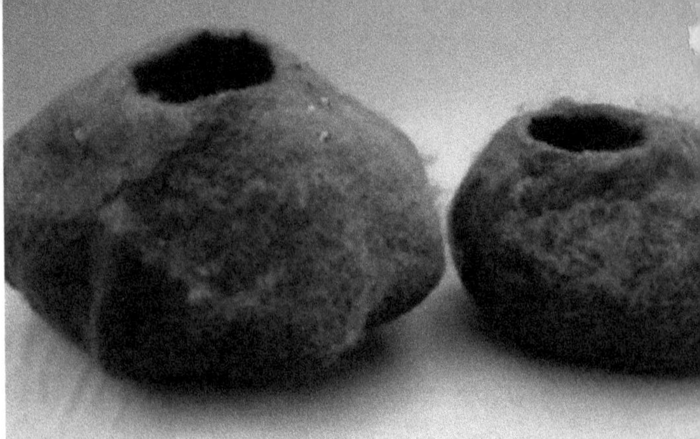

Gwyn Kirk, *Felted Pots*, wool batting and roving, seed beads, embroidery thread, 2016

Also, I've continued to write. This year, I've worked on an anthology about ecofeminism with a co-editor, to be published in spring 2021. I'm very excited about how it has unfolded. Even close to the end, the book was still evolving. And our understanding of what we were trying to do was still growing. We're planning a website to post photos and videos of the projects that contributors write about, to expand the work and to help create a community beyond the pages of the book.

Talking about creativity would not be complete without mentioning the garden here. I'm hoping to make a book about that too, with writing and photos. For me, gardening is a marvelous, restorative thing. I like to sit out there and notice what's happening: watch clouds of little birds pick over seed heads or listen to the rustle of fallen leaves as the wind blows them down the path. I scatter seeds, water and feed them, leave cabbages to go to seed, or deadhead roses to force new growth. My interventions make me feel involved, but plants are their own living beauty, of course. Unlike other creative activities, the garden grows whether I work at it or not. Its magnificence has very little to do with me.

GARDENING IS A MARVELOUS, RESTORATIVE THING

I lived in San Francisco before moving to Oakland. Two friends invited me to look for a place here. We got a duplex together with a joint mortgage. This has also been a creative process that none of us could have accomplished on our own. Several things drew me here, especially the possibility of having a productive garden while I had the health and strength to enjoy it. This was an interest we shared.

What's so great about this location is that it's a long, thin plot. The house sits at the back. You come in off the street and walk through the garden to get to the house. This makes us much more connected to the garden since we're always walking through it.

I've been here twelve years now. The space feels like having a big canvas. We planted a lot of bare-root fruit trees early on. We put in a greenhouse that's big enough for people to sit in and eat meals together. It's become a magical place that changes with the seasons and from year to year. Now, I'm much more aware of something that I only used to understand intellectually, which is the whole cycle of seeding, growing, flowering, dying, and reseeding. I really feel part of these processes. It's a wonderful experience.

I WANT TO SURPRISE MYSELF

The next thing I want to learn is how to combine text and images, maybe learning Photoshop or InDesign. Beyond that, I don't really know what I'll do creatively throughout the rest of my seventies and into my eighties. I hope some aspects of the kaleidoscope will continue to inspire and hold me. I think I'd benefit from being challenged by peers and teachers to stretch my imagination and grow my skills. I have no idea what my art would look like, but I'd love to see what I could do.

As I get older, I expect I'll have to make adjustments. You don't know how your heart is going to hold up, your mind, or your bodily strength. For now, I can still thread a needle. I can use a hammer. I can learn new skills.

I'm planning to move to an intentional community in Southern California that I believe will support me in this. This new home will be both a physical space and a community of people. It will be a huge wrench to uproot from here, especially this garden and my friends. But I hope to grow there in terms of expressing myself creatively. I'll continue to engage with what gives me pleasure, and maybe what I create will give other people pleasure. There's a lot of beauty and satisfaction in that.

I read something recently by Hilary Mantel, a British novelist. She was asked a question like, "What's your next project?" She didn't have a very clear answer, but she said, "As I grow older, I hope I'll be able to surprise myself." I just love that idea. Yes, I want to surprise myself with the new stuff I'll do. ❖

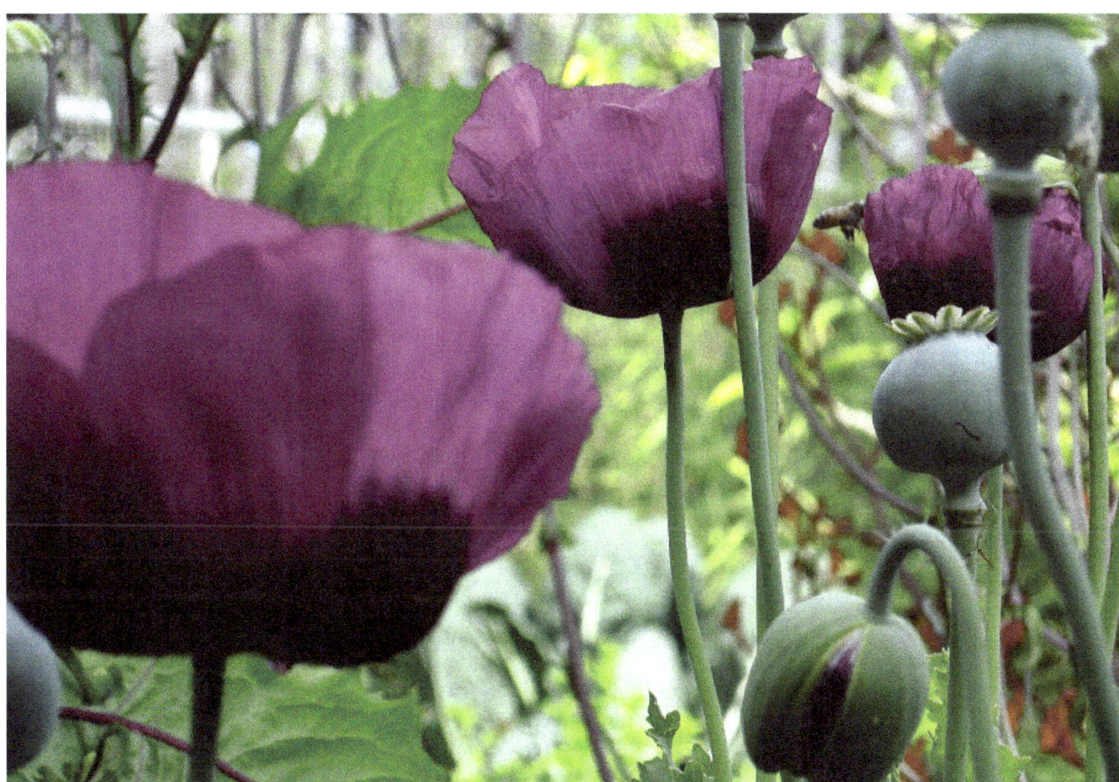

Gwyn's Garden in Oakland, 2019

See *Pacifico,* page 33

LAUNA D. ROMOFF

Visual Artist I Model I Actress
Place of Birth: Los Angeles, California
Current Location: Los Angeles, California
Age: 76
www.launadromoff.com

WHEN I WAS a younger woman, I never thought my life would be how it is now. When I was working in different office jobs, it was just a grind. I often worked long hours from the early morning until seven at night. With work like that, you're exhausted. It's the same thing every day. You're lucky if you have enough energy to get up and exercise before work. The weekends were spent cleaning the house, doing laundry, and going to the market. I used to think, "Is this what life's about? This grind? All the time?" I never thought beyond it. I didn't know what the possibilities were. I certainly never thought about acting or anything like that, even though I grew up in Hollywood.

Now, because of my life as an artist and being a cancer survivor, I've been asked to speak about my experiences. The main thing I want to tell people is that they can start something new at any age. Here I am. I'm a two-time cancer survivor, and now I'm an artist, model, and actress. I never thought I would be any of these things.

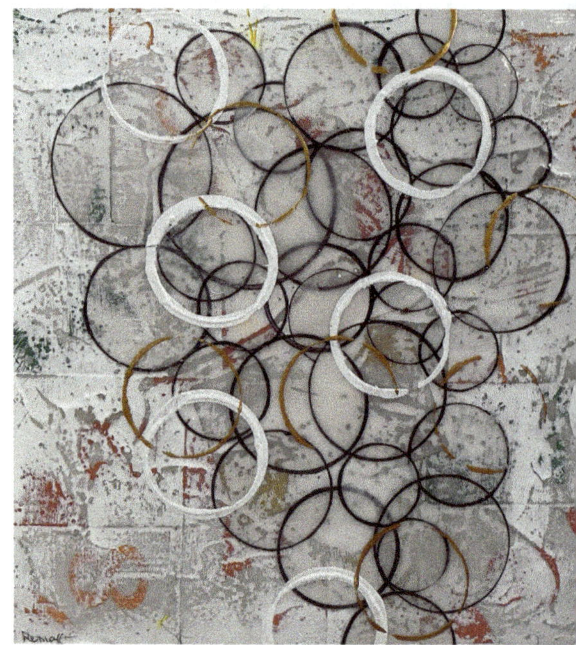

Launa D. Romoff, *Untitled*, mixed media collage on wood, 10" x 10", 2021

I KNEW I HAD FOUND MY VOICE

For most of my life, I did arts and crafts-related things. I enjoyed this but didn't think it made me an artist. I never thought I was an artist because I couldn't draw. My brother drew, and he was the artist in the family.

When I was age fifty, I met the artist Mitzi Trachtenberg. She was a sister-in-law of a good friend. I was familiar with Mitzi's work and thought it was amazing. I didn't know much about collage until I first saw her art.

My friend had a housewarming, and Mitzi came. At the time, she would have been in her late sixties. I sat down with her, and we talked for hours about art, architecture, and design. We had the same sensibilities and feelings. She mentioned that she taught a class in San Francisco. I was so fascinated by her. I said, "Would you teach me?"

Mitzi said she would fly down to Los Angeles once a month and teach me if I could gather six people and have a place to make art. I was so determined that I found a small group of people and a place. In the very first class, I knew I found my voice. I knew that I could make art. There was a place inside of me that needed to come out, and I was blown away by it. That's how my journey started. I did my first class with Mitzi in 1997. In 1999, I had my first show of my collages. At this first show, I sold five pieces.

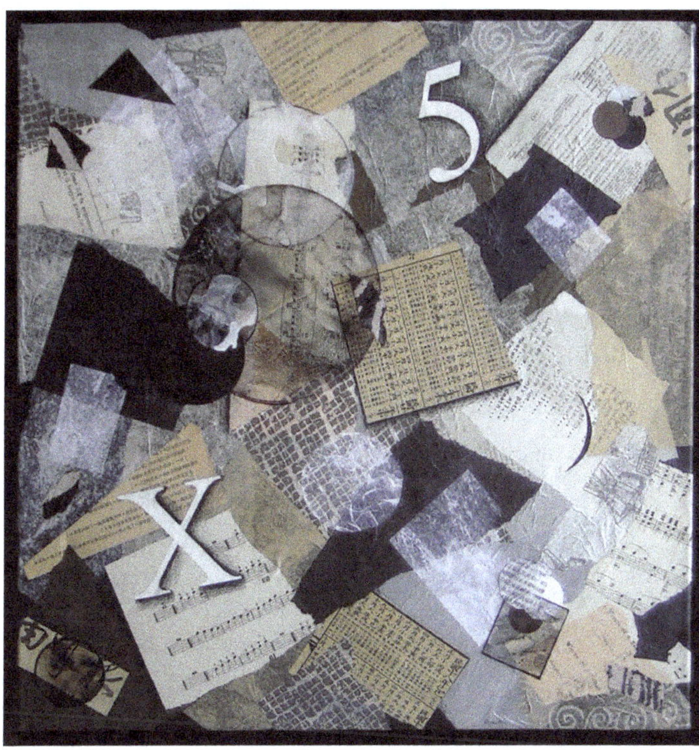

Launa D. Romoff, *Circles & Music*, mixed media collage on canvas, 20" x 20", 2016

I KNEW IN MY BODY THAT I WAS AN ARTIST

Mitzi, being close to age seventy at the time she taught me, had more energy than you could possibly imagine. She would call me from San Francisco and say, "You need to go to this show," "You need to see this museum," "Go see this artist," or, "Get a book on this artist." I never had a mentor in my life. This woman was my mentor. She was constantly calling me and giving me things to study. She'd say, "Don't come to class unless you know all about the artist that I'm going to talk about." She'd fly down with books on different artists for us to look at. I found my voice. I knew in my body that I was an artist once I started studying with her. Mitzi has since passed away, but I still hear her voice at times when I am making art.

I continue to work with collage today. I use anything that I can find, including a lot of paper, sometimes objects, and I now incorporate paint. I used to travel a lot, and wherever I would be, if I saw something that inspired me, I would take it or buy it. These elements from my travels also appear in my collages.

Before I met Mitzi, I worked in business. I was an executive secretary. At one point, I managed my brother's business, but I never liked it. I never felt that I belonged there in that career, but it paid the rent, paid my bills, and provided me medical insurance. I was good at it, but I never identified with it. Once I had my first show and I called myself an artist, it resonated in my body. I knew that was truly me. Since I started, I have created over five hundred works of art.

What I love about collage is that there are so many facets to it and different directions and possibilities. I love the experimentation and all it offers me. I honestly cannot say there is anything I would change with my art practice. It has taken me on an amazing journey.

I believe anybody can start a new career at any time in their life. You can follow your passion at any age. Sadly, a lot of people don't. I believe they are frightened of something new, of change, or that they will fail. When I got to a point in my life where I was sick, I also became game for anything. "Why not try the things that I always wanted to try?" I asked myself.

In 2004, I finished the Los Angeles Marathon for the second year. I was excessively tired with a low-grade fever. I went to the doctor, and they did a bunch of tests. To make a long story short, by the time I got to my oncologist, I had stage four lymphoma. It progressed very quickly. I was in treatment for six months. I was age fifty-eight when I was diagnosed and started chemotherapy.

EVERY DAY, I COULD GO INTO MY STUDIO AND MAKE SOMETHING

When you undergo chemo, the thing that gets you the most is fatigue. Sometimes, I just couldn't get out of bed even if I woke up early. I was so tired. I used to lie in my bed and think about what I wanted to make. When I finally had the energy to get up, I'd come into my studio and work on my art. Even if it was just for half an hour, it was something I had. Every day, I could go into my studio and make something instead of dwelling on, "Oh, poor me," which I don't do.

Then, after I overcame the lymphoma, I was diagnosed with cancer again in 2006. This time, it was lung cancer from smoking even though I quit in 1982. I was lucky though because I never pitied myself, and I never thought I was going to die. I really went into myself at this time and

Launa D. Romoff, *Untitled*, mixed media collage on wood, 10" x 10" 2021

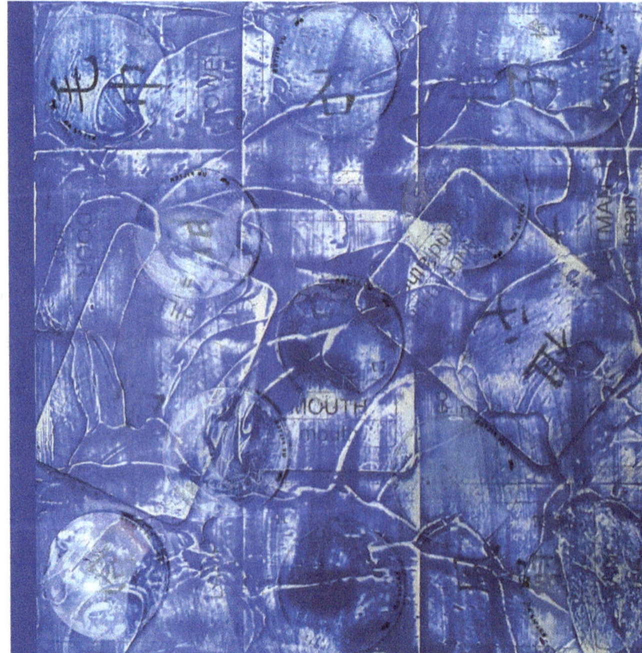

looked at what I needed to do to change. Getting cancer for the second time was like going ten steps forward and seven back. I didn't want to be sick again, so I really changed my life a lot after that. I believe much of it was putting up boundaries with people. I was attracting people who were into drama all the time. I got rid of the drama and now have a wonderful tight group of friends who are loving and supportive.

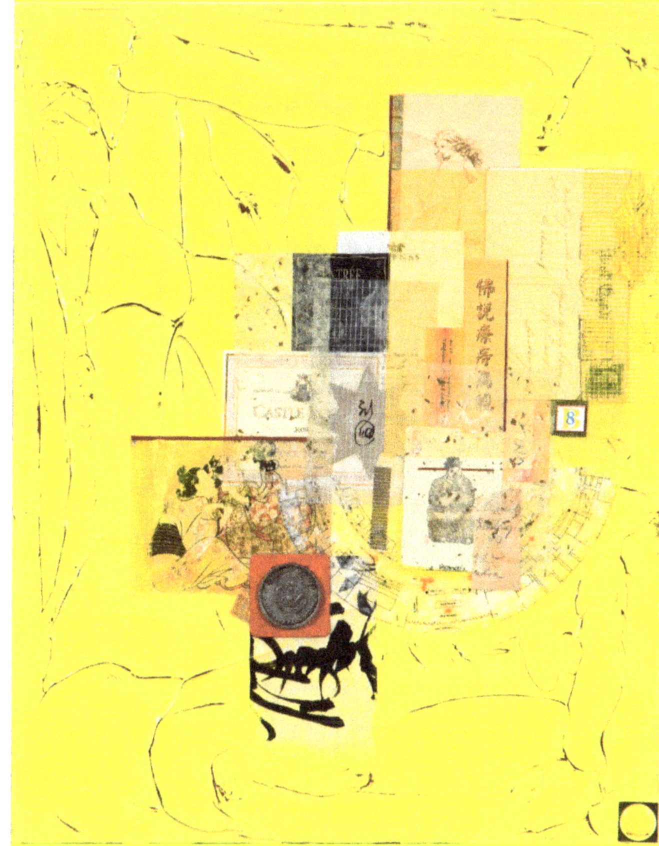

Launa D. Romoff, *Travelling Companion*, mixed media collage on canvas, 20" x 16", 2017

I also noticed things about my art at the time. I work in a series. What I mean is that I will do between five to ten pieces and then I'm spent. I have to go out into the world and fill up again on whatever is out there. I love being in an urban environment, so I will go outside and spend time in the city. Then something starts to bubble in my body, and I know something wants to come out, and I'll do another series of something totally different. At the moment, I'm into circles. I know I'm not finished with this because I just want to keep making more circles.

As an artist, it's important for me to explore different things. Some artists do the same thing over and over again. They may be popular with that, but where's the adventure? Where is the pushing? I want to always try something new. I don't want to be safe with my art.

ADVENTURE LEADS TO ANOTHER PART OF MY STORY

This sense of adventure leads to another part of my story. I was at an art opening, and the artist and photographer J. Michael Walker came up to me. I was sixty-eight at the time. He said he was doing a project and he wanted me to become involved. I asked him to tell me more. He said, "I'm photographing women in the nude." My initial response was to not accept. After chemotherapy, the body changes a lot. As I sat there thinking about this invitation, I thought, "Oh my God, this scares the shit out of me." Ultimately, I said, "Michael, this scares me so much. I'm going to say yes." I recall he said, "It's going to transform your life." I said, "Yeah, right."

There were a lot of delays, and we finally made a date. I was beyond nervous. I totally trusted him though. I looked at his work of other women he had done, which is all so beautiful. It took my breath away.

The session was four hours long, and he took three hundred and fifty pictures, but I had no idea four hours had passed. After, we sat down at the computer together. I come from a very critical mother, so I'm very critical of myself. At first, seeing these photos, I was saying things like, "Oh, God, look at my breasts. Oh, my thigh! Oh, my arm!" He told me I had to stop and try to relax. I decided to look at the photos from an artist's point of view. I got out of the critical mindset and started looking from this different perspective. At one point, I said out loud, "She's a very beautiful woman." And he said, "That's you." This experience was life-changing. He was right: it was transformative.

OLDER WOMEN ARE HOT

Following the session, Michael posted a headshot of me on Facebook. The response was amazing. People were commenting that I was elegant and beautiful. One guy said, "Older women are hot." Although I was someone who had always been shy of cameras, after receiving different forms of encouragement, I ended up posting my images on Models Mayhem, a modeling community website that connects models with work assignments. This led to a photographer from Austria reaching out to me. She wanted to put older women in her portfolio. She took photos of me when she came to Los Angeles. Like before, I was first critical when I looked at them, but I walked away and came back to view them differently. The photos were stunning!

From that, I started to also get into acting and making commercials. I believe my work as an actress started at age sixty-nine. I just think, "This is such an adventure." I can say that I'm always recreating myself and having a lot of fun doing it.

I BELIEVE THAT LIFE ABSOLUTELY KEEPS GETTING BETTER

The wonderful thing about being a certain age is that I can try whatever comes up that interests me, but if I don't like it, I don't have to continue. This is part of the adventure. If I take a class and I don't like it, I don't need to stay until the end. I'm in a book club. If I don't like the book, I don't have to finish it. I can try anything, but I don't have to do anything I don't want to do.

I believe that life absolutely keeps getting better. We all have our little side roads in life. Every once in a while, there's that left turn. The thing is that we're not supposed to be happy all the time. I'm grateful that I've done all the things that I have done. I'm grateful for my life. When I have the little side roads come up, I just say, "You need to come through it." Some of them are harder than others. I've been asked a few times, "If you could change something in your life, what would you change?" The thing is, I like who I am. If I changed anything in my life, I wouldn't be who I am now. I needed all of those things to happen to become the woman I am. What I like to think about is not something I could change; I like to think about gratitude. I have a lot to be grateful for. ❖

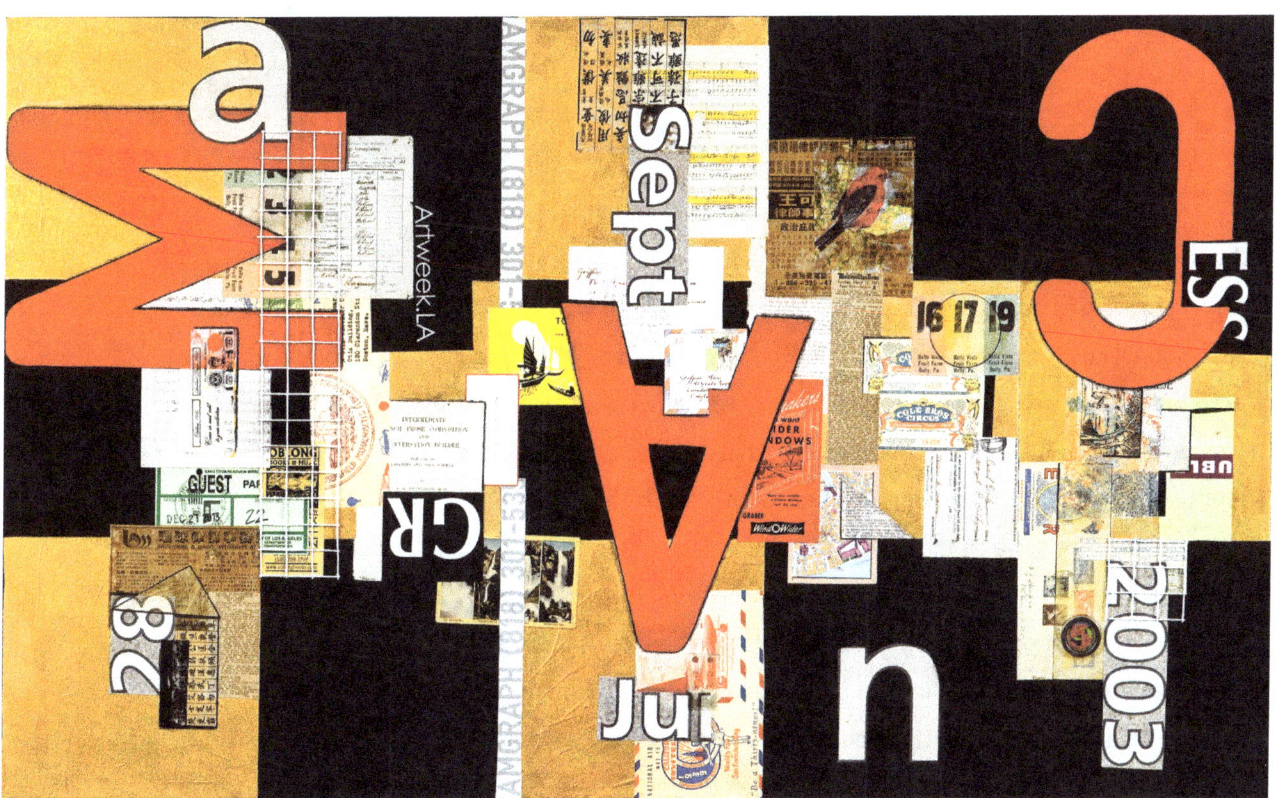

Launa D. Romoff, *Red Letters*, diptych, mixed media collage on canvas, 30" x 50", 2018

See *Kath performing with guitarist,* page 34

KATH BLOOM

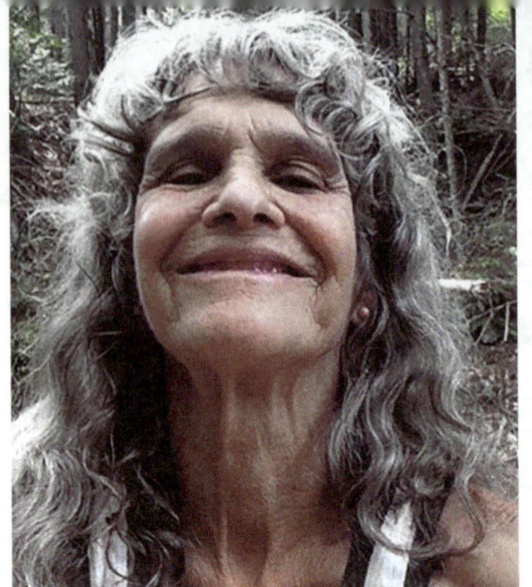

Musician
Place of Birth: Huntington, Long Island, New York
Current Location: Litchfield, Connecticut
Age: 70

I DON'T FEEL old, even when I'm around young people. I feel the same as I always did. If they need any wisdom from me, I'll try to dig some up.

I started writing songs out of my love for music, including the music of Bob Dylan, Joni Mitchell, Janis Joplin, Jimi Hendrix, Neil Young, and so many others. I feel blessed that I have lived, since I was very young, around a tremendous amount of creativity and energy that came out of popular culture. Music was also part of my family. My father, Robert Bloom, an oboist, was a famous classical musician.

I ALWAYS GRAVITATED TOWARD MAKING MY OWN CREATIONS

I always gravitated toward making my own creations since I was never good at figuring out other people's songs, but I don't have a memory of exactly when I began writing music. In my early twenties, I started singing with a boyfriend. We traveled around performing. He sang and played while I did harmony. Eventually, I ended up getting a guitar and started fooling around with it. I would have been around twenty-four when I was first plucking and learning some chords. Then I started playing more.

Kath performing, circa 2015

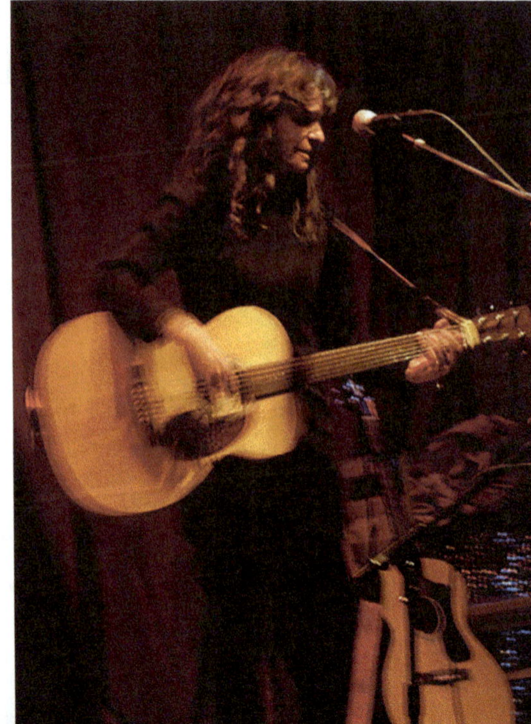

When I was twenty-six, I met Loren Mazzacane and Tom Hanford, who were to become very important for my development with music. They both studied with a visual artist named Mike Skope and were deeply affected by his teachings on creativity. They taught me what they discovered with him. I started playing a great deal with Loren around 1979 and the early 1980s. We made several albums together in the 1980s, including *Sand in My Shoe*, *Sing the Children Over*, *Restless Faithful Desperate*, and *Moonlight*. We didn't perform very often.

To be truthful, it was uncomfortable for me. I felt shy, and I never felt like people wanted to hear us, whether that was true or just my feelings. I don't have many positive memories of performing, but I believe we did have our good moments.

THROUGH MUSIC, I WORKED THINGS OUT

I still kept writing music over the years, but I also became very interested in becoming an actress. With others, I formed a little theater group, and I studied acting in New York City. I was also doing visual art at the time, and then I got married during this early period of creativity. Seeing how I could create was a real rush, and I was dedicated to it all: writing songs, painting, and acting. Even when my marriage started to not work out and ultimately ended, I kept everything up. I took classes and went into New York a lot. My songwriting was constant. Through music, I worked things out. It was therapeutic.

By the time I got married to my second husband, Stan Bronski, who I am still with now, I was writing songs all the time. I have memories of sitting in a field while playing and writing my music. I had one child with my first husband and then two more with Stan. I was always writing, but children were such a part of my life too. I became very fond of working with kids and playing music with them. When my children were still young and we were then living in Florida, I started playing music at a little daycare up the road from our home. I loved it.

Kath with her granddaughter Jade, 2020

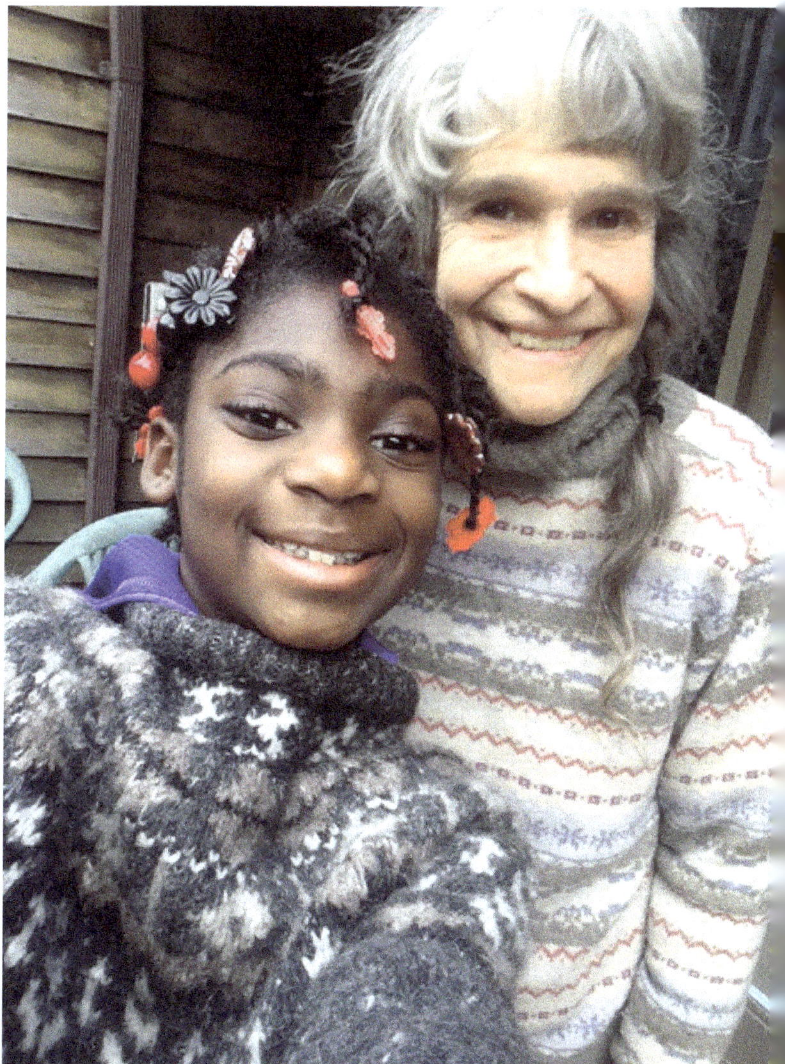

In the 1990s, I worked with a man named Javier Del Sol. Around 1997 or 1998, we obtained a grant to work with children, and we formed an after-school program for doing art, music, and theater. I also formed a women's band, which was another part of my life there in Florida.

Eventually, Stan and I moved back to New England and bought a house in Connecticut. I continued to work a lot with children. I reconnected with Tom Hanford, and I also kept writing and making self-produced albums. For the past two years, I've been working with a wonderful daycare where I am kind of the music teacher. I sit in a circle with the children and jump around like crazy. We dance and move to the music together. I also play music with my granddaughter, who is the real light of my life.

[MY] SONG WAS USED IN THE FILM *BEFORE SUNRISE*, DIRECTED BY RICHARD LINKLATER AND STARRING ETHAN HAWKE AND JULIE DELPY. IT WAS A TRIP!

I have a very good story about my song *Come Here* that happened before we moved back to Connecticut. This was in 1994. I didn't have a computer and was somewhat divorced from pursuing a career in music, although I did write my favorite album at this time, *It's Just a Dream*, with my husband Stan and a guitarist named Peter Friedman. I was living in the middle of nowhere in the orange groves in Florida. We were eight miles from the nearest paved road. I was a horse trainer. I especially liked working with horses that were considered problems because they were scared or difficult in some way. The horses made me strong, and working with them was my favorite thing, which I ended up doing for many years, until I was into my sixties. It became my medicine.

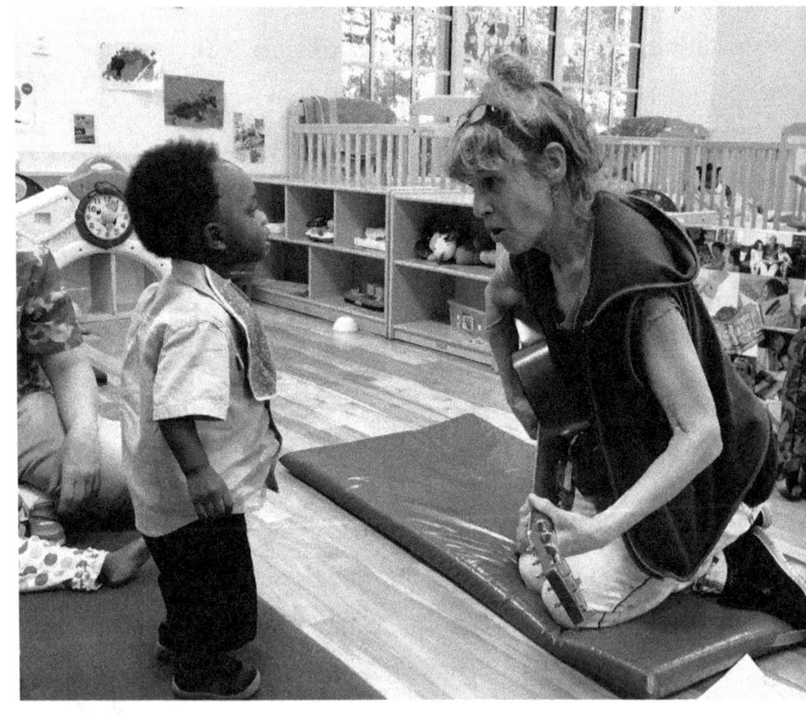

Kath teaching at a daycare, 2015

So, one day, while out there in the Florida orange groves, I got a call that somebody wanted to use my song *Come Here* for a film. They wanted me to record it again. We ended up going the whole way back to Connecticut, and I re-recorded it in 1994. The song was used in the film *Before Sunrise*, directed by Richard Linklater and starring Ethan Hawke and Julie Delpy. It was a trip!

I experienced an odd coincidence when the film was released. Stan got a job playing bass for a theater in Vienna, and I went with him for two weeks. Although I didn't know it at the time, they had just finished filming *Before Sunrise* in Vienna the week before Stan and I arrived. I didn't know where the film took place. It felt like synchronicity when it was released and I saw that it had been filmed in Vienna and so close to the time I had been there.

Years later, in 2009, covers of my songs by various artists were compiled on a tribute album titled *Loving Takes This Course*. These things just happen, and people get a hold of me. It's only been recently though that I've become serious about my music career.

I'M READY FOR MY CAREER AT THIS AGE

There were times when opportunities developed around my music that I was unable to act upon because of my second son Jack's journey into schizophrenia. He ended up experiencing crises and being in different hospitals. I found myself driving all over Connecticut and New York for several years during this time. He still has crises, but he is much better now. I could not apply myself to my career when I was helping him. It was hard enough keeping up with the music classes for children.

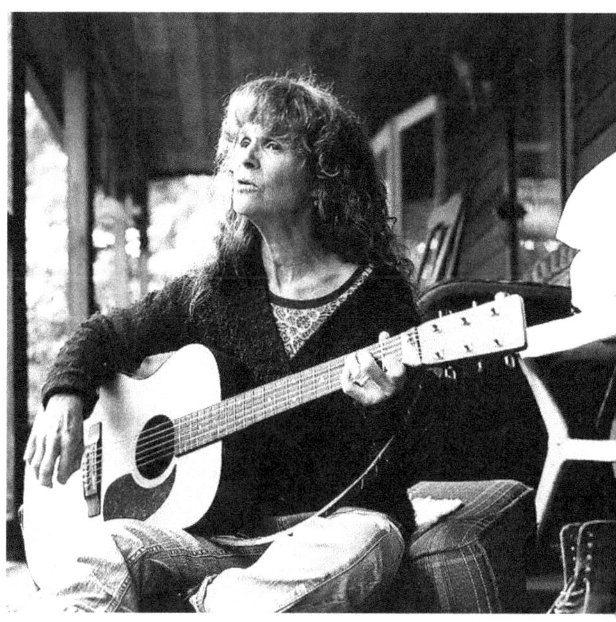

Kath on her porch at home in Connecticut, 2011

In the early 2000s, we moved back to Connecticut, and I reunited with different people. My main job was working with children, and I was performing locally. Around 2009, I started to get invitations to play around the world. I went to England a bunch of times and also performed in Spain, Japan, and Australia. Starting around 2013 through 2017, I went out to Los Angeles maybe five times to record with a wonderful man named Jeff Hassay. We made a few albums together. I didn't try to have a career though. I just went where I was invited, played, got stoned, and had fun. It was good to get away.

Now is different though. I play with my friend Flo Ness on percussion and a young guitarist named Dave Shapiro. We just started touring the past few years, and I realized at this age that I really love this! I love going to bed and waking up knowing that I'm going to go out and play. Because of how good I feel about it, I decided I'm ready for my career at this age. I'm no longer such a private person. Right now is the happiest I've been with my music career.

THERE'S A PLACE IN ME WHERE THE SONGS ARE SITTING AND WAITING

I'm grateful that I am able to play music, and I feel so positive about my career. I'm also grateful for listening. I believe in the power of listening. When I speak of being able to listen, I mean listening in general to everything: nature, the birds, the wind. Listening is part of the creative process. Listening, writing, creating. It's what I live for.

Every medium is different, but I think the creative impulse is the same.

You just have to believe in your feelings and that you can work with them. Some people are never able to learn how to deal with their feelings in this way. Our feelings are the best thing we have and also the most dangerous. The majority of art comes from there.

It has been about five years since I created visual art. I used to paint outside at different places we lived, including the orange groves. I believe that I will return to it. Sometimes, there are detours in life. I don't have the energy to do all of the art forms, and I've been focused on my music. I'm looking forward to getting out on the road and performing more.

A difference with how I am now is that I'm able to be critical toward the work, such as the melody and words, but I'm no longer critical of myself as I used to be. Why would I want to do that? I suppose when I was younger, I didn't understand where the songs were coming from, but I felt I had to create them. I still feel that I have to create, but now it is a good thing, and I enjoy it more. I guess you could say I'm a bit more measured at this age and with my experience.

I can also now work slowly with my creativity, although it's the same process as when I was younger. It still feels like something is going through me when I create. When I begin writing a song, the melody is what comes first. The melody comes together with the lyrics, and they kind of repeat in my subconscious and conscious. I can feel a shadow of a song when I'm working on it. It's like there's a place in me where the songs are sitting and waiting. I'm ready for the pandemic to be over so I can get out there and do more. ❖

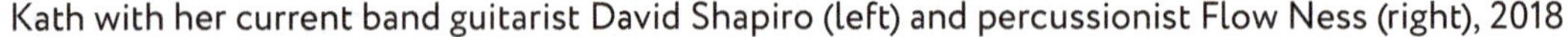

Kath with her current band guitarist David Shapiro (left) and percussionist Flow Ness (right), 2018

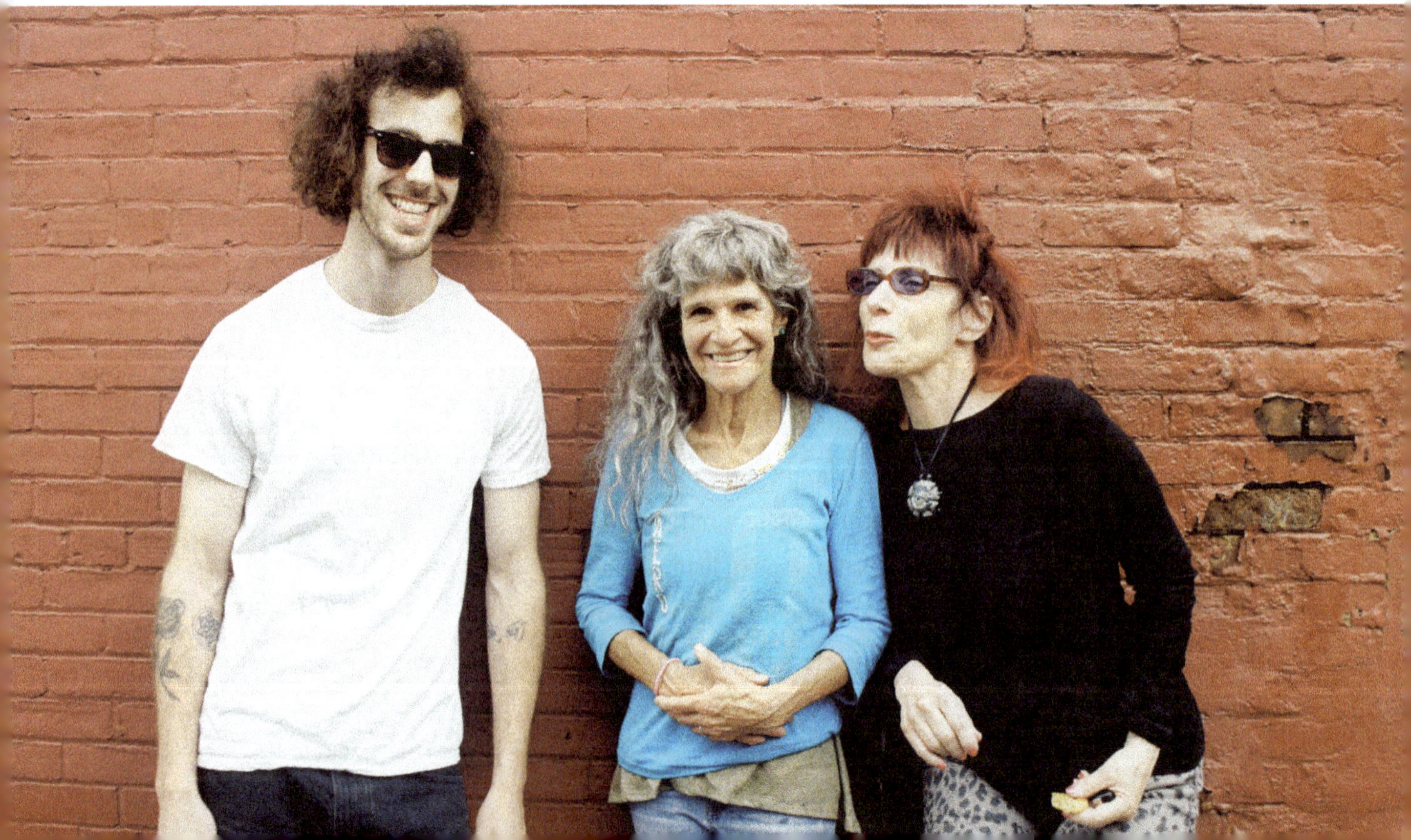

See *A Certain Loneliness,* page 35

SANDRA GAIL LAMBERT

Prose Writer
Place of Birth: Hamilton Air Force Base, California
Current Location: Gainesville, Florida
Age: 70
www.sandragaillambert.com

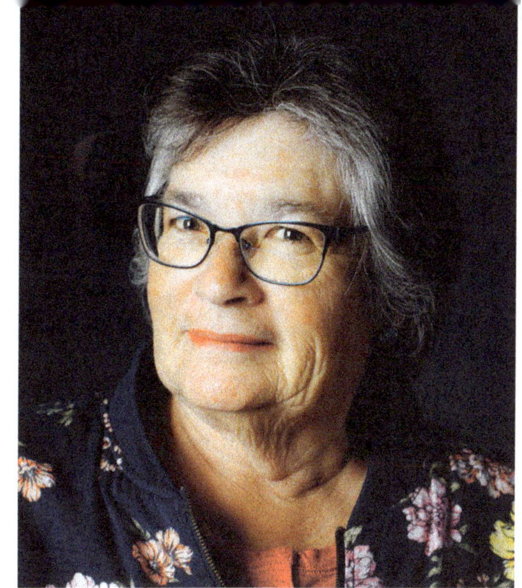

I ALWAYS START the story of my journey as a writer from my early forties. That's when I began writing seriously and thinking of myself as a writer. Lately, I've been confronting the question of why I wasn't a writer before that. All the signs were there. I always helped out in the library and had crushes on the school librarians, which was a sign of a writer and also of my early attraction to women.

I read by flashlight late into the night. My mother would yell at me about ruining my eyesight. I'd call in sick to work to finish reading a novel. And then I ended up running a feminist bookstore for most of the 1980s. Considering all of this, why was I not one of those people who wrote their first little story in crayons, edited the high school yearbook, or whatever other narrative we hear about writers?

I've come to understand that those years of not writing weren't just an accident. They weren't happenstance. They had to do with shame and secret-keeping. Somehow, I knew that if I was going to be a writer, I had to be honest to myself and the world. And I wasn't willing to do that for many years. Growing up disabled involved surviving through surgeries as well as enduring the loneliness of being the only one—the only disabled kid I knew. Fitting in became my goal. It was an unobtainable goal, but I chased after it for decades. When emotional and physical survival is primary, creative energy can be sucked into nothingness.

Yet there I was, at Charis Books in Atlanta, a feminist bookstore, for most of my thirties. I was part of a vibrant lesbian feminist community in my work and personal life. Everyone around me was

A WRITING COMMUNITY ...OPENED UP [A] SPACE FOR ME

writing. So many women were creating small presses and journals. It was an exciting time. Everyone was telling their stories in this multitude of voices. It was a writing community that often found content more important than skill, craft, or training. For someone like me who had no training or academic background in that way, it made me brave enough to try. It opened up that space for me.

I started by writing blurbs for our store catalog. In fifty words, I had to describe the book accurately and with enough enthusiasm that people would buy it. There's really not much better training for a writer. At this same time as I was beginning to write, I started experiencing the effects of post-polio syndrome. I had polio as a baby, and I used braces and crutches all my life. It had always just been how things were. I figured out how to do what I wanted and I didn't think that much about it, but now, I was having all this weakness, pain, and a strange diminishment of mental focus. Sometimes, I would be talking to a customer, and I would fall over right in front of them. For the first time that I have a memory of, I had to pay attention to my body. I think this was significant in not only becoming a writer but also in how I write. Whether I'm writing a fantastical short story with alligator women or a personal essay about kayaking on my own in the Everglades, the body is always central to my work.

There have been ways that age helped me become a writer who put my work out into the world. Writing and publishing is a rough-and-tumble place. No matter how decent your work is, for many of us, it will still be rejected again and again. Being older helped me to recognize the first thing I needed to know, which was that I just wasn't good enough. I know we women aren't supposed to disparage ourselves in this way, but it's a simple fact that I was not good enough. I was learning and doing something new. It would be ridiculous to think I was some sort of brilliant genius of a writer right off the bat. I don't know if I would have been able to accept that and then go out and learn what I needed to if I was younger.

WRITING AND PUBLISHING IS A ROUGH-AND-TUMBLE PLACE

There's no way that you can enter into the world of publishing or learning anything new without many embarrassments and small humiliations. It helped that I was older and had a long history of living through moments like those. I knew that these embarrassments weren't about me. They didn't affect who I was. I had a sense of who I was in the world that I wouldn't have had earlier in my life. This creates a bulwark against humiliation.

I didn't have enough money or physical stamina to go get an MFA even if I'd known what one was, so I showed up at all the author events. I was that annoying white lady in the front row that asked too many questions and took too much time from the author. To this day, I am grateful for those generous and patient authors who were simply kind or understood that I wanted to learn something from them and I didn't know what it was yet.

I would get rejection letters for writing about my body. I was told I didn't know what I was talking about or that what I was writing wasn't interesting enough. I applied for residencies that no one with my lack of credentials had any business applying for, and I was rejected over and over, but sometimes, every now and then, I got a yes.

There are a few things that I believe would help writers be more successful. This includes mentorships, information about navigating the publishing world, and other forms of support for new (not necessarily young) writers, especially those of us who are learning our skills and making our way outside of an academic community. These forms of support would have saved me a lot of floundering.

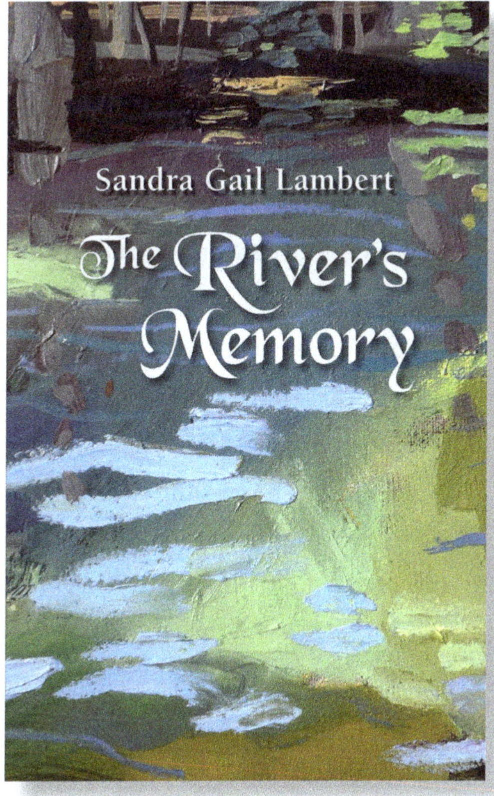

Sandra Gail Lambert, *The River's Memory* published 2014 by Twisted Road Publications

I ALSO HAVE VALUE IN THE WORLD

It took me about a decade to write my first published novel. I was in my early fifties when I started, and it took me a long time to figure out what I was doing. I lived in Florida, and I loved doing research about the state. Since I lived on Social Security disability and didn't have much money, I couldn't travel far, but I could travel around the area I lived in. I picked a locale close to where I live to set the novel, and I would visit state parks and local history museums. Down the street from my house was a used bookstore with a Floridiana section. I was using a wheelchair now, and I would reach way over my head to get books off the higher shelves. Sometimes, the information I needed would literally fall onto my lap. My novel slowly took shape.

When you're creating the story of a place over time, there's this strong pull to make it genetically connected. It's satisfying to do that. For example, someone's grandchild is the main character in the next chapter. But I thought about how I'm a genetic dead end, and yet I also have value in the world. The word for a woman like me is barren, with the idea that we don't pass anything on. I know that's not true, so I made all of my characters—each woman in each chapter and each time period childless. The connections were all about their art or their impact on the environment or some other way of creating change in their world.

At this moment in my life, I want to get back to the wildness in my writing. Have you ever had the experience of reading an author's first book and being thrilled by the exuberance and momentum of the writing, and then you read the second book and it's much better, as far as craft, skill, and structure, but that original wildness just isn't there? I think it's inevitable. Sometimes, I feel like that about my writing. These days, I want to get that back—the wildness.

I WANT TO GET THAT BACK–THE WILDNESS

I was sixty-six when my memoir, *A Certain Loneliness*, was published. I was ready. I had been awarded a National Endowment for the Arts grant and had used part of it to hire a publicist. We had a plan. Hah. The day the advanced readers copies arrived, I had my first breast cancer surgery. In the next six weeks, I had another surgery, a heart attack, and a GI bleed. The publicist arranged interviews and podcasts I could do from bed. With the help of friends and my beloved, I made it to the book fairs I'd been invited to and traveled on a reduced book tour. Despite all of these excellent excuses, I felt like a fraud when I was asked to make presentations and talk about writing, since I wasn't writing. Finally, now, in these pandemic times, I'm writing again. And this gets back to the wildness.

Four weeks after I went into lockdown, I hired a writer I know to teach me a short story writing class. Her expertise is magical realism, fairy tales, and absurdist short stories, which are things I knew nothing about. I read her recommendations—which was a long list—and started writing stories in that genre. It is as if I'm going back. I'm learning new things again, and it's exciting. I've written three short stories so far as a result of that class. I don't care that none of them have been published yet. I'm enjoying it so much. When I was a kid, I loved science fiction. It was one of the few places where disability was presented as just a regular thing without it being negative or positive. Learning this genre has given me the opportunity to go back and reclaim some of that old wildness and excitement in my writing. It makes me happy.

EVERY DECADE HAS BEEN BETTER THAN THE LAST

I had no imaginings about my future when I was younger. I wonder why I didn't, because these days, I do. I think it had to do with being a disabled kid. When you are a disabled kid, you don't get asked regular questions. We don't get asked, "How many kids do you want to have?" or, "Do you have a crush on anyone?" "What sort of wedding do you imagine?" or even, "What do you want to be when you grow up?"

I just had to fill out an application that had a question about the future related to my writing career. It asked, "What do you want to accomplish in the next ten years in your writing life?" I think there was an assumption that a younger person would be answering the question. And they'd be imagining an expansive future and their place in it. But to me, that question was asking how I want things to end. I'm not suggesting that I plan on dying by the time I'm eighty, but it could easily happen. I have to say that the question took me back a bit. It made me aware, for the first time, that there's a time limit on my writing. I asked myself, "What would be enough as far as my writing life is concerned?"

I know about limits and how not to be constrained by them. When you are disabled, you need to be very clear about what you want, to take the direct path to whatever that may be, and to not mess around. For me, there's always been a honing down of what is possible to what is most important. Unbeknownst to the creators of the application, they were asking me what I want to accomplish before I die. I needed to be specific. I wrote that in the next ten years, I want to complete a second collection of essays, prepare a manuscript of short stories, and write another novel. That will be enough.

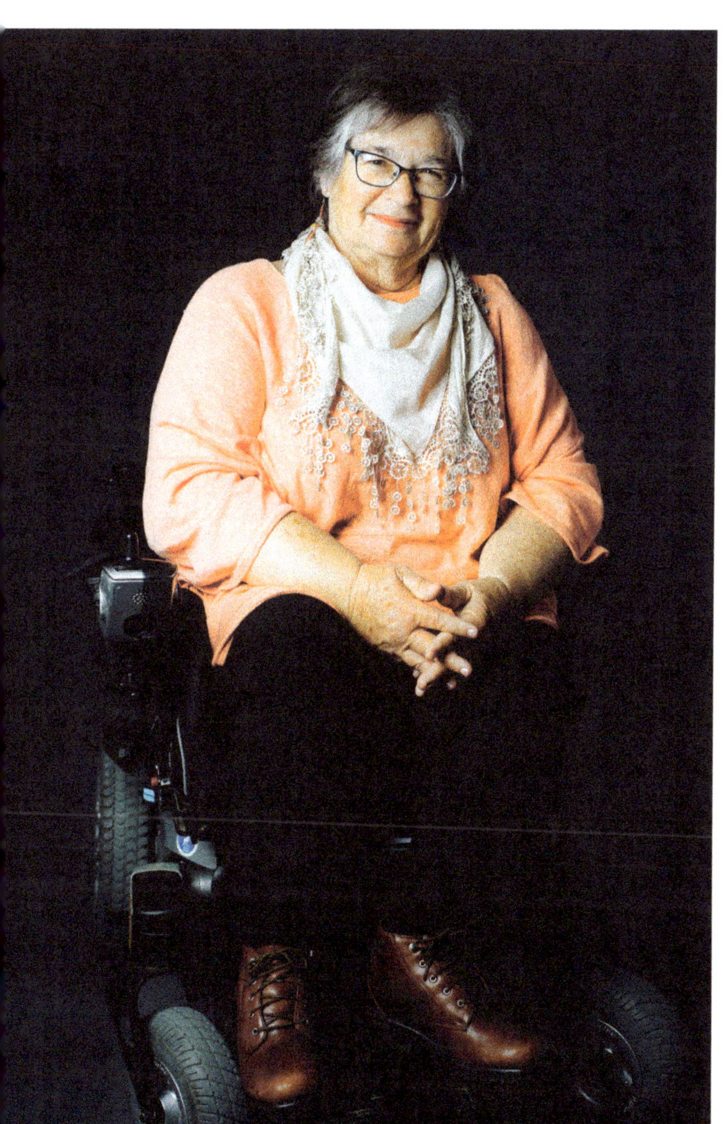

The truth of my life is that every decade has been better than the last. This doesn't mean that only good things have happened, but as I've grown older, I have more of that sense of who I am. I feel I have purpose and that I can help in the world. This has increased with every decade of my life, so I'm looking forward to the next one that's coming up.

I like considering what I would do if I had the means to do anything, with absolutely no restraints, to change my writing practice. I would change nothing. These days, I have the writing life I want, along with a community of support and encouragement. ❖

DISCUSSION QUESTIONS

1) Did reading these women's stories make you think differently about age and what is possible beyond the age of seventy?

2) Are you aware of any biases you may carry regarding age and the value of older women's lives?

3) Being creative is definitely a key element to the vitality of the women featured in *BEYOND 70*. What role does creativity play in your life? When answering this question, consider other forms of creativity beyond visual art, writing, and music.

4) If you are an artist or writer, which of the stories most resonated with you and why? Will you look further into any of the women featured here to discover more about their work?

5) Some of the women featured in the book, such as Phyllis I. Thompson, PhD and Judy Bowman, started out as artists but then had long gaps in which they did not practice their art. Phyllis described becoming ill because she was not creating art. Is there a calling in your life that you've put on hold? If so, can you start making changes, even small ones, to return to this calling?

6) During her interview, Launa D. Romoff stated, "I believe anybody can start a new career at any time in their life. You can follow your passion at any age." Do you agree with Launa?

7) Judy Bowman, Ofelia Esparza, Pat B. Allen, and other women in this collection discussed ways to assist artists in the United States. Do you believe individual artists and the arts in general should receive funding through the government or by other means? Do you have any ideas?

8) Several of the women interviewed mention influential people who provided them support. Some of these people helped the women to realize their calling and embrace their identities as artists.

Who has been a mentor in your life that provided support and encouragement of your talents and dreams?

9) Suellen Cox and Wendy Tigerman imagined meeting with artists and writers, past and present. If you could meet with people from the past or present to ask them questions, who would they be and why?

10) Sandra Gail Lambert says, "The truth of my life is that every decade has been better than the last. This doesn't mean that only good things have happened, but as I've grown older, I have more of that sense of who I am." Has this been the same for your life?

11) The title of Della Wells' exhibition that then became the title for a play about her life is *Don't Tell Me I Can't Fly*. What would a play about your life be titled?

12) In Launa D. Romoff's interview, she discusses a personal transformation after posing for nude photographs for the first time in her life at age sixty-eight. Have you ever done something completely out of character, perhaps something that took a good amount of courage, that transformed your life?

13) Young Yun Summers shared, "As I've gotten older, I'm able to loosen up more. I used to be so careful and fearful of the imperfection and loose ends... Now, I've gained enough confidence to use my own judgment." Have you loosened up more like Young as you've aged? Are you becoming more courageous as you get older? If you've had a harsh "inner critic" throughout your life, has this voice softened?

14) Suellen Cox discussed how her life has turned out quite differently than she expected. Have you had to make significant changes in your life that you were not anticipating?

15) Some of the women offered dreams of what they would do if money was not an issue in their lives. What would you do?

ENDNOTES

Introduction, pages 8-11

1 "The Painter and the Planetarian: Luchita Hurtado in Conversation with Andrea Bowers about History, Nature, and Art as a Form of Shouting," *Ursula*, Spring 2019, 37.

2 Jenn Pelly, "Recalling a Life of Defiance and Song," *New York Times*, February 14, 2021, AR 11.

3 Siddhartha Mitter, "At 86, She's Still Cutting Into the Culture," *New York Times*, February 21, 2021, AR 6-7.

4 Emily Urquhart, *The Age of Creativity: Art, Memory, My Father, and Me* (Canada: House of Anansi Press, 2020), 3.

5 Stacy Russo, *A Better World Starts Here: Activists and Their Work* (Switzerland: Sanctuary Publishers, 2019).

6 Mary Catherine Bateson, *Composing a Further Life: The Age of Active Wisdom* (New York, NY: Knopf, 2010), x.

7 Pat B. Allen, *Art is a Way of Knowing: A Guide to Self-knowledge and Spiritual Fulfillment Through Creativity* (Boston, MA: Shambhala, 1995), 21.

ACKNOWLEDGMENTS

Thank you to the Rancho Santiago Community College District Board of Trustees and my faculty peers at Santa Ana College for recognizing the value of this project and the role of oral history and story-gathering projects within the field of librarianship. The sabbatical leave I was granted for the 2020–2021 academic year allowed me the time to conduct research and interview the phenomenal women who appear in this collection.

Much gratitude for the exceptional editorial services of Bryony Leah.

Thank you to Karyn Kloumann, founder and publisher at Nauset Press, for believing in this project.

ABOUT THE AUTHOR

Stacy Russo is a California writer, poet, and artist who is committed to creating books and art for a more peaceful world. She serves as a librarian and associate professor at Santa Ana College. Stacy is the author of several nonfiction books, the editor of two essay collections, and a published poet. She is the author and illustrator of the children's picture books *Poetry Hounds* and *Wild Librarian Bakery and Bookstore*. Her writing has appeared in *Feminist Teacher, American Libraries, Library Journal, Serials Review, Counterpoise*, and *Feminist Collections*. Stacy's books have been adapted for university classes and featured on various media channels, including National Public Radio, Pacifica Radio, the Canadian Broadcasting System, Sirius XM Radio, KCET Artbound, and LA Weekly. She is the former chair of the Association of College and Research Libraries, Women and Gender Studies Section. She holds English degrees from the University of California, Berkeley, and Chapman University, and a degree in library and information science from San Jose State University. Stacy is currently pursuing a PhD in transformative studies through the California Institute of Integral Studies. She lives in a house full of books and art with her dog Walter. Stacy takes her coffee black, eats chocolate before noon each day, and walks around her neighborhood with Walter every morning.

www.stacy-russo.com

ALSO BY STACY RUSSO

EDITED COLLECTIONS

- *Feminist Pilgrimage: Journeys of Discovery*
- *Life as Activism: June Jordan's Writings from The Progressive*

NONFICTION

- *A Better World Starts Here: Activists and Their Work*
- *We Were Going to Change the World: Interviews with Women from the 1970s and 1980s Southern California Punk Rock Scene*
- *The Library as Place in California*
- *Love Activism*

FICTION

- *Stella Peabody's Wild Librarian Bakery and Bookstore*

POETRY

- *The Moon and Other Poems*
- *Everyday Magic*

CHILDREN'S BOOKS

- *Wild Librarian Bakery and Bookstore*
- *Poetry Hounds*

www.ingramcontent.com/pod-product-compliance
Lightning Source LLC
LaVergne TN
LVHW081300100826
845148LV00005B/931

* 9 7 9 8 9 8 5 9 6 9 2 1 4 *